T0305459

The Materials of Service Design

The Materials of Service Design

JOHAN BLOMKVIST

Assistant Professor in Design, IDA, Linköping University, Sweden

SIMON CLATWORTHY

Professor in Design, Institute of Design, The Oslo School of Architecture and Design, Norway

STEFAN HOLMLID

Professor in Design, IDA, Linköping University, Sweden

Cheltenham, UK • Northampton, MA, USA

Published by
Edward Elgar Publishing Limited
The Lypiatts
15 Lansdown Road
Cheltenham
Glos GL50 2JA
UK

Edward Elgar Publishing, Inc.
William Pratt House
9 Dewey Court
Northampton
Massachusetts 01060
USA

A catalogue record for this book
is available from the British Library

Library of Congress Control Number: 2023946826

This book is available electronically in the **Elgar**online
Business subject collection
http://dx.doi.org/10.4337/9781802203301

ISBN 978 1 80220 329 5 (cased)
ISBN 978 1 80220 330 1 (eBook)

Typeset by Cheshire Typesetting Ltd, Cuddington, Cheshire
Printed and bound by CPI Group (UK) Ltd, Croydon, CR0 4YY

Contents

Acknowledgements

Never judge a book by its cover, the saying goes. In this specific case, judging by the cover, it is a three-person authored book. In some sense this is true, but there are more contributors in the book, and of course, seen over a longer period of time, many more contributors to the topic of the book.

We wish to extend our gratitude to all the contributors and participants in the multitude of processes, which was the starting point for the making of the material descriptions. Your contributions in dialogues leading up to the joint discussions, as well as those joint discussions, gave food for thought, inspiration to pursue with the book and not the least kickstarted parts of the contents of the book. We admire the critical thinking, openness and mutual curiosity with which you all engaged in those dialogues.

We also wish to extend our deepest gratitude to the contributors of material descriptions to the book. You all took on the task of writing down, in a succinct manner, a description of a design material of a non-material nature.

Some of the dialogues around materials turned into longer pieces, fitting into the book as reflective interludes. We are grateful to all contributors to those interludes, in the form of texts and interviews, for the considerable time and brainpower spent reflecting on the topics and our questions. Whether read as critical perspectives or experiential notes, they provide new openings for questions about materials of service design.

A big thanks to the cover designer, Teis Casperson, who managed to make sense out of visualising the immaterial in a meaningful way.

To us, the engagement we were met with is a reminder to continue working with the materials of service design in a crowdsourced and co-creative manner.

Preface

If design is about forming materials, then what are the materials of service design? This was the start point for our collaboration several years ago and the basis for a conference paper at ServDes in Copenhagen (Blomkvist et al., 2016). The theme struck a chord with the participants at the conference and we were invited to develop a journal article to discuss it in more detail. When we got going on the journal article, we started to realise that it would perhaps be better as a whole book – the book you are now holding.

Materials are central to design, and design schools have invested considerable resources in the development of workshops for clay, wood, plastic, metal and 3D printing. They are occupied night and day by students investigating form, forming and constructing materials, or simply exploring the characteristics of materials. This is because it is in the very nature of design to form, and although what is being formed has changed, the desire to explore through forming has not relented.

Service design researchers have increasingly based their conceptualisation of service on theories from service marketing and management. Recently, this has been influenced by theories of service logics, where the focus has been resource integration, value exchange and phenomenologically derived value. Service logic theories have been valuable for design theory in many ways, but have perhaps shifted the focus away from a conceptualisation of service as a design material. This book deliberately takes a design approach, and highlights the material constituents of service design from various designerly perspectives. We argue that a discussion about service as a design material also needs to have a design foundation, and we would like to promote conceptualisations that come from design theory. This book aims to initiate such a discussion.

Service design is expanding, and now encompasses healthcare, social innovation, design for policy and environmental change. Exploring and understanding service as a design material may contribute to these areas and help us understand how design can better contribute to such developments.

Each characterisation of a design field carries with it some indication about what should be emphasised in the practice of design and, looking at other fields of design, a discourse regarding materials has contributed to the development of each field, its research direction and its educational foundations.

This book specifically establishes a discourse around the materials of service design. The intention is not to develop an exhaustive list of materials but rather to discuss it as a means to explore what service design is, might be and might not be. Such a discussion gives new insights into service, since something has to be combined, formed, customised and produced to provide service. We believe that these 'somethings' have not yet been fully identified and that a discussion about them might provide new insights into design for service.

Our ambition with the book is to give some new insights into the field of service design at a time when it has become well established as a field, and perhaps ready to push on in new directions. We are unsure what direction this will be, but we have a sense that change is about to occur. This book might be viewed either as the closure of a first period of service design or the handover between old and new. We also hope that the book can contribute to the development of education within service design. The number and type of materials being described here point to a broad and diversified service design field, which is developing multiple voices. To plan and run a course requires some choices in course profile and content, and we hope that this book can help course leaders navigate a path to their own service design view, one that fits the context of the institution holding the course.

So, together we have questioned what is being formed by service designers and in the design of service, and have reached out to the service design community to find out if we were onto something or not. The response has been immense and the enthusiasm motivating, however, it was not without critics of the material approach to service design. But, even those critical to the term material have been enthusiastic about this project and have taken part in the nerding that was central in the making of the book.

In this book, we develop ways of seeing the materials of service design, to give new insights and understanding into the nature of service itself, to bring leverage for service design in terms of vocabulary and repertoire and to research and educate in terms of framing and concepts. This is done through a foundation in design, here conceptualised as transforming the materials of a design situation. Within service design, the discussion within this book relates not only to the interactions at a granular level, but a meta-discussion regarding material in an essentially immaterial service. This can be framed as a move from forming materials as matter to forming materials that matter.

We have used a lot of time and energy attempting to create a structure for materials, hoping for some inspirational breakthrough, and this in itself has led us to explore and understand more. In this way, we have followed a typical design process. We started with explorations without having a clear end goal in sight but with optimism that exploration would suggest multiple solutions and important insights. We have considered alternative ways of categorising and grouping materials and structuring the book, again with an aim to understand more about our topic. We have approached this from the nature of the material, the type of forming, who is involved, when it occurs in the design process or type of outcome. However, we found no clear categorisation that nicely fits with these, and have to conclude that materials for service are a messy contextual mix of all of these things. We do, later in the book, reflect and suggest some frameworks for viewing the materials of service from a design perspective, however, these are suggestions aimed at reflection rather than a presentation of rigid taxonomies. The book does not conjure a rabbit out of a hat, but instead presents a broad range of materials and lays out multiple interpretations of material. We think this is the best approach to encourage the many strands of service design that are now appearing. However, we have to acknowledge that the three co-authors share many factors in terms of history, experience and context, all coming from Nordic service design groups. To counter this, we encouraged input from around the world, but still recognise the heavy European influence. This, we appreciate, can be a double-edged sword and has led to us sometimes think that our insights are simplistic, and other times that they are new and valuable. We leave that judgement to you, and hope that you can enjoy following the journey that is this book.

Structure of the book

The book begins with Part 1, consisting of an introductory foundation and positioning to establish a platform that can be used later to analyse, reflect and conclude about the materials presented in the book and about materials in service design as a whole.

The introductory foundation is then followed by Part 2, containing material descriptions from invited authors that aim to stretch our understanding of materials for service. There are a lot of them. Some of them may be core materials in your mind, and some of them may challenge your thinking a bit. This is deliberate and the goal has not been to create an exhaustive list of materials. Instead, we have aimed to map out some of the contours in what is a large and growing material space. In addition to this we have interviewed key people from practice in service design, to give a perspective from practice.

In Part 3 we take a step back and reflect on what the material descriptions tell us about the materials of service design. This starts with immediate reflections and a description about our (failed) attempts to categorise the materials. We use concepts from New Service Development to sort the materials, and we try a bottom-up approach based on different design contexts. We also view the materials in terms of Buchanan's four orders of design (1992) and through that identify the strategic and tactical importance of service design. Part 2 then continues with a chapter on service as a hypermaterial, in which matter, time and immaterial aspects melt together. This chapter discusses the implications of hypermateriality and what this means for service design. Part 3 concludes by looking at how service materials can be understood as layered materials.

Finally, Part 4 takes a broader view to reflect on what this means for service design and the service designer's repertoire. One aspect of this is the need to focus on aesthetics within service design, and Simon Clatworthy discusses what that might mean. Another aspect is how designers come into contact with materials of service through representations of them, and Johan Blomkvist explores this relationship further. A third perspective is brought into the picture by Stefan Holmlid, on how one could view service designing as a work with bricolages and rhizomatic structures. These reflections are then translated into suggestions for service design in terms of developing research, education and practice.

We see this book as part of a conversation about the materials of service design, and further, the materials of service itself. During the book's development, we have been in touch with many service designers and have had fantastic conversations with them. We would like to continue this dialogue, so please continue to the companion website at servicedesignmaterials.ep.liu.se to add your thoughts and perhaps add some new materials. In that way, we hope that this can become an evolving discussion.

References

Blomkvist, J., Clatworthy, S., & Holmlid, S. (2016). Ways of seeing the design material of service. ServDes2016, 24–26 May, Copenhagen (125, pp. 1–13). Linköping University Electronic Press.

Buchanan, R. (1992). Wicked problems in design thinking. Design Issues, 8(2), 5–21.

Prologue: defining material

If design, as Schön (1983) would argue, is about a 'conversation with materials', then what are the materials of service – something that is commonly described as immaterial? What are the shapes that these conversations take when forming the material of the immaterial?

The core premise of this book is that a central concern for any design discipline must be its relationship with the qualities and properties of its design material. A designer's understanding of what should be designed influences how they go about designing. This in turn decides who is involved and why. It also influences for whom design is carried out and what is included in the perceived design space, i.e., what someone expects to be able to change.

We start here with a dictionary definition of material to expand the concept of material and broaden the view on what materials can be.

Definitions of the term material

What is material, or a material, and are they different? The term material is often considered to be something that is physically formed as part of the design and production process but not commonly defined as part of design, and instead taken for granted. Therefore, we believe it is worthwhile exploring the term material based on its usage in the English language. The following dictionary definition of material is taken as a starting point to explore and consider the nature of material and to show that it is a broad and rich term, with relevance to the design of 'immaterial' services:

(1) the elements, constituents, or substances of which something is composed or can be made (2) matter that has qualities which give it individuality and by which it may be categorised <sticky material> <explosive materials> (3) something that may

be worked into a more finished form (4) something used for or made the object of study <material for the next semester> (5) a performer's repertoire <a comedian's material>. (Merriam-Webster, 2014)

This definition clearly defines material as something that does not necessarily have physical form and this makes the definition interesting as a basis for a discussion of service design. Based on the definition, we can immediately ask, what are the 'constituents' of service, what is the 'object of study' and what is a service designer's 'repertoire'? Further, when relating to Schön's conversations with material (1983), we can contextualise this as being the designer's conversations with the constituents of services. In this way, an exploration of materials helps us get closer to not only service design, but service itself.

The constituents of which something is composed

This definition is perhaps the one that is easiest for a designer to relate to, particularly if they have some relation to product design. Generally, we would view this as being some form of tangible formable material, but now, with both interaction design and service design, we need to broaden the approach and look more at the essence of service.

We know that in design, in a broader sense, the designer has to focus on both the whole and the parts. Schön (1992) describes how the designer must shift stance and 'oscillate between the unit and the total … and between involvement and detachment' (p. 102). To be able to answer this we need to ask what 'service' is composed of, and to deconstruct the whole and the parts. This is something we return to later in Part 1.

Matter that gives individuality

A second definition of material is that of 'matter that has qualities which give it individuality and by which it may be categorised'. The term individuality when applied to services can be understood to relate to novelty, uniqueness, differentiation and perhaps the value proposition. This implies a relationship to innovation as well as categorisation, and also points towards service genres.

Each service is unique, but unlike other materials it is unique because the material constantly changes depending on who takes part in it, at what time and at what location. As we will see later, the aspect of individuality and material can be viewed through the lens of invention (Manzini, 1986). Within service, it could be said that materials appear as new, not only due to the invention of a new material, but also through the recognition of 'something' being a material for the designer or through new combinations of materials. This book suggests new types of material that allow you to question and explore the materials of invention in service.

Something to be formed

This third definition of a material, 'something that may be worked into a more finished form', relates to its use as part of the design and development process – as an exploration and forming material. Such material is used in design to explore a problem and model and express characteristics of the final solution. In service design, this raises two questions: negotiation with whom, and using which materials?

First, the nature of service development places the designer into a cross-functional team. This brings with it specific needs in terms of ways of working (collaborative) and the challenges this brings. The second challenge for the designer is that of engaging with the problem and solving it through exploration, representation and testing. Schön (1992) describes this as a reflective conversation with the problem and, more specifically, as a 'conversation with the materials of the situation' (p. 78). Materials for collaboration and materials for representation are both discussed and suggested in the book.

Service as the object of study

A fourth definition of a material is 'something used for or made the object of study'. This definition is singular, implying that there is an object of study, and therefore in relation to design may relate to high-level concepts in design. The interpretation of the object of study could also be viewed in a contextual sense as the object of 'design' study at any particular moment. In this interpretation it could be viewed as the designer reflectively asking, 'what do I need to be my "object of study" at precisely this stage of the project?'. We could analyse this through the lens of what a service designer focuses on during the design process, in a series of connected, time-based activities.

A further interpretation of this can be seen as the object of study through education and research. This partially crosses over with the next piece, the service designer's repertoire, but can also be described as a need for discourse regarding materials. Essentially, this is arguing for the content of this book and the discussion it might generate.

The service designer's repertoire

The final definition of a material is that of 'a performer's repertoire'. In the same way that a comedian may have their 'material', or 'repertoire', there is a need to develop the same for service design, both as a practitioner set of competencies and as part of education programmes. At present, there is limited agreement regarding what service design and its constituent parts are. The landscape of service design education is also changing, with an increasing diversity of institutions offering service design courses, ranging from design schools, information technology schools, universities to business schools. Each of these has their own institutional logics behind curriculum development and develop courses based on this. We hope that this book can assist in the choice of materials to be a part of an individual professional profile and for the development of existing and future curricula.

This broad view of material, based on its definition, is central to our thinking, and is used to form the structure of the book itself. From materials being worthy of study (Part 1), to being the constituents of something (Part 2), being categorised (Part 3) and, finally, discussed as a performer's repertoire (Part 4), the parts of the book move through the facets of material using a service design context. Hopefully, taken as a whole, this closes the circle to cover material and service design in all of its richness.

References

Manzini, E. (1986). The material of invention. Milan: Arcadia.
Merriam-Webster. (2014). Material. www.merriam-webster.com/dictionary
Schön, D. A. (1983). The reflective practitioner: How professionals think in action. New York: Basic Books.
Schön, D. A. (1992). Designing as reflective conversation with the materials of a design situation. Research in Engineering Design, 3, 131–147.

PART 1

INTRODUCTION: SOMETHING MADE THE OBJECT OF STUDY

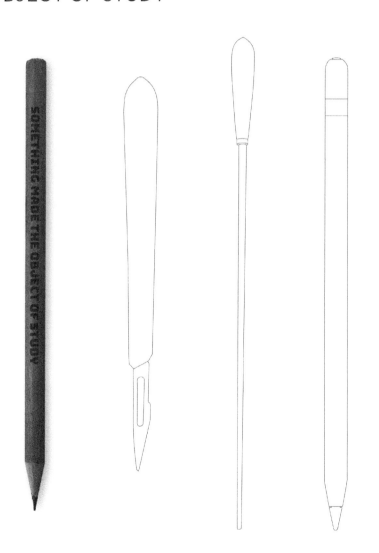

Introduction to Part 1

Part 1 of the book is an introductory foundation and positioning, to establish a platform for the remainder of the book. It shows how material is worthy of study in design, particularly service design. It considers the general move from the material to the immaterial within art and design, and then considers what it is that designers do with materials during the design process. This is then followed by a chapter about the importance of representation in design, particularly service design, before concluding with a chapter about service as a material.

1 The move away from matter in art and design

Simon Clatworthy

This part of the book looks at what designers do in relation to materials, then relates this to service design and service itself. It concludes with a leftfield view, with an invited chapter from Yoko Akama and Cameron Tonkinwise about bodies. But first, a very short view of how art (and design) has, at times, specifically focused on the materials of the immaterial and how it makes sense for service design to do the same.

Any discussion of the materials of service design needs to look at how other creative fields interpret the immaterial and perhaps ask why this questioning of design materials has emerged now. We can clearly see a move from the material to the immaterial in art and design during the past hundred years, and could say that perhaps service design has arrived late to this discussion. However, it is interesting to note that, until recently, the materials of design have not been fundamentally questioned, and the questioning of materials in design really started after the advent of digital design and the emergence of new design fields. Although the desired outcomes of a design solution have been discussed and debated during this time, with a move from the functional to the experiential (and societal), the materials of the situation seem to have been taken for granted.

My brief historical investigations into the emergence of the immaterial start with art, since questions relating to the material object perhaps have the longest history here. Technological development and social change at the beginning of the twentieth century encouraged artists to explore new materials such as light and film, and this brought about a discussion on materiality. Using the term 'materialised energy', Vesnin (1922, p. 68) described how the inter-relations between human beings and the material elements of art were being reconceptualised, and that material was disappearing. The introduction of the term 'immaterial materiality', used by Lissitzky in 1925 in relation to light, is the earliest direct discussion of the immaterial as material I can find. Dadaism focused on conceptual and contextual art, right up through the 1950s,

3

questioning 'the object' in art. The Fluxus movement in the 1960s further developed this, and ushered in a period where the concept, the happening and cultural commentary were considered as important or more important than objects themselves. The art was often a concept, where the associations were dependent on 'the viewer'. With the increasing use of technology artists started to specifically question materials, particularly once art gained a digital component. Burnham (1968) described the transition in art in the following way: 'We are now in transition from an object-oriented to a systems-oriented culture. Here change emanates, not from things, but from the way things are done' (p. 24).

Similar discussions and transitions have been visible in design disciplines with movements that have had ambitions to transcend the object, to change and improve the human condition. These aimed to change the role that the discipline played in society and can be traced back to movements such as the garden city movement, design to influence social change and design and democracy. However, although enthusiastically discussing utopian contributions and outcomes of design, there was little or no discussion specifically regarding the materials of design. It seems that the materials were taken for granted, and it is only relatively recently that the materials of design have been questioned.

When considering the development and treatment of materials in design, we have to give special mention to the book by Manzini, titled *The material of invention* (1989). He describes material not in terms of physical characteristics, but in terms of how it can support desired new outcomes. Thus, his chapters are titled 'Transparent matter', 'Creating the light and resistant' and 'Hot objects' in a way that could be described as almost experiential in nature. Rather than describe materials in terms of their tangibility or formability, he instead describes the materials of design as being an embodiment of what is both thinkable and possible. His focus on materials as supporting invention has great relevance to this book, since service designers have fundamentally the same ambitions as those mentioned by Manzini – material exploration is key to invention.

Dilnot (2016) takes a design history view, and describes the recent societal development, where the 'artificial and not nature, is the horizon, medium and prime condition of human (and not only human) existence' (p. 117). He stresses therefore our dependence on the ideas of relation, mediation and the propositional as being core to design. Although Dilnot describes the difference between matter and mattering in his article, he does not exemplify new materials of design, and stops short of including new areas of design such as services and policies. He therefore gives us a societal context of the artificial, but does not indicate what we as designers will form as part of this. Dilnot's view is perhaps a reason why the materials of design are being questioned now, and we can ask the question: what are we forming when working with the ideas of relation, mediation and the propositional?

One design field that has specifically questioned the materials being formed is interaction design. Since service design is considered by many to have emerged from interaction design, this is worth exploring. Here, an extended discussion specifically regarding materials occurred during the first part of this century and has helped define the field. Löwgren and Stolterman (1998) describe information technology as a material without qualities, expressing that digital artefacts do not have given physical qualities in the same sense as traditional design materials. Blevis, Lim and Stolterman (2006) discussed software as a material of interaction design, and Gaver (1996) discussed the social as a material for design. Hallnäs and Redström (2006) explored deep into the foundations of interaction design through various materials, and Nordby (2011) specifically carried out a large research project exploring the materials of interaction design.

What is interesting from reading this work is that whilst the material might change, it seems that the designerly approach employed by the designer remains relatively unaltered. This closes the loop back to the materials of invention, since Manzini (1989) does not question the designerly approach when relating to new materials, but instead focuses on the designerly drive to innovate. It seems therefore that although there has been a move away from matter in design, the fundamental way of designing still matters. This makes it worthwhile to consider essentially what designers do with materials, to be able to relate this to the suggested materials in the book. This is the focus of the next chapter.

Later in Part 1, we transition to the materials of service design and service itself. This can be seen as a logical continuation of the discussion, since it could be said that art and design has, for the past century, been transitioning from product to service. If we use the broad definition of service as being the application of competences for the benefit of another (and/or self), it can absolutely be argued that art from the 1920s has increasingly moved towards being a service rather than a product, without explicitly formulating this. It has moved from being an object to being an experience evoked in a specific context, where its value is phenomenologically derived. This makes the many considerations of materiality in art and design of relevance to service design.

References

Blevis, E., Lim, Y. K., & Stolterman, E. (2006). Regarding software as a material of design. DRS2006 – Wonderground.

Burnham, J. (1968). Systems esthetics. Artforum, 7(1), 31.

Dilnot, C. (2016). The matter of design. Design Philosophy Papers, 13(2), 115–123.

Gaver, W. (1996). Affordances for interaction: The social is material. Ecological Psychology, 8(2), 111–129.

Hallnäs, L., & Redström, J. (2006). Interaction design: Foundations, experiments. Borås: University College of Borås.

Lissitzky, E. (1925). A. and pangeometry. The Structurist, 15, 56.

Löwgren, J., & Stolterman, E. (1998). Design of information technology: Material without qualities. Lund: Studentlitteratur.

Manzini, E. (1989). The material of invention. Cambridge, MA: MIT Press.

Nordby, K. (2011). Between the tag and the screen: Redesigning short-range RFID as design material. Oslo: Oslo School of Architecture and Design.

Vesnin, A. (1922). Credo. Reprinted in M. Kalinovska & R. Andrews (Eds) (1990), Art into life: Russian constructivism, 1914–1932. Seattle, WA: Henry Art Gallery and New York: Rizzoli.

2   The core of design is in the making

Simon Clatworthy

This chapter goes back to the basics of how designers design, to understand and highlight the long heritage that design has in working with materials and how this can influence our understanding of service design materials. It concludes, not unsurprisingly, that design, at its core, is a making profession with a long heritage of balancing function, aesthetics and structure. These three pillars have been resilient and adapted to new contexts of designing, however, the recent move towards design thinking can be viewed as a break with this tradition. The consequences of this are discussed and there is a call to refuel the design school approach towards service design.

The chapter takes a personal view and is based on recent events at the Oslo School of Architecture and Design. Service design has been taught at the School since 2004 and has always recruited students from a bachelor-level education in product design. We found that these students had core competencies that were relevant and useful for service design but never really had time to reflect on what those were. There were of course some things that were missing (including an understanding of *service*), but their core approach was highly relevant to service design. Recently, a total rethink of the bachelor-level education allowed us to explore this, and to develop the core competencies that we wanted from a broad design curriculum. This forms the basis of this chapter because in essence we concluded that at its core, design relates to a way of forming, where the materials and application field are secondary to the core ambitions and approach. We also found a long heritage in design school design that should be preserved and can be enriched as we move from product design to interactions, services, systems and transformations.

The integration of function, aesthetics and structure

In the 1980s there was a clear focus on the pillars of industrial design being function, aesthetics and structure (including construction for manufacture). This can be traced all the way back to the Roman architect Vitruvius, and his core architectural attributes of *firmitas*, *utilitas* and *venustas* (strength, utility and beauty). I focus on this because these three aspects have been a core of design in one form or another for centuries. The designer at that time had a focus on the integration of what something does, how it looks and feels, how it works and how it could be manufactured. Finding the sweet spot of these was the challenge, and I still see the heritage of Vitruvius in the product design education of today. This is not to say that the user was not a central part of design at that time. During the 1970s, design was characterised by the rise of ergonomics (Valtonen, 2005) and the user-centric approach was derived with input from human factors and ergonomics. This was not just anthropometrics in terms of designing for bodily dimensions, but also look-ing at user needs. This approach also started to work with new technology, and worked to balance human capabilities with technological capabilities (human–machine systems) and even worked with organisational design to fit people (e.g., Tavistock Institute in London). It is difficult to identify when *designing with* took over from *designing for*, but in my own experience, I saw a dramatic shift in the early 1990s. This was variously described through human factors, democratic processes and design participation (for example, Ehn, 1988; Sanders, 2002).

Designerly ways: solution orientation, synthesis and balancing

In the early 1990s there was a great deal of interest in understanding the dis-cipline of design and an exploration of how designers design (Cross, 1990; Buchanan, 1992). This built on the work carried out by Donald Schön, Herbert Simon and others, but with greater focus on design rather than architecture or technology. This period identified the way the designer worked and solu-tion orientation, and wicked problems, metaphorical thinking and abductive thinking started to become part of the description of how designers approach projects.

Cross, building on earlier work by March and Marple, identified that the designer has a focus on a conjectured solutions as a way to gain an under-standing of the design problem. In other words designers design as much to understand a problem as to solve (or in the case of wicked problems, resolve) it.

Horst Rittel introduced the relationship between design and wicked problems (Rittel & Webber, 1973) and described the characteristics of wicked problems in a way that could well be a description of design for service. In terms of design, Rittel (1988) argued that there is no clear separation between problem definition, synthesis and evaluation in real-world design activity and this can be seen as a support for the designer's solution orientation and abductive approach. It has also perhaps been visualised in the design squiggle (Newman, 2010), where the designer jumps between stages as a means of sense making as much as ideation (Figure 1.2.1).

This is later unpacked more by Kolko (2010), who describes in depth the relationship between wicked problems and design synthesis, and describes how 'Synthesis requires a designer to forge connections between seemingly unrelated issues through a process of selective pruning and visual organization'. Synthesis reveals a cohesion and sense of continuity; synthesis indicates a push towards organization, reduction, and clarity (p. 18).

Kolko describes how, during synthesis, designers organise, manipulate, prune and filter (material) to create a structure. Salustri and Eng (2009) describe design as balancing, characterised by the designer responding to multiple inputs and attempting to find a best balance through an integrated solution. I like the term balancing when related to service design since it links synthesis and aspects of wicked problems together. I am not sure if the concept of balancing as a design

Source: Image drawn by Frida Almquist.

Figure 1.2.1   The way that the designer works is often described as messy and chaotic and visualised as a form of a squiggle

activity is new; it most likely can be traced back to balancing the different aspects of beauty, strength and structure from Vitruvius.

Buchanan (1992) shows how design does not follow a linear model for resolving problems and criticises the two-phase definition-solution model:

> such a model may appear attractive because it suggests a methodological precision that is, in its key features, independent from the perspective of the individual designer. In fact, many scientists and business professionals as well as some designers, continue to find the idea of a linear model attractive believing that it represents the only hope for a 'logical' understanding of the design process. However, some critics were quick to point out two obvious points of weakness: one, the actual sequence of design thinking and decision making is not a simple linear process; and two, the problems addressed by designers do not, in actual practice, yield to any linear analysis and synthesis yet proposed. (p. 15)

Buchanan explores design and wicked problems and describes how design, due to its approach, could work with almost any project area: 'The subject matter of design is potentially universal in scope because design thinking may be applied to any area of human experience' (Buchanan, 1992, p. 16).

I would like to just pause a little here, and summarise the state of knowledge at this time:

1.   The design approach does not follow a linear definition-solution approach.
2.   Its core is the integration of aesthetics, function and production.
3.   It attempts solutions as a way of understanding the problem.
4.   It has a relatively strong focus on users.
5.   It is solution oriented and is suited to resolving wicked problems.
6.   It relies on the synthesis or balancing of multiple inputs.
7.   There is no clear separation between problem definition, synthesis and evaluation.
8.   It can be applied to different levels of project complexity.

I admit to this being painted with broad brush strokes, but around the turn of the century, a step change occurred in design through the identification of the business value of design. The designerly way was clearly understood to have economic value and its societal value was quantified in many countries (e.g., Cox, 2005). Design not only started to approach new subject areas, but also became embedded into strategy and tactics. Valtonen describes this as a period in which the designer moved from designing the product (product definition) into designing roadmaps and product portfolios and then further towards designing strategy (Valtonen, 2005).

Enter Tim Brown stage right – exit Vitruvius?

It's perhaps not surprising, then, that at this time Tim Brown, from consultancy IDEO, wrote an influential article in the *Harvard Business Review* about design thinking. He did not invent the term, but he certainly was a catalyst for the uptake of design thinking in relation to business. Tim Brown defined design at this time as: 'it is a discipline that uses the designer's sensibility and methods to match people's needs with what is technologically feasible and what a viable business strategy can convert into customer value and market opportunity' (Brown, 2008, p. 86). This has had a profound effect on the broader understanding of design, but there were several interesting aspects in the article. Firstly, Brown highlighted the changing role of the designer in taking a role moving from tactics towards strategy (Figure 1.2.2). Secondly, the role of aesthetics is played down and barely mentioned. Thirdly, design thinking was described as a collaborative innovation activity and eschewed the rockstar designer idea that was pervasive at the time. Further, the 'messy' design squiggle was played down and replaced by a streamlined predictable process. However, most importantly, Brown almost exclusively used examples of services in the article to exemplify design thinking. There are some images of products, but in almost all cases, the examples are of services or product service systems. Taken together, this can be seen as a pivot away from the three pillars of design mentioned earlier. This pivot was later further supported by the book design thinking by Thomas Lockwood (2010), which

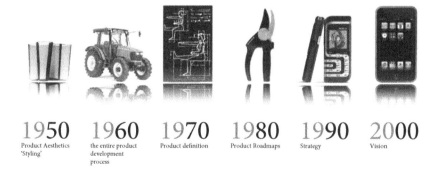

1950 — Product Aesthetics 'Styling'
1960 — the entire product development process
1970 — Product definition
1980 — Product Roadmaps
1990 — Strategy
2000 — Vision

Source: Valtonen (2005); visualised by Judith Gloppen and Maria Elskær.

Figure 1.2.2   The changing role of design

had a whole section on service design, and then multiple books from business schools on design and business (Martin, 2009; Liedtka & Ogilvy, 2011).

This pivot makes perfect sense. Design was embedded into business, was creating value, moving from products to interactions and services, and was increasingly collaborative. Design was increasingly being seen in relation to business value. However, the pivot is significant. Not because design has moved up the Buchanan scale of orders of design or that it has moved into services and servitisation. No, these are new areas of application and already described by Buchanan as being related to the core of design. It is significant, I believe, because it transformed the centuries' old pillars of design. The three aspects of aesthetics, function and production were now replaced by desirability, feasibility and viability (Brown, 2009). This redefined design was oriented towards successful business implementation and, notably, the focus on aesthetics disappeared. It can be argued that it didn't disappear totally and become incorporated into the term desirability, but it is notable that since that time, aesthetics as a core element of design has disappeared within design thinking. It is unknown if Tim Brown deliberately played down the role of aesthetics or whether he found it difficult to discuss the aesthetics of service (and how many people are comfortable doing just that). Design thinking as a term has increasingly distanced itself from the term aesthetics and I believe that service design has followed suit.

Did the baby go out with the bathwater?

I personally believe that we are risking throwing the baby out with the bathwater by accepting and deepening the pivot away from some of the core aspects of design. There are two aspects that I think we are at risk of losing. Firstly, I think the design approach itself is being eroded. Secondly, the pillar of aesthetics seems to have gone missing and I would like it back.

The first aspect relates to the design approach itself. With the advent of design thinking in its business-oriented clothing, I have seen the emergence of service design and design-thinking courses popping up in business schools and universities. When looking closer, it is clear that they do this with their own institutional logic as a backdrop, which means that they do not take the core of the design approach (as described in this chapter) on board. I have taught on multiple courses in both business schools and universities and see that they often utilise a linear process (separated definition-solution phases). There seems to be a tendency for the double diamond to be strictly applied, leading to a non-iterative and rigid phase-based interpretation of the design process. As an example, I was recently told by some master students in design (on a university course) that they were not allowed to generate ideas during the insight phase, because idea generation was a phase they moved to when all insights were captured. In such situations, we risk losing critical aspects that have made design relevant for such schools; the designerly way of thinking through the designerly way of doing.

The designers' orientation towards 'forming as a means of understanding' is in danger of disappearing. This makes design vulnerable to losing its forming skills and places a formulaic two-stage straitjacket on something built up over centuries. Therefore, I would like the reader to bear in mind when reading this book not only the materials of service design but also how they are formed. Any talk of materials and forming need to highlight that design *is in the making*. In this way, we will not only support an understanding of the materials of service design, but we will also support the design-making approach. Indeed, I do not believe it is possible to consider the materials of service design without considering the core design approach through making.

The rebirth of the cool (apologies to Miles)

An aspect that I feel we are increasingly neglecting when deepening the design thinking direction is that of aesthetics. I am not alone in identifying that we are moving away from the aesthetics pillar of design. Cameron Tonkinwise commented: 'What must be removed from designing to make it appropriable by managers is rather, it seems: aesthetics, by which I mean, anything to do with form-giving, the pleasing appearance and feel of a design' (Tonkinwise, 2011, p. 534). Tonkinwise criticises the pivot away from aesthetics in design thinking, and this unresolved relationship between design thinking and aesthetics seems to have carried over into service design. There is perhaps a need for the cool to be reborn within design thinking and service design?

Making interactions matter

As mentioned earlier, interaction design has discussed the aspects of material and immaterial, and I will focus a little here on some work that specifically focuses on design and immaterials. Kjetil Nordby completed his PhD specifically exploring issues of material/immaterial related to interactions and RFID (Nordby, 2011). He suggests that the designerly ways described above are still central, but identifies some aspects with design for interaction that are of importance when designing for the immaterial. These are listed here, since they have relevance for the materials of service design.

Material affordance from a designer perspective

Nordby uses the term material affordance in a design perspective (2011, p. 33) to relate to the affordance a material offers to the designer for forming, rather than using affordance in the commonly used sense of end-user affordance as part of usability. He argues that in the same way that materials such as metal, wood and plastic have a material affordance, so too do interaction materials. It can be argued that Nordby is both relating to the materials of the situation (context) but also underlining the qualities of the material in what it affords for designing. This suggests that to design with the materials of service design we need to not only identify the material but we also need to understand the affordances these materials offer to the designer in a forming context.

Temporal behaviour as a material

Nordby clearly identifies time as being key to interaction design, and this is not new. However, he focuses on temporal *behaviour* as being central to materials in interaction design, rather than time itself. He claims that computational materials relate primarily to behaviour, rather than their composition as matter. This resonates with service design due to the important role of people, and also when considering the behaviour of touch-points during a journey. Time and behaviour are also of importance when considering relationships between users, and between users and their service providers. As an example, the relationship we have with the tax system lasts a whole lifetime, and at the same time can relate to a few minutes filling in a form. The long-term relationship has to take account of various life changes, such as first job, unemployment, marriage, illness and death. The temporal-behavioural aspect of materials therefore has implications for both short-term interactions and also for long-term relationships.

Conceptual, experiential materials

Nordby uses the term 'conceptual material' and is clear that interaction design materials can be seen as conceptual in nature. Key to this is the designer's role in 'shaping the effect of technologies rather than the technologies themselves' (2011, p. 75). This can be seen to echo the term used by Manzini (2015) and later Blevis et al. (2006), of materials of invention, in which the concept is in focus. For Nordby, however, the invention lies not only in the concepts that new technologies afford, but additionally how the concepts are experientially evaluated. This can be seen to give a direct connection to the zooming in and zooming out of service design, where the service concept and individual touch-point interactions are in focus. Further, it implies that the materials of the conceptual are experientially evaluated.

Forming forwards for future situations

Nordby describes a move from a focus on directly forming the material itself to forming a future activity. Material has thus become something that is formed to enable rather than an end point in itself. This points to a greater focus on the experience and the context for the experience. In this way, the service designer is forming forwards, forming for future states, rather than directly forming the materials of the present.

Representations and mediation as a means of exploring immaterials

One thread of interaction design discourse regarding materials has focused on the role of representation and mediation as a way to understand the materials of interaction. This is the work of Timo Arnall, who coined the term immaterials (Arnall, 2014). In a way similar to Dunne and Raby (2001), Arnall focused on addressing sociocultural concerns through a discursive design approach in what is described as a 'reflexive and iterative interplay between materials, experimentation, and use' (Morrison & Arnall, 2011, p. 226). Arnall uses this to specifically focus on exploring the possibilities that the materials of interaction design offer, whereas the goal of Dunne and Raby (2001) has been to provoke discourse about the social consequences of technology solutions in a broader sense. Arnall focuses on using photography, animation, filmmaking and social media to develop discursive material to specifically explore the characteristics and possibilities of his 'immaterials'. This can be described as understanding the immaterial by mediating alternative value propositions enabled through interactions with it. We see this as being a useful direction to explore in service design, particularly as we are talking about immaterials with a time component. Therefore, time-based media such as animation, comics and cinema have particular relevance.

How does this relate to the materials of service?

If we take the view that the service designer is forming the materials from which the service is co-produced, then we can say that the service designer is forming for the application of a complex set of competencies that provide valued experiences over time. Not only this, the service designer forms, together with a team, in a co-design approach so the forming activities occur both at the individual designer level and at the team level. This in itself is a novel (for design) approach, a co-forming activity. The designer could therefore be seen to be an orchestrator of competencies and in this context the competencies are the materials of the service situation. However, the designer is designing for a future state and representations of how the competencies can be applied become a design imperative.

What, then, makes the designer's contribution different to that of any other participant on the project team? Surely anybody can combine competencies? This is where the core elements of designing through making become relevant and this is how design differs from many other disciplines. Forming and synthesis are inseparable and the design approach uses this as a means of identifying and synthesising the multiple elements needed to both understand a situation and as a means to resolving a problem. Forming is therefore as much about exploration as it is about the solution. Indeed, forming and synthesis are possibly the core elements of designing as the designer attempts to bring together the many aspects of design into an integrated solution. This degree of integration or synthesis will vary, depending on what is formed, and is part of the designer's tactical approach to resolve a problem through a combination of aesthetics, use and structure (in the traditional design sense) or desirability, feasibility and viability (in the design-thinking sense).

For design to be able to capitalise on its forming competences it has to have something to form – it needs material. This is why it is important to identify the materials of service design now and to discuss what is formed, how it is formed, when the forming occurs, with who and with what consequence. I believe this is a fundamental aspect of service design that we now need to establish as a means to fuel the next stage of service design. I have no clear evidence that can prove that we are at a new pivot point in service design, but I sense a Schumpeter-like step change coming to service design. As part of that, I would like to ensure that the long design heritage that goes back centuries can be a part of it. Since forming is the fundamental approach that design takes, and is a core part of synthesis, then forming materials should be central in service design. This is the core of what the book, and the following chapters with material descriptions, aims to explore. The material descriptions later in the book offer some answers to these questions.

Johan Blomkvist to the rescue?

Since service design is mainly about forming immaterials, together with others, I think that the focus that Johan has in the next chapter regarding representation is key to retaining the forming tradition in design. Johan shows that designers still form materials, but that this is forming forwards using representations. Service design needs to represent the multiple facets of service and the forming skills necessary for these representations might well be the key arena where the design approach is applied. To be able to represent service during the early stages of a project utilises the core design skills of exploration, forming and synthesis. The customer journey, a classic representation in service design, combines all three of these. An increased focus on representation in service design could well be the vehicle to retain the designerly way of thinking, and that is why this book on materials can be useful. I am hoping that we will find that the materials identified here are formed and represented in various new ways by designers that allow us to embed the designerly way into a new phase of service design representation.

Conclusion

The core competences of design are found to be in the making approach, with a focus on a solution orientation that requires the synthesis of multiple aspects. The historical heritage towards creating solutions that embody structure, function and aesthetics is still visible, although it has been added to over time. In this view of design in the making, materials are viewed as supporting the approach and, as such, the core competencies are a good foundation for service design. The move toward design thinking, however, has the potential to disrupt this, and although not intentional, there is a risk that the designerly way, and the traditional pillar of aesthetics, has been weakened.

When it comes to service design, we see that materials can not only be viewed as the constituents of the final service, but also the multiple representations of service that are developed during design. Further, materials can be viewed as supporting, or possibly affording, the designerly way of designing.

The chapter shows that any discussion about the materials of service design cannot solely focus on the characteristics of the material. It has to also focus on the design process and core ethos. This has important consequences for teaching, and also for practice and research. We will return to this later in the book and what I hope I have given you here in this chapter are some reflections that you can take with you when thinking about materials and the future direction of service design.

References

Arnall, T. (2014). Exploring 'Immaterials': Mediating Design's Invisible Materials. International Journal of Design, 8(2).

Blevis, E., Lim, Y. K., & Stolterman, E. (2006). Regarding Software as a Material of Design. 2006 Design Research Society International Conference, Lisbon.

Brown, T. (2008). Design Thinking. Harvard Business Review, June, 86.

Brown, T. (2009). Change by Design. HarperCollins.

Buchanan, R. (1992). Wicked Problems in Design Thinking. Design Issues, 8(2), 5–21.

Cox, G. (2005). The Cox Review of Creativity in Business. https://webarchive.nation alarchives.gov.uk/ukgwa/+/https://www.hm-treasury.gov.uk/coxreview_index.htm.

Cross, N. (1990). The Nature and Nurture of Design Ability. Design Studies, 11(3), 127–140.

Dunne, A., & Raby, F. (2001). Design Noir: The Secret Life of Electronic Objects. Springer Science & Business Media.

Ehn, P. (1988). Playing the Language-Games of Design and Use: On Skill and Participation. Proceedings of the ACM SIGOIS and IEEECS TC-OA, April, 142–157.

Kolko, J. (2010). Abductive Thinking and Sensemaking: The Drivers of Design Synthesis. Design Issues, 26(1).

Liedtka, J., & Ogilvy, T. (2011). Designing for Growth: A Design Thinking Tool Kit for Managers. Columbia University Press.

Lockwood, T. (2010). Design Thinking. Allworth.

Manzini, E. (2015). Design, When Everybody Designs: An Introduction to Design for Social Innovation. MIT Press.

Martin, R. (2009). The Design of Business: Why Design Thinking Is the Next Competitive Advantage. Harvard Business Press.

Morrison, A., & Arnall, T. (2011). Visualizations of Digital Interaction in Daily Life. Computers and Composition, 28(3), 224–234.

Newman, D. (2010). The Process of Design Squiggle. http://cargocollective.com/central/ The-Design-Squiggle.

Nordby, K. (2011). Between the Tag and the Screen: Redesigning Short-Range RFID as Design Material. Oslo School of Architecture and Design.

Rittel, H. W. (1988). The Reasoning of Designers. IGP.

Rittel, H. W., & Webber, M. M. (1973). Dilemmas in a General Theory of Planning. Policy Sciences, 4(2), 155–169.

Salustri, F., & Eng, N. (2009). Designing as Balance-Seeking Instead of Problem-Solving. Design Principles and Practices, 3(3), 343–356.

Sanders, E. B. N. (2002). From User-Centered to Participatory Design Approaches. In J. Frascara (Ed.), Design and the Social Sciences (pp. 18–25). CRC Press.

Tonkinwise, C. (2011). Unrepressing Style in Design Thinking. Design Studies, 32(6), 533–545.

Valtonen, A. (2005). Six Decades – and Six Different Roles for the Industrial Designer. Nordes.

3 Representations in service design

Johan Blomkvist

This chapter builds on the previous chapters regarding design and the immaterial and looks at the different ways in which materials can be represented during service design. To start with, it is important to recognise that service design is predominantly a co-design activity involving 'immaterials' that cannot be formed directly. Instead, the designer forms, conceptualises and mediates and does this together with a team. This makes shared understanding central, and as we will see in this chapter, representations, both individual and collective, are central to this co-design process. In my view, the designer has a key role in this, by, amongst other things, externalising service representations.

This chapter also looks forward and acts as a primer for the second part of the book. The next part of the book contains suggested materials of service design; each material you read about can be represented, and many are routinely visualised or prototyped as part of design activities. Take for instance customer experiences: they can be researched and visualised using customer journey maps, scenarios, storyboards and so on, or they can be summarised as bullet points or cells in an Excel sheet. Even though they are immaterial, designers interact with them constantly through their representations.[1] This is true for many, if not all, of the materials included in the book – they can be given physical form in one way or another during design, often appearing in different shapes and representational states as the design process progresses.

Current and future states

In any design project, people bring in versions of the world as it is and as it could be and these versions can be more or less elaborate. During design research, knowledge is internalised by participants and shared through conver-

---

1   This is a simplification that we will return to and expand on later in the book.

sations and other external representations of findings, such as written accounts, maps, Excel sheets, field notes, databases, etc. In this way, individual representations become externalised and contribute to a collective internal representation, which itself might be externalised for others to understand. This might include aspects such as an understanding of the interplay between different actors, physical spaces, forces that influence hospitality, care and so on.

There is an important difference between representations of current situations (what is) compared to future situations (what could be). The difference is that when design deals with current situations, representations of that situation generally can be examined and verified by returning to the actual, real-world situation. It is, however, far from unambiguous, since services include human beings with their own internal motivations and experience and services also exist in a dynamic and changing time continuum.

Representations of the future depend much less on observational skills than on the ability to imagine. For example, when we represent what a future insurance service should be like, we have no available real-world referent before the service has started. The representation represents something that does not yet exist. Representations of the future play an important role as a stand-in for what the future might look like and in creating a shared, collective understanding. This stretches the formal meaning of the term representation, but it would be inaccurate to refer to the external material (the non-existing service) as reality.

Although described here as two different states, we have already argued in the book that designers fluidly move between them, for example, by representing a possible future state as a way of better understanding the current state. These different states should therefore be considered as fluid approaches that the designer can use to both understand an existing situation and to improve on it.

Different kinds of representations

Representations can be internal or external. Internal representations are in someone's head and until they are externalised cannot be shared. Externalisation can be done through physical media such as paper sketches, models or prototypes, or it can be verbalised and even expressed in other ways with the body (e.g., Kirsh, 2011). The main point is that an external representation is not in someone's head, but rather in the world where it can be perceived by others. On a very general level, external representations in design can be divided into visualisations and prototypes. Representations that are based on the current situation, 'what is', are often referred to as visualisations, and those that represent the future, 'what could be', are often referred to as prototypes.

In Table 1.3.1, I present a taxonomy of representation. The table does not suggest that some representations are better than others, but instead allows us to consider how a material can be represented, or in other words, how people might encounter different expressions of service during a design process. All representations can be placed in this table, and often designers will work to externalise internal representations so that they may be shared, discussed and improved.

Individual, internal representations

Individual, internal representations are in the head of each person, be they project participants or users. We all represent aspects of phenomena like service in our minds as a means of trying to understand the world around us. In situated theories of cognition, the internal representations depend on previous experiences and internal processes of simulation. Individual internal representations of the current situation can be verified by referring back to the existing situation, although they will always be partial, since service is situated in a time and place and never totally repeatable.

Individual imagined future situations are highly influenced by the creativity of individuals and the scope of projects. It is important to be aware that any internal representation is always influenced by individual differences such as focus, background, role and goals of a person. In a co-design project there will be multiple individual, internal representations, and this can lead to problems and increased project risk if they do not become externalised, aligned and shared.

Table 1.3.1   A taxonomy of representation showing how a current or future situation can be represented internally or externally with various degrees of overlap between individuals

Referent		Modes of representation		
Current situation / What is	Actual service	Individual / Internal	Shared / External	Overlapping / Internal
Future situation / What could be	Imagined future situation			

Shared, external representations

If thought processes are not externally represented and shared in some way, it can lead to considerable risk during development and delivery. Internal representations are often fragmented and flawed, and they do not have to follow principles and limitations set by the external world. For example, we can imagine a world where gravitation is inverted, or a structure that in reality is impossible. At the same time, externalising can reduce cognitive load and the process of externalising often brings with it a questioning of characteristics of a situation, and this will usually improve the understanding thereof. Externally representing our internal representations in the world forces us to be explicit and to relate to the frames set by the external world. It also invites co-design processes. External representations are by their nature collective and available to others since they are shared in the world where they can be perceived. External representations of current situations is especially important for understanding experiences, behaviours, flows and attitudes that are otherwise difficult to capture. Translating internal representations into external representations is therefore important in service design. Accurate descriptions of 'what is' creates favourable conditions for externalising 'what could be'.

It can be argued that a core design skill is to understand a situation through attempting a solution. This can be seen as creating a representation of an imagined future situation, (a prototype of some kind). The accuracy of future service representations are not decided by referring back to the actual service (since it does not exist yet) but rather by inclusion of potential customers, users and people with relevant knowledge and background. External representations of future situations make coordination and collaboration possible and are enhanced by being physically manifested. By being given form, the shared point of reference becomes less vague and abstract.

To understand and explore future situations with external representations, prototypes are often used. Prototypes exist in special circumstances where the normal rules do not apply. Dyrssen (2010) has called this a liminal state. It is a state where time and the laws of nature can be manipulated in the interest of exploring a situation. For instance, in a roleplay we can jump immediately from one interaction to the next, we can replay conversations or imagine a world where technology has made it possible to ride a car without a human driver.

Overlapping, internal representations

Overlapping, internal representations when taken as a whole can be considered to be a shared view of representations within a group. For example, within a project team, each individual will have a different internal representation of the same thing, although aspects may well overlap. Overlapping representations bring a degree of risk during a design process, and due to individual differences will always exist. The degree of overlap can be improved by externalising representations and making them shared. However, this only creates new internal representations in each participant, albeit hopefully closer to each other with a greater degree of overlap.

Material representations

There are materials that can never be truly represented, since they are only constituted during service provision, for example, an important sales conversation that takes place in an insurance service is not a representation. The conversation can be externally represented, for example through a customer journey map, and prototyped through roleplay or enactment, so that what is desired from such a conversation becomes shared. The involvement of salespersons in the design will give access to the detailed and elaborate internal representations of those conversations and allow them to be externalised, thus minimising risk. However, these representations do not form the actual conversation, and this example highlights the importance of representing pivotal parts of a service. The designers need to ensure that these parts are represented during design and therefore available for collective action. This includes ensuring that the right people are involved and that relevant internalised knowledge becomes externalised through representation.

There are multiple aspects of a service that can be represented, and in a project, participants should be aware of what should be represented and how at any particular time. In a service design context, this may be a combination of spontaneous externalisations (for example, to create clarity in a meeting) or pre-planned representations such as customer journey maps.

What is represented as part of service?

As part of my focus on representations, I took an interest in service representation techniques and described how representations were considered material versions of services or service elements (Blomkvist, 2015). By examining the representations resulting from service design techniques mentioned in the book *This Is Service Design Thinking* (Stickdorn & Schneider, 2010), a list of aspects of service that are materialised was generated:

1. components;
2. things;
3. locations;
4. actions;
5. procedures;
6. interactions; and
7. experiences.

Today, I would add to this aspects from the following material descriptions, such as time, social norms and concepts. However, the aspects remain useful, since they allow us to understand what they afford for representation, and they allow a discussion of when it is appropriate to represent them during the design process. For example, procedures afford representation using flowcharts of some kind or other, whilst concepts might afford representations using metaphor.

Different expressions of materials

All materials can and will be represented in different ways depending on where, when and how they occur in the real world or future worlds and each version has its own set of attributes. Hence, every material mentioned in this book can have multitudes of expressions that influence how it is perceived and understood. For example, a roleplay of an insurance sales meeting has a very different material expression than a circle denoting a touch-point in the customer journey. From a representational perspective, visualisation and prototyping are both processes of externalisation. Notions, information or ideas are all transferred from an internal state into an external state. As Schön (1983) and Gedenryd (1998), among others, have suggested, the process is also interactive, meaning that the material takes shape based on interplay between the internal and external world and between people involved in designing (with their own, partially overlapping, internal representations). Skills of working with these types of representations must be learned and practised to be able to craft them and use them to collect relevant and meaningful knowledge for design processes. This means that the designer has to be both well versed in the tools of representation and also able to recognise what needs to be represented at what time and in what way.

As the number of materials increases, this places emphasis on representation being increasingly important for service design.

Representations also have different degrees of fidelity. For example, an inter-active prototype of a smartphone app has greater fidelity than a touch-point designation on a journey map. The designer has to therefore choose the right degree of fidelity according to the context. Similarly, a representation might vary in its degree of abstraction, depending on what is important to commu-nicate. Here, the choice of representation has to be relevant to the context and what the designer wants to achieve at any given time. A quick sketch during a workshop may be good enough for that context, but not good enough for a final specification. Therefore, the designer needs contextual sensitivity in addition to representation skills.

Conclusion

Representations are a central part of service design and have many forms and facets. For the service designer, there is one central question that should continually be asked during the design process: what needs to be externally represented right now, and how can it best be represented?

Service design, as a co-design activity, involves different disciplines and dif-ferent organisational functions, so it is natural that there are multiple internal representations within a group that may or may not overlap. This can repre-sent a risk, and formalised externalisations, for example in deliverables, are one way an organisation manages this risk. However, this is an imperfect way to align representations and there are benefits to be gained from continually being aware of representational differences. The service designer has an important contribution in this task by being able to externalise representations through visualisation and prototypes. The communication skills of the designer are cen-tral to this, although I would like to underline that the designer needs to have a contextual awareness such that representations occur at the right time, in the right form and together with the right people. This is not a trivial task, and therefore demands skills of reading a situation and, further, being able to exter-nalise what needs to be represented and to communicate this in an effective way.

Although representation in service design has been described here in a co-design context, it is also something that the service designer does alone in order to be solution oriented and to be able to represent possible futures to better understand 'what is and could be'. Representation is therefore a fluid endeavour, moving from the individual to the collective, and between 'what is and what could be'.

I would therefore encourage you, as you read on, to view the material suggestions in the next chapter through a representational lens and ask yourself:

- Is this material a representation in itself?
- How should this material be externally represented?
- When do the representations of this material occur and are they internal or external?
- What does this mean for service design competencies?

References

Blomkvist, J. (2015). Ways of Seeing Service: Surrogates for a Design Material. *Proceedings of the Nordic Design Research Conference (Nordes)* (pp. 1–4). Stockholm.

Dyrssen, C. (2010). Navigating in Heterogeneity: Architectural Thinking and Art-Based Research. In M. Biggs & H. Karlsson (Eds), *The Routledge Companion to Research in the Arts* (pp. 223–234). London: Routledge.

Gedenryd, H. (1998). *How Designers Work: Making Sense of Authentic Cognitive Activities*. Lund: Lund University.

Kirsh, D. (2011). How Marking in Dance Constitutes Thinking with the Body. *The Extended Mind*, 183–214.

Schön, D. A. (1983). *The Reflective Practitioner: How Professionals Think in Action*. New York: Basic Books.

Stickdorn, M., & Schneider, J. (Eds). (2010). *This Is Service Design Thinking: Basics–Tools–Cases*. Amsterdam: BIS Publishers.

4 Service as material

Stefan Holmlid

Throughout the years there have been multiple attempts, more or less explicit, at describing service as a general phenomenon, but less about what it is that is being formed, and the multiple practices engaged in that forming. This is not surprising considering the complexity and scope of service, the various types of service around us and the forming practices that at the surface seem to be needed, spanning from physical resources, spaces, interfaces, etc.

In this chapter a short retrospect of how service has been viewed as a material, in different fields, will be followed by a development of two theoretically founded designerly points of view on service as a material.

The retrospect covers how service has been understood as a material from the field of service management and marketing, as well as how service has been viewed from a design point of view. The first perspective on service as a material focuses on situated action, a concept that includes interactions, mediation, as well as joint and individual action. The second highlights collaborative resource integration as a central material of service, that frames processes, interactions and competencies in service.

Splitting and merging service and product

The foundation for 'service' as a separate entity from products was laid firmly during the 1970s and 1980s in studies of service marketing and management (Fisk et al., 1993; Edvardsson et al., 2005; Gustafsson & Lervik-Olsen, 2018). A couple of general ideas were founded then, and became widely spread, such as the molecular model (Shostack 1977), the experiential perspective (Czepiel et al., 1985), as well as a process-oriented view (Shostack, 1982). They were all concentrating on a need to distinguish 'service' and 'product' as separate categories for marketing and management.

This period was a turning point when enough effort and interest coincided to start an institutionalisation of the field.

Four characteristics were often used to identify service, to shape marketing and management specifically for services. Services were said to be *intangible*, their composition *heterogeneous*, their production *inseparable* from their consumption and *perishable* in the sense that they cannot be stored. This was referred to as the IHIP model (Zeithaml et al., 1985; Lovelock & Gummesson, 2004).

However, a shift occurred in the early–mid-2000s, following a longer period of research and development that had taken other starting points, such as relationships, value constellations and value creation (Berry, 1983; Normann, 1983; Normann & Ramirez, 1993; Grönroos, 2006). In marketing and management research, the perspective shifted from distinguishing service and product as top-level entities to suggesting a logic where value creation through service was the main category (Vargo & Lusch, 2004; Grönroos, 1988).

During this period, very little was explicitly focusing on service as a material, although indirectly one can find discussions that relate to this. One example is that in Shostack's early work intangibility is under scrutiny:

> It is wrong to imply that services are just like products 'except' for intangibility. By such logic, apples are just like oranges, except for their 'appleness'. Intangibility is not a modifier; it is a state. Intangibles may come with tangible trappings, but no amount of money can buy physical ownership of such intangibles as 'experience' (movies), 'time' (consultants), or 'process' (dry cleaning). (Shostack, 1977, p. 73)

A second example is regarding the conditions for materials at different times in a service development process, here exemplified by Gummesson: 'In service design an element of improvisation forms a symbiotic relationship with standard procedures. This makes service design different from product design' (1990, p. 97).

Shifting between designing of and for service

It is necessary to say that the design of services has a long history, in many cases longer than the design of the products we are surrounded by today. Many of these products had a precedent that was a service, and they were crafted and formed, not by a designer from a design school, but often by someone who cared about the service experience, the cultural aspects and the service system. One example is the design of hotel experiences in the early twentieth century

(Lee, 2012), but several others would be possible to find, especially if using a social innovation lens.

Ideas about service from the 1970s and 1980s were picked up by early service designers and service design researchers, for example at Cologne and Milan (Erlhoff et al., 1997; Pacenti & Sangiorgi, 2010). The IHIP conceptualisation heavily influenced these early proponents of service design. The object of service design, and hence the material, was considered to be 'the interactivity dimension of services' (Maffei et al., 2005, p. 5), which included experience, interface and identity. These are all visible parts of a service. Similarly, the interface perspective was highlighted in early practice-driven knowledge development on service design, emphasising the interactivity through touch-points (Parker & Heapy, 2006).

In many senses, early service design focused on services as something that could be designed in themselves as if they were material objects, the design *of* services.

In parallel with this, an understanding of service design as a practice focusing on designing *for* service was developing. A similar shift had been part of the development in interaction design (Forlizzi, 1997; Forlizzi & Ford, 2000), where 'designing for' was starting to be established. With the focus on designing for service, the material focus shifted from the interface and the interactions to the conditions for value co-creation (Kimbell, 2011; Meroni & Sangiorgi, 2011). Earlier work in service design that created a foundation for this also touched on activity theory and systems perspectives (Sangiorgi, 2004; Sangiorgi & Clark, 2004). Materials that were highlighted in this view were, among others, experiences, assemblies of relations, business models and mediated action (Kimbell, 2009).

An example that amalgamates multiple views is how Clatworthy (2013) approached the issue in his dissertation, with an experiential point of view but also focusing on interactions. He described service experiences through the lens of brand, service personality and how meaning is transformed to be experienced through touch-points. In this way, perceived and expressed meaning become materials of service design, and the service designer is viewed as transforming meaning into material.

A short backdrop and nod to design

Throughout the growth of design since the nineteenth century, design has been touching on topics about the design material, the material that designers engage in forming. Just as in art and the art world, there is a 'design world' with its institutionalised structures, norms and approaches to breaking and maintaining design and the design world, that can be used to understand what kinds of conversations and radical shifts are possible. Some of these discourses within design have relevance for how materials and objects of service design can be understood. For example, the Swedish design pioneer Ellen Key developed the idea about how purpose and beauty were connected, although asymmetrical. This can be understood as Key suggesting that purpose, the offering or meaning if you will, is what designers should spend more effort forming: 'Be it ever so useful, each man-made thing must, like each beautiful thing in nature, serve its purpose with simplicity and ease, with delicacy and expressivity, or it will not have achieved beauty. Thus though utility is a prerequisite for beauty, beauty does not guarantee utility' (Asplund et al., 2008, p. 34; Swedish original Key, 1899).

The debates during the twentieth century around form and function touch on similar issues, certainly if function is seen as something immaterial, and form something material. Another Swedish design pioneer wrote in the 1950s about how products are servicing people (Hård af Segerstad, 1956). Similar suggestions and discussions can be found in many other places, of course.

Later, the design process movement balanced between other categories as the focus for forming: object and process, solution and problem, as well as problem definition and problem framing. Two design fields developing during the last decades of the twentieth century that contemporary design owes a lot of intellectual development to are interaction design and participatory design. Apart from the connections made between interaction design and service design, on for example material and aesthetics, in the paper by Holmlid (2007), the two fields provide several connected concepts and foundational theories for service design (Gaver, 1996; Löwgren & Stolterman, 1998; Hallnäs & Redström, 2006; Nordby, 2011). Worth mentioning is what was called contextual design, with its roots in the late 1980s, that highlighted the need to work with the physical surroundings, systems of artefacts, as well as with culture, as part of and objects of design work (Holtzblatt & Beyer, 1997). When it comes to participatory design, with its early focus on forming workplace democracy, central questions were highlighted on what it meant to work with material design practices in cooperative settings (Greenbaum & Kyng, 1991; Binder et al., 2011). Questions as to whether the object of design should be the material outcome of the design process or should be about use before use and design after design were raised (Ehn, 2008; Redström, 2008). Through these two fields the materials of design were given an expanding frame that service design directly or indirectly heavily relies on.

The object(s) of service design

There have not been many design research texts dedicated explicitly to service as a material, even though some hints were given in some earlier papers (Holmlid, 2007; Blomkvist et al., 2016). Two interesting pieces of work that focus on the object of service design come from Secomandi and Snelders (2011) and Kimbell and Blomberg (2017).

Secomandi and Snelders identify the concept of the service *interface* as the main object for design efforts. The interface they claim includes tangible as well as intangible elements, and are in themselves heterogenic. They also identify a couple of other concepts coming from service marketing and management that are relevant to service design, such as exchange relations, interface and infrastructure and materiality. These support their general concept about service as manifested through an interface.

Kimbell and Blomberg cast a wider net around research disciplines to also include participatory design, systems design and science and technology studies. They identify three approaches to understand the object of service design: the service encounter, the value co-creating system and sociomaterial configurations. There is an increasing complexity from the service encounter to sociomaterial configurations, but the approaches are not mutually exclusive. With the former approach, the materials become the interactions, the touch-points, the servicescape and other aspects that are close to the people in the service. The latter approach highlights materials such as participation, engagement and other aspects that are dependent on and form the social fabric of service.

The materials of service

Even though designers use different kinds of representations, such as customer journey maps or actor maps, to materialise some understanding of a current service, or to visualise a suggested future service, they at the same time know that this is not the way the service works, or how it will be in the future. Many of the things in those maps are beyond the competence of the designer to work with or design. And everyone also knows that some of what seems to be already designed will not be done in that way in reality, because the actors in the situation will make in situ decisions that are better informed than the designer. The kind of design work using such materialisations is there to open up the possibilities for multiple actors to contribute in designing the future frames and possibilities for a new or improved service. In many senses, this creates a design situation very similar to those in the rich tradition of Scandinavian participatory design, where the design object could be for example co-determination or citizen empowerment, which was achieved through engagement in transformation processes, supported by enactments and material explorations.

As a starting point, it has to be established that there is no service until it happens. Before this it is merely preparations and something conceptual. The hotel is an architectural manifestation that embodies some of the spatial preparations for a hotel stay. The service offering is conceptual in relation to the later service experience, be it ever so material in its presentation. A service, or the service system, becomes material in the moment. Which means that the final design decisions of any service are made in the service situation. This is fundamental and every service designer knows this, but not all service organisations recognise it. Moreover, the final design is made not only by the providing actor, but by each actor of the service system in co-creation, even those that are not part of a specific service moment. There are connections over time and spaces, as well as transcending time and space. The consequences of this are far-reaching for designing and designers, which also will be touched upon later in the book. What are the materials that are under the forming power of the designer and what materials are under the forming power by others? How are these materials being made and made available in and for designing? At what points in time does the forming of certain materials play different kinds of roles in the distributed designing that service design is? How can and should we as designers direct our efforts in designing? How can designing be seen in terms of before and after, that is, design before design and design after design, and how does the knowledge-intensive design practice relate to those in service design?

Two perspectives on service as a material can give directions for design. The first, service as situated action, is rooted in activity theory and advanced cognitive science. The second, collaborative and deliberate resource integration, is rooted in service research. Some of the questions above will be discussed in the following two sections.

Service as situated actions

It is not controversial to claim that there can be no service unless there are humans involved.[1] Nor that it is their actions situated in time, space and

---

[1]   Two more observations connected to this are: (1) there are no all-digital services, and the probability that there will be such services in a near- or medium-range future is close to 0; and (2) in some areas 'human

context that constitutes service. Through the years the idea of what service 'is' has meandered, and currently the idea of value co-creation in a system is dominant. However, this high-level idea suffers from a vague conceptualisation of 'value' as well as a vague conceptualisation of 'co-creation'. Focusing on service as *situated action* is one way of getting closer to reality, and to find materials that can be made part of designerly forming and manipulation.

Approaching service as situated actions means caring about the everyday activities of persons in a setting, with all its richness of actors, artefacts, knowledge, social relations, practices, values, norms and institutions (Suchman, 1987; Lave, 1988). In these situated actions multiple actors are engaged in joint or collective action, directed by objects/objectives and mediated by artefacts or regulations (Wertsch, 1981; Kuutti, 1991; Engeström, 1993). An important consequence of this is that a service does not have a user or users, only actors that participate and contribute to value creation. Some of the artefacts in the situations will have users, but not the service per se.

In service situations, activities are performed jointly, or collectively. There is a net of actors, or system of actors if you will, that are engaged in the situated actions. Actors here refer to actual people, rather than the more abstract entities sometimes referred to, such as an organisation or type of organisation.[2] The people involved will embody the abstract entities in the situations through actions. That is, a meeting between a patient and a doctor is as much a meeting between two individuals as a meeting between institutionalised categories, and they are often tightly embedded in other relations on which the situated action depends. It is not uncommon to use the idea that the right actor should be in the right place at the right time. But, what does 'right' mean in such a statement? In a situated action perspective, also the situated actions are connected in one or several systems. What is 'right' then will not only be determined in the particular situation, but also by differences between actors, for example in value perspectives and logic, by the structure of the actions, and by the pluralistic objectives of the actors joining. Under a certain logic, meeting specialist after specialist in a chain of healthcare meetings is considered 'right', while under another logic, meeting all specialists upfront is 'right'.

---

in the loop' is a concept, in a service setting it may be more meaningful to think in terms of 'machine in the loop', as the basis for value creation is that there is a human that understands and can assess and have intentions about values and their creation.

2   However, in the more abstract view, the conception of a system of actors is still valid. A recent view is that the minimal system consists of three actors, connected in a transitive or intransitive triad, and not the dyad from traditional marketing (Kowalkowski et al., 2016).

For service design, the materials related to situated actions come in at least two categories: (1) the materials that equip the actors in the situated action with the knowledge, resources and mandates to jointly move towards pluralistic objectives; and (2) the materials that equip designing with the capability of contributing to transforming a service system.

An example of the former could be collected from situated learning (Lave & Wenger, 1991). Each actor has their own practice, professional or everyday, and each of them enters the situation with their general and practice-based knowledge, and knowledge from their own process before the situation. Few of them will know what the others know, but there will be preconceptions between actors. In each particular situated action, they are all becoming what is called 'legitimate peripheral participants' in each other's practices. The doctor does not become the patient, or vice versa, but the doctor will be a peripheral participant in the everyday practice of the patient. The materials here would be the understanding of these relational conditions, the making of peripheries and legitimate participation. Moreover, the resources they use should support them both being professional practices in their own right Another manner of thinking is to view the situated actions from the lens of action nets (Czarniawska, 1997; Lindberg & Cziarnawska, 2006). Action nets are the actions that require interdependent actors (formal as well as informal) in joint action to achieve outcomes. Action nets can be seen as the ongoing organising, the forming, the stabilisation and the dissolving of actors, organisations and actor networks. From a design material perspective the processes of forming these action nets are important. That is, for each situated action, there will be formed an action net, and the capability of actors to take part in this forming will in turn be a design material. Some of these action nets will be institutionally pre-formed, and therefore open for breaking and maintenance (Wetter-Edman et al., 2018). Some of the action nets will be partly populated with actors that can be presumed, and partly actors that emerge in the forming of the action net. Some of these, the presumed or the emergent, would be actors that actively steward the forming of the action net. Some of the action nets will mainly be populated by actors based on the outcomes sought. For example, in the case of midnight football (Ekholm & Holmlid, 2020; Holmlid et al., 2021), the joint forming and maintenance of the action net around the football activity is of absolute importance to the success of the social entrepreneurship as well as the societal objectives.

An example of the latter, equipping designers with transformational power, is the concept of action space (Rodrigues et al., 2021). Action space refers to a particular actor's possibilities to act in situations. This includes the actor's knowledge, the mandate assigned to the actor, the processes and relations within which actors act, the resources the actor can activate in a situation and the capability of the actor to reshape action space. By reshaping action spaces, the interstices and interactions between action spaces, designers can contribute to the transformation of service systems. From a situated action point of view, it does not make sense to see each of the aspects as individual materials, but instead view them either as interdependent parts of the material 'action space', as something that can be formed, or as tools that are shaped, through for example design, that in turn form the material 'action space' and thus through their power of tools will contribute to transforming service systems. Another example comes within the context of creating inquiry into and within service systems, and the many different materials that design equips itself with to achieve these. These often materialise as design tools, where experiential and aesthetic knowledge is central. The former is dominant in for example design probes (Gaver et al., 1999) and design games (Vaajakallio & Mattelmäki, 2014), while the latter is dominant in for example aesthetic disruptions (Wetter-Edman et al., 2018).

Given all these perspectives on situatedness, one can view situated action as *making*, and the actors as *makers*. That is, the service, in whatever definition one fancies, is under making. This making is done in the situation, using resources that are materialised in and through action and action nets in emergence. When successful, the making is done where it matters, where values are supported, and where the sought effects are fulfilled. With a critical, or constructive, point of view, the making is done in a material world, where there is envy, consumerism, capitalism, etc., creating possibilities as well as frictions. Some acts of making will follow patterns and some will have formal procedures, but there will be a lot of room for different kinds of improvisation. When approaching service as making in situated action, one important set of materials for service design will be the structures, resources and conditions for such making, such as organisation, collaboration, mandates and improvisation skills.

Service as collaborative and deliberate resource integration

In addition to situated action, focusing on *resource integration* gives another perspective of materialities of service (Maglio & Spohrer, 2008). In service we assume that resource integration is done in collaboration or even in collectives. The resources integrated are operand as well as operant resources (Constantin & Lusch, 1994). That is, resources such as material, time, tools, knowledge, processes, norms, etc. are made available in a situation for integration. That is, only resources we know of, and believe are important for the situation, we will make available; other resources may be withheld from sharing (deliberately or not), and some resources will be shared without us knowing it, such as norms (Vink & Koskela-Huotari, 2021).

Resource integration could be seen as a subset of situated action, in the sense that resource integration is actors doing things together, collaboratively. Holmlid (2012) described a case where the Customs Office was in conversation with an importer of goods, in order for their customs declaration to be correct. They were integrating their different knowledge resources about what goods were to be imported with knowledge resources of what codes needed to be on the declaration form, with a regulatory process of declaring goods, etc. The case also showed that by changing the call-in structure, from a direct line to a sector specialist for the specific importing companies to a general line for companies from any sector, the integration of both actors' knowledge resources was demoted.

The material that is manipulated are the acts of resource integration, by manipulating who is participating in the integration activity and what resources they have at hand to share. These actions are collaborative and deliberate, rather than anything else. In the case above, at least one can say that had resource integration been in focus as a material, one would have been able to expect longer calls and less satisfied clients.

Sharing resources and integrating them does not happen by itself, though. Service isn't just made, or doesn't just happen to you. Resource integration must be done deliberately by people. There is a deliberate choice of selecting resources to be shared, and deliberate choices made on when to share the resources and with whom. There is also a deliberate choice to utilise a resource shared by someone else. The material here is the resources in themselves, but also the reflective knowledge of the individual to understand their own resources, when and how to share them, and their attitude and skill to understand these things in relation to other people. Resource integration as a material, then, also concerns the relational and reciprocal. Or, put more radically, reciprocity is the material, that is formed by designing possibilities for resource integration, and manipulated by the actual acts of resource integration. With reciprocity also comes mutual dependence; resource integration creates a dependency between actors. The material also becomes the organisation, structural support and mandate that allow for resource integration and the necessary improvisation in service situations.

A trivial example is a visit to any institution where the visitor has limited or unstructured knowledge, and the professional that the visitor is meeting is knowledgeable with structured knowledge, such as a visit to a library, museum, or primary health-care centre. The visitor may ask a question, based on unstructured knowledge, and the professional answers with a follow-up question, to get an understanding of what the visitor knows and at the same time move value creation forward.

The collaborative and deliberate acts of resource integration are connected to each other in intricate structures. Blomkvist et al. (2016) provide an example where 'phrases' are used as a way of describing structure. This opens up for material concepts such as timing and rhythm to be used. The Storybraid tool (Holmlid, 2018) focuses on service moments as systems, and maps the processes that each actor has been involved in before coming to that specific service moment, showing how resource integration in the different service moments are intricately structured and (dis)connected. This opens up for working with knowledge and knowing as a material, what actors know, or need to know, before they enter into a resource integration activity, and what they know after being in the activity. Or, flipping the design work a bit, what knowledge is needed in the different service situations in sequence to make for a well-designed service. This idea was also captured in the service information canvas tool (Holmlid & Björndal, 2016), where we explore what different actors know about an external event at specific points in time.

Resource integration materialises in the activity and acts of resource integration where the resources that people have are key; where the intricate structures of connections between integration, resources and actors give form to activities; where relations, reciprocity and collaboration are formed; and where knowledge of the actors is shaped before and through resource integration.

As designers, we only have access to certain aspects of this very rich material, and even when doing cooperative design, the possibilities of forming and shaping the material have to focus on designing for resource integration. The actual resource integration happening in the service will in the end be a situated creative act of knowledge and reciprocity.

Conclusion

Service as a design material has taken on many guises and conceptualisations. Here, the main focus has been on situated action and collaborative resource integration, and these are also proposed as the main frames for understanding service as a material in service design. This view is closely related to materials being systemic, and to the two approaches of value co-creating systems and sociomaterial configurations.

A consequence for the understanding of materials in service design is that there are materials that are manipulated and formed in design situations but, given the nature of service, there are also activities of forming and making in the actual service situations. The forming of materials in the service situation are sharp-end design activities that ultimately distinguish between a service that is well designed and one that is not. As a consequence, the materials and design activities in the design situations should aim towards making those sharp-end design activities possible and possible to do well. Apart from the specifics of situated action and collaborative resource integration, the relationship between materials of the design situation and the service situation is one way of reflecting over the materials in Part 2; is this material part of the design situation, and how does that relate to the materials and forming in the service situation?

References

Asplund, G., Creagh, L., Kåberg, H. & Lane, B.M. (2008). Modern Swedish design: three founding texts/by Uno Åhrén, Gunnar Asplund, Wolter Gahn, Ellen Key, Sven Markelius, Gregor Paulsson and Eskil Sundahl; edited and with introductions by Lucy Creagh, Helena Kåberg, and Barbara Miller Lane; essays by Kenneth Frampton. New York: Museum of Modern Art.

Berry, L. L. (1983). Relationship marketing. Emerging Perspectives on Services Marketing, 66(3), 33–47.

Binder, T., De Michelis, G., Ehn, P., Jacucci, G., & Linde, P. (2011). Design things. Cambridge, MA: MIT Press.

Blomkvist, J., Clatworthy, S., & Holmlid, S. (2016). Ways of seeing the design material of service. In Service Design Geographies, 125, 1–13.

Clatworthy, S. (2013). Design support at the front end of the New Service Development (NSD) process: The role of touch-points and service personality in supporting team work and innovation processes. The Oslo School of Architecture and Design.

Constantin, J. A., & Lusch, R. F. (1994). Understanding resource management. Oxford: The Planning Forum.

Czarniawska, B. (1997). Narrating organizations: Dramas of institutional identity. Chicago: University of Chicago Press.

Czepiel, J. A., Solomon, M. R., & Surprenant, C. F. (Eds.). (1985). The service encounter: Managing employee/customer interaction in service businesses. Lexington books.

Edvardsson, B., Gustafsson, A., & Roos, I. (2005). Service portraits in service research: A critical review. International Journal of Service Industry Management.

Ehn, P. (2008). Participation in design things. Participatory Design Conference, Bloomington.

Ekholm, D., & Holmlid, S. (2020). Formalizing sports-based interventions in cross-sectoral cooperation: Governing and infrastructuring practice, program, and preconditions. Journal of Sport for Development, 8(14), 1–20.

Engeström, Y. (1993). Developmental studies of work as a testbench of activity theory. In S. Chaiklin and J. Lave (eds), Understanding practice: Perspectives on activity and context (pp. 64–103). Cambridge: Cambridge University Press.

Erlhoff, M., Mager, B., & Manzini, E. (1997). Dienstleistung braucht Design: Professioneller Produkt-und Marktauftritt für Serviceanbieter. Munich: Luchterhand.

Fisk, R. P., Brown, S. W., & Bitner, M. J. (1993). Tracking the evolution of the services marketing literature. Journal of Retailing, 69(1), 61–103.

Forlizzi, J. (1997). Designing for experience: An approach to human-centered design. Master's thesis, Carnegie Mellon University.

Forlizzi, J., & Ford, S. (2000). The building blocks of experience: An early framework for interaction designers. Proceedings of the 3rd Conference on Designing Interactive Systems: Processes, Practices, Methods, and Techniques, 419–423.

Gaver, B., Dunne, T., & Pacenti, E. (1999). Design: Cultural probes. Interactions, 6(1), 21–29.

Gaver, W. (1996). Affordances for interaction: The social is material. Ecological Psychology, 8(2), 111–129.

Greenbaum, J. & Kyng, M. (1991). Design at work: Cooperative design of computer work. Hillsdale: Lawrence Erlbaum Associates.

Grönroos, C. (1988). New competition in the service economy: The five rules of service. International Journal of Operations and Production Management, 8(3), 9–19.

Grönroos, C. (2006). Adopting a service logic for marketing. Marketing theory, 6(3), 317–333.

Gummesson, E. (1990). Service design. TQM Magazine, April.

Gustafsson, A., & Lervik-Olsen, L. (2018). The past, present and future of service marketing: From understanding quality to understanding customers. In A. Sasson (ed.), At the forefront, looking ahead: Research-based answers to contemporary uncertainties of management (pp. 251–266). Oslo: Universitetsforlaget.

Hallnäs, L., & Redström, J. (2006). Interaction design: Foundations, experiments. Borås, Sweden: University College of Borås.

Hård af Segerstad, U. (1956). Tingen och vi [The objects and us]. Stockholm: Nordisk rotogravyr.

Holmlid, S. (2007). Interaction design and service design: Expanding a comparison of design disciplines. Nordic Design research conference, Nordes 2007, Design Inquiries.

Holmlid, S. (2012). Designing for resourcefulness in service: Some assumptions and consequences. In S. Miettinen & A. Valtonen (eds), Service design with theory (pp. 151–172). Rovaniemi: Lapland University Press.

Holmlid, S. (2018). Storybraids: Material exploration of a service system visualization technique. Proceedings of PIN-C.

Holmlid, S., & Björndal, P. (2016). Mapping what actors know when integrating resources: Towards a service information canvas. In Service Design Geographies, 125, 544–550.

Holmlid, S., Ekholm, D., & Dahlstedt, M. (2021). Practice occludes diffusion: Scaling sport-based social innovations. In A. Tjønndal (ed.), Social innovation in sport (pp. 57–77). Cham: Palgrave Macmillan.

Holtzblatt, K., & Beyer, H. (1997). Contextual design: Defining customer-centered systems. Amsterdam: Elsevier.

Key, E. (1899). Skönhet för alla: fyra uppsatser [Beauty for all: four essays]. Stockholm: Bonnier.

Kimbell, L. (2009). The turn to service design. In Julier, G. and Moor, L. (editors), Design and Creativity: Policy, Management and Practice, (pp.157–173). Oxford: Berg.

Kimbell, L. (2011). Designing for service as one way of designing services. International Journal of Design, 5(2), 41–52.

Kimbell, L., & Blomberg, J. (2017). The object of service design. Designing for Service: Key Issues and New Directions, 27, 20–34.

Kowalkowski, C., Kindström, D., & Carlborg, P. (2016). Triadic value propositions: When it takes more than two to tango. Service Science, 8(3), 282–299.

Kuutti, K. (1991). Activity theory and its applications to information systems research and development. In H.-E. Nissen (ed.), Information systems research (pp. 529–549). Amsterdam: Elsevier.

Lave, J. (1988). Cognition in practice. Cambridge: Cambridge University Press.

Lave, J., & Wenger, E. (1991). Situated learning: Legitimate peripheral participation. Cambridge: Cambridge University Press.

Lee, K. (2012). Hospitality service as science and art. Touchpoint, 4(1), 26–31.

Lindberg, K., & Czarniawska, B. (2006). Knotting the action net, or organizing between organizations. Scandinavian Journal of Management, 22(4), 292–306.

Lovelock, C., & Gummesson, E. (2004). Whither services marketing? In search of a new paradigm and fresh perspectives. Journal of Service Research, 7(1), 20–41.

Löwgren, J., & Stolterman, E. (1998). Design of information technology–material without qualities. Lund: Studentlitteratur.

Maffei, S., Mager, B., & Sangiorgi, D. (2005). Innovation through service design. From research and theory to a network of practice. A user's driven perspective. Joining forces, University of Art and Design Helsinki, September 22–24.

Maglio, P. P., & Spohrer, J. (2008). Fundamentals of service science. Journal of the Academy of Marketing Science, 36(1), 18–20.

Meroni, A., & Sangiorgi, D. (2011). Design for services. Farnham: Gower.

Nordby, K. (2011). Between the tag and the screen: Redesigning short-range RFID as design material. Oslo School of Architecture and Design.

Normann, R. (1983). Service management. New York: Wiley.

Normann, R., & Ramirez, R. (1993). From value chain to value constellation: Designing interactive strategy. Harvard Business Review, 71(4), 65–77.

Pacenti, E., & Sangiorgi, D. (2010). Service design research pioneers: An overview of service design research developed in Italy since the '90s. Design Research Journal, 10(1), 26–33.

Parker, S., & Heapy, J. (2006). The journey to the interface. London: Demos.

Redström, J. (2008). Re:definitions of use. Design Studies, 29(4), 410–423.

Rodrigues, V., Blomkvist, J., & Holmlid, S. (2021). A designerly approach to exploring disruptions in service: Insights from employing a systems perspective. International Journal of Design, 15(3), 61–72.

Sangiorgi, D. (2004). Il Design dei servizi come Design dei Sistemi di Attività. La Teoria dell'Attività applicata alla progettazione dei servizi. PhD dissertation, Disegno Industriale, Politecnico di Milano.

Sangiorgi, D., & Clark, B. (2004). Toward a participatory design approach to service design. Artful Integration: Interweaving Media, Materials and Practices, Participatory Design Conference, Toronto, 27–31 July.

Secomandi, F., & Snelders, D. (2011). The object of service design. Design Issues, 27(3), 20–34.

Shostack, G. L. (1977). Breaking free from product marketing. Journal of Marketing, 41(2), 73–80.

Shostack, G. L. (1982). How to design a service. European Journal of Marketing, 16(1), 49–63.

Suchman, L. (1987). Plans and situated actions. Cambridge: Cambridge University Press.

Vaajakallio, K., & Mattelmäki, T. (2014). Design games in codesign: As a tool, a mindset and a structure. CoDesign, 10(1), 63–77.

Vargo, S. L., & Lusch, R. F. (2004). Evolving to a new dominant logic for marketing. Journal of Marketing, 68(1), 1–17.

Vink, J., & Koskela-Huotari, K. (2021). Social structures as service design materials. International Journal of Design, 15(3), 29–43.

Wertsch, J. (ed.). (1981). The concept of activity in Soviet psychology. Armonk: M. E. Sharpe.

Wetter-Edman, K., Vink, J., & Blomkvist, J. (2018). Staging aesthetic disruption through design methods for service innovation. Design Studies, 55, 5–26.

Zeithaml, V. A., Parasuraman, A., & Berry, L. L. (1985). Problems and strategies in services marketing. Journal of Marketing, 49(2), 33–46.

5 Cultural bodies empowered to perform services: a critical perspective

Yoko Akama and Cameron Tonkinwise

Authors' note: We invited Yoko and Cameron to provide a critical perspective on the materials of service design, and we include it here in the book to transition towards service design and service materials.

The materiality of service design lies with the people involved in service interactions. Services are people's daily jobs, things that structure their lives, roles they play when collaboratively creating value. Services are experienced through bodies, from the fingers and eyes that trace lines around screens to the weary legs that have hurried along train station platforms to get to a store before closing. Services are maintained by bodies that clean sheets, that fetch a heavy object, that respond politely to rude requests so that they can avoid poor reviews.

Before proceeding, we offer two notes about materiality.

The first is a philosophical point about materiality. What does it mean for something to be material? It is hard to ask this kind of question because the answer seems to lie in rapping your knuckles on a table (Edwards et al., 1995). This is the point, though. The materiality of a material lies in the resistance it offers, the force with which it pushes back, holding its shape, or allowing itself to be reformed into only some shapes but not others (see Miller et al., 2005; Ingold, 2007). Materials make their presence felt through bodies, and bodies are themselves material. Sometimes, non-physical things like an idea or a memory can transfix us, guiding what we do. In these cases, those attitudes and feelings have a kind of material force; they are a matter of concern for us (Latour, 2008), constraining our bodies and giving form to how we act.

The second related point is that designers manipulate materials to create overall affects. The materials they select and the form they give them, as well as the context in which a product will be used, will have a particular quality, by design. For an industrial designer, that affect has been called the product's character (Janlert & Stolterman, 1997); for a fashion designer, it is the outfit's style; for the interior designer, a space's atmosphere (see Griffero, 2017; Sumartojo & Pink 2018). These overarching qualities are, strictly speaking, immaterial, especially as they are in part subjective experiences that are hoped for in the users of the designs. Nevertheless, done well, these qualities should have a presence that endures and can be felt, that resists change and even orients or directs the people experiencing them.

Services have a formable materiality, qualities that can be designed to resist change, an overall affect that gives form to the bodies that perform those services. Interaction design has started to document several qualities that can be evaluated as part of the atmosphere or style of an interactive domain (Bardzell, 2009; Löwgren, 2009; Mõttus & Lamas, 2015), and the situation is related for service design. In summary, services are sociomaterial, but where that term in science and technology studies (Star & Ruhleder, 1996; Suchman, 2000) tends to foreground the social aspects of the material, in service design, the term should perhaps more signal the material aspects of social interactions.

In this chapter, we wish to describe elements of the sociomateriality of services, and show how service designers must negotiate their ethics and politics (Butler, 1993; Costanza-Chock, 2020).

Bodies

It is one thing to design a service hypothetically; it is quite another to get people to perform the service as 'designed', meaning with intended outcomes. If the essence of a service is the interactions that happen between people, those immaterial interactions are undertaken by material bodies. Those bodies will be required to fit more or less well with what they are being paid and asked to do, and that level of fit can be sensed by all involved, contributing to the particular material quality.

The French sociologist, Pierre Bourdieu (1987), argued that society involves people making evaluations of each other via correlative factors. A central evaluation judges a person's level of cultural capital. The working hypothesis is that people of one particular cultural class (a measure not just of wealth but also level of education) like similar kinds of things across different categories of consumption (e.g., food, music, sport, books, etc.). If someone enjoys something in one area of life, like their musical taste, that requires some expense, but more importantly, some knowledge, to enjoy (for example, nineteenth-century Italian opera), then that person will most likely enjoy things of similar expense and knowledge in other areas – Michelin-star restaurants, political biographies, etc. In so doing, he explains how unconscious stereotypes work, especially when based on appearance and limited understanding. Bourdieu makes the point that being in society means we ungenerously develop a capacity to 'read' and classify other people. These classifications structure interactions to tacitly influence which strangers at a function would be pleasant to talk to, which person in a street to ask for directions from and who to sit or stand next to on crowded public transport (especially when concerning safety).

Bourdieu argues that these correlative judgements also apply to people's bodies: not just their dress style, which should be a strong indicator of their wealth and cultural capital, but also their posture, movements and body language. It is, according to Bourdieu, possible, and an important part of how our societies function, to discern manual workers from office workers; and among the latter, people who play a team sport for leisure from those who prefer gardening or reading.

Services makes explicit use of these Bourdieu-like judgements of 'distinguishing'. The functional version is hiring people to perform physical work whose bodies appear to evidence their capabilities. There is then 'aesthetic labour' (Warhurs et al., 2000) – hiring someone to do a job because their body and the way they carry and fashion themselves fits with the brandscape of the service. 'Do sexy flight attendants really sell more seats?' quips a CNN reporter on seeing worrying patterns of how women are hired and advertise for airlines (Ramy, 2013).

These judgements always involve stereotyping. Bourdieu's argument is that we can unfortunately be observed making these kinds of discriminatory judgements all the time, often without thinking. It is ethically problematic (an implicit bias if not explicit prejudice, whether racism, sexism, ableism, classism, etc.), and we will always get it wrong – how often have we used pronouns, ignorantly, in this way? This is precisely the point we want to make. Service designs call on bodies to perform roles, to present themselves in particular ways that allow the service experience to proceed smoothly, as expected.

All of our social existence involves negotiating the many roles we are expected to play in everyday interactions – think of the effort that goes into choosing the right attire for a job interview. Service provision might involve extensive bodily learning and adjusting – becoming skilled at balancing several plates through a crowded restaurant, or at voice modulation and ways of speaking when working at a call centre. Over time, a service provider's body might itself be restructured by the skilled work they provide. Bourdieu argues that it is often possible to read somebody's work from the way they carry their body, even when not in the uniform of their job – to pick who at a party is a nurse or an architect or a politician. These are the material effects of services.

Power

A key dynamic in any service relation is power. Traditionally, to be of service is to be subservient; to be a servant to, if not a slave of, some master. These days service designers are hopefully designing services that allow more equal relations between all involved. However, in any service there will always be someone with a need and someone with the capacity to help with fulfilling this need. The way these differences are communicated to facilitate service interactions is part of the materiality of services.

Consider, for instance, the power dynamics of a professional service; the service provider is an expert to be accorded status even though they are there to help the service recipient. In a non-professional commercial context, a service worker, such as someone in a retail store, tries to be of assistance, but can do so when the customer asks for help, providing the right kind of information at the right time. In either case, power is dynamic, changing hands as the service unfolds.

Service designers might use particular material touchpoints, such as uniforms or visually communicated instructions, to help service recipients and deliverers negotiate that power dynamic. A service designer can materialise those power dynamics in ways that feel fixed or fluid. A service's atmosphere can be designed to signal that roles can shift and change depending where in the service you are, or what kind of service request you need. A service that shows that interactions have been modified in the past – one that signals through interior design that it is open to dialogue and that the organisation providing the service is not time-pressed – would create an atmosphere of power negotiability; whereas a service that makes its history of consistent service evident – that has solid fixtures as part of its servicescape and that involves standardised greetings – creates a structured atmosphere. Either could be a pleasant service to engage with, as long as you (whether service provider or recipient) know how to behave, given the material style of the service's feel. The overall affect associated with the servicescape and flow of the service would materially afford or disafford renegotiation of the roles in the service.

Power dynamics of any situation are felt and manifest in bodies; someone's posture and voice, for example, will signal their status, but also whether they are comfortable playing that role. Service designers have to pay attention to the material consequences of how services are structured, and should be guided by deeper understandings of the sociocultural conditions that services are nested within.

Emotions

Emotional labour is a term coined by Arlie Horschild to describe when a service worker is being paid not only for their skills at servicing customers, but also for delivering the service with a specified mood. These moods are defining of the materiality of a service, that is, the aesthetics of service, how it feels to be a part of it. Hochschild notes that emotional labour requires a high level of skill. Emotional labour refers to three different things:

1. Emotional self-control: the requirement that a service worker leave their personal life and its emotions at home when commencing work.
2. Emotional performance: the requirement to adopt a particular demeanour while working, irrespective of particular service interactions with customers.
3. Emotional intelligence: the ability to read the emotions of customers and interact with them in ways that manage them into more productive interactions with the right temperament.

In strictly managed services, service workers are often directed through rituals before beginning work that aims to cultivate 'the right' emotional attitude. Removing personal clothing and putting on a uniform is a way of getting service workers to divest themselves of their personal life before taking up their role in the performance of a service. These acts put them in a service 'frame of mind' before commencing work. Less prescriptively, service designers can signal various emotional ranges that are considered appropriate for a service. These mood settings can make use of what social psychologists refer to as 'ensemble perception' (Whitney & Yamanashi Leib, 2018). Similar processes can be designed for customers to dispose them appropriately to the service before the service interaction commences, like anticipating long queues. This would reduce the emotional labour required of the service worker by ensuring that the service recipient is sharing those interpersonal requirements.

There is clearly an overlap between issues of emotional labour and how empowered that person feels with respect to how the role is performed. Service workers can sometimes feel empowered by having a restricted role to perform without the need for emotional labour requirements. To leave your complicated personal life behind for a while and engage in service work can be liberatory if the work can be done routinely, without having to negotiate the emotional demands for customised service delivery. This is the power of the disempowered to say: 'I am afraid I am not allowed to do that' or 'Hey, this is just a job for me'. Or, in another direction, it can be entertaining for someone to role-play being someone other than they are, performing emotions that they do not necessarily feel (Hochschild (2003 [1983]) calls it 'surface acting').

Culture

Our discussion of Bourdieu indicated, insensitively, that the materialities of a service quality are cultural. We mean this in the sense of organisational culture, but there will always be a relation between this and the habits and values of the places and communities where services are being offered. We emphasise this because to design a service is usually to assume that existing cultural ways of people helping each other are in need of improvement. The quality a service designer materialises as a service will either build on those existing norms of collaboration (power, and demeanour toward those you may be obliged to service or will be obliged to after they help you) or attempt to be separate from them, a site with its own particular power and demeanour. Service designers need to be very attentive to local cultural practices, and ignore or change them with great care and responsibility.

This means service designers taking account of their own bodies and cultures, their own materiality. The service designer's positionality is frequently scrubbed out of service design research reporting, in an attempt to achieve universality, neutrality and purity (Akama, forthcoming). We must foster cultures of service designing that do the opposite, encouraging designers to build critical awareness of their own positionality: what habits, values and expectations about being of service materially structure their own ways of working?

References

Akama, Y. (forthcoming). Reciprocities of decay, destruction and designing. In S. Heitlinger, M. Foth, & R. Clarke (Eds), Designing more-than-human smart cities: Beyond sustainability, towards cohabitation. Oxford University Press.
Bardzell, J. (2009). 'Interaction criticism and aesthetics'. Proceedings of the SIGCHI Conference on Human Factors in Computing Systems.
Bourdieu, P. (1987). Distinction: A social critique of the judgement of taste. Harvard University Press.
Butler, J. (1993). Bodies that matter: On the discursive limits of 'sex'. Routledge.
Costanza-Chock, S. (2020). Design Justice: Towards an intersectional feminist framework for design theory and practice. Proceedings of the Design Research Society.
Edwards, D., Ashmore, M., & Potter J. (1995). Death and furniture: The rhetoric, politics and theology of bottom line arguments against relativism. History of the Human Sciences, 8(2), 25–49.
Griffero, T (2017). Quasi-things: The paradigm of atmospheres. Suny Press.
Hochschild, A. R. (2003 [1983]). The managed heart: Commercialization of human feeling. University of California Press.
Ingold, T. (2007). Materials against materiality. Archaeological Dialogues, 14(1), 1–16.
Janlert, L.-E., & Stolterman. E. (1997). The character of things. Design Studies, 18(3), 297–314.
Latour, B. (2008). Powers of the facsimile: A Turing test on science and literature. In S. J. Burn & P. Dempsey (Eds), Intersections: Essays on Richard Powers (pp. 263–292). Archive Press.
Löwgren L. (2009). Toward an articulation of interaction esthetics. New Review of Hypermedia and Multimedia, 15(2), 129–146.
Miller, D., Meskell, L., Rowlands, M., Myers, F. R., & Engelke, M. (2005). Materiality. Duke University Press.
Mõttus, M., & Lamas, L. (2005). Aesthetics of interaction design: A literature review. Proceedings of the Mulitimedia, Interaction, Design and Innnovation, 1–10.
Ramy, I. (2013). CNN travel report. http://edition.cnn.com/travel/article/asia-flight-attendants/index.html.
Star, S. L., & Ruhleder, K. (1996). Steps toward an ecology of infrastructure: Design and access for large information spaces. Information Systems Research, 7(1), 111–134.
Suchman, L. (2000). Located accountabilities in technology production. Centre for Science Studies, Lancaster University. www.comp.lancs.ac.uk/sociology/papers/Suchman-Located-Accountabilities.pdf.
Sumartojo, S., & Pink, S. (2018). Atmospheres and the experiential world: Theory and methods. Routledge.
Warhurst, C., Nickson, D., Witz, A., & Cullen, A. M. (2000). Aesthetic labour in interactive service work: Some case study evidence from the 'new' Glasgow. Service Industries Journal, 20(3), 1–18.
Whitney, D., & Yamanashi Leib, A. (2018). Ensemble perception. Annual Review of Psychology, 69, 105–129.

PART 2

THE CONSTITUENTS OF WHICH SOMETHING IS COMPOSED

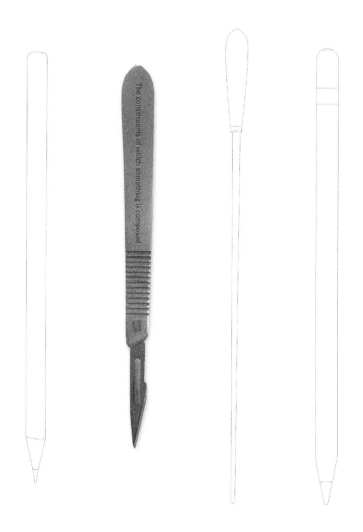

Introduction to Part 2

This is Part 2 of the book where we start with a recap of the previous part and a primer for the contents of this part. That content consists of suggestions for what the material in, of or for service is, and why it matters for design. We like to see this as the beginning of a library of materials in service design, much like other design disciplines have their own material libraries. In total there are 18 materials suggested by different authors. The materials you will see are based on a symposium held in September 2021 where service design researchers and practitioners were invited to 'pitch' materials for consideration and discussion. Each author or pair/group of authors are introduced in the beginning of the respective chapters. We also have three interludes based on interviews with leading service design thinkers and doers, where the issue of service materiality is discussed in a freer format.

1   Introduction to a library of materials

Previously in the book we examined definitions of material and broadened our focus from giving form to matter to also include aspects of individuality, meaning and material as a collection of competences. We start this part of the book by summarising some of the main takeaways from the previous part and by priming for what is to come. Most of all, however, this part of the book is about service materials and you will read about many different suggested materials of interest for people working with service. In other words, we are going to explore the constituents of which something is composed. We begin with a look back at making that something an object of study.

One of the starting points in making something the object of study was to look at other design disciplines and their relation to materiality. Based on that, we suggested that materials are used in other design disciplines as a way to invent, and that 'forming' materials can be seen as a means for understanding material affordances. Not only this, but also the exploration-through-forming approach is broadly conceptual in nature and requires a high degree of representation and mediation to succeed. From this, it is clear that to explore the materials of the situation it is not forming the material directly that is key, but instead forming the final outcome that the material manipulation affords. This has relevance for service design and amongst other things highlights the focus on representations, simulations and prototypes as a means of material exploration, perhaps in greater detail than we do now.

From material of invention to material of innovation?

It seems, therefore, that we need to focus less on the material and more on what the designer wishes to achieve through the conversations that take place with material. Manzini[1] talks about the material of invention, and moving into 2024 we would probably term that the material of innovation. However, the key element that makes Manzini's book so interesting is his focus on the creative impulse to explore the possible and to match it to the doable. It is this creative dance that he explains is core to design, especially as new materials appear – how the designer can expand on the possible with the materials now at hand. This has great relevance to service design. It is also supported by the movement towards immateriality in art, in which the focus is on finding new ways of expressing something through the materials of the time, and in a new way. Whether we call the materials of service design 'immaterials', 'intermaterials', 'neomaterials' or 'hypermaterials', we need to view them as being part of the designer's drive to expand the possible and to explore the context and constraints that make this possible. Thus, material is viewed in this book as being related to the possible in its context.

A need for material awareness

From the definition of material, service designers need to have an understanding of how they use and relate to materials as part of their design process (forming), as a specification (e.g. touch-point journey map) and as a competence (the service designer's repertoire). We consider these three dimensions to be of interest and valuable for the future discourse, since they help us understand and perhaps further develop the field of service design. In many ways, it might seem obvious to discuss and categorise service design in terms of process, specification and competences. However, it is a reflection on the field at present that this view does not exist but is called for. Perhaps it is time now for service design to look at itself and summarise best practice within each of these three areas.

The importance of materialisations of existing and future states

A further aspect worth discussion is how service designers use materialisations of immaterial aspects of service during the design process as representations. These can be toolkits developed specifically for a project context, or generic toolkits, or ready-mades that are supposedly applicable to all of service design. These strategies for manifesting service are something that characterise service design, and can be seen as both a way for the designers themselves to explore a situation but also as the development of boundary objects as part of a co-design process. Upon inspection, it seems that the service designer oscillates between material and immaterial representations of

---

1   Manzini, E. (1989). The material of invention. MIT press.

the same things, moving between the abstract (immaterial) and the concrete (material). The different moves in service design are between the actual and the represented. This can be described as 'traversing a virtual cleft' in which something in the world is virtualised using visualisation techniques. We end up with a tangible surrogate of a service, or some aspect of a service. When we do something with the surrogate it can be seen as a move back across the virtual cleft and trying to say something about what reality we want the service to exist in. Perhaps this is the conversation with the materials in a service context? Instead of trying to make a strict division between tangible and intangible we could talk about the transitions, traversing and translations between them. This can, in turn, be a way to discuss the techniques, the competences required to work with them (including the repertoire) and the output in terms of the actual resulting material.

A need for a service design terminology around materials

There is a need to further develop a vocabulary and a discourse around materials in service design, which goes beyond trivial tangible design specifications. Well-designed touch-points are important for service, but are not in themselves the key to understanding service as a material for design. Not only experiential aspects of time and collaboration become integral, but also how agents, resources, institutions and integrative actions interact to form service. Service designers form aspects of the material to result in a rhythm, tempo, intensity, phrasing, etc. But also aspects such as how initiative is structured, how power is shared and distributed and levels of engagement. Instead of focusing on instants, we could focus on pluralistic value creation, dynamic integration of evolving resources as well as actors as resourceful interpreters of assumed service.

Service as a material may be difficult to grasp as a concept. It might seem illogical to devote a whole book to the material of the immaterial. However, we feel that by starting to articulate how service is manifested in design work and in service co-creation, we may form a starting point to go beyond reductionist ideas of the material–immaterial dichotomy, and open up new constructivist perspectives.

A suggested way to view materials in service design

To summarise, and move on to the next part of the book, we have developed a summary set of characteristics that could be used to discuss materials in service design. It is presented here as a way to help the reader view the following content and to be an aid in reflection and discourse around materials in service design. In this book, materials are therefore viewed in the following way:

1. Materials of service design and service are worthy as an object of study.
2. Exploring materials in design is a way to invent and innovate. This is likely also true when considering invention and innovation in service.
3. The recognition that something is a design material allows it to be consciously formed.
4. The materials in service design have an affordance for the designer, and identifying this affordance can unleash its innovation potential.
5. Materials in service design and service are related to the designer's context and change over time.
6. Identifying, forming and representing the materials of service are part of the service designer's repertoire.
7. The way a designer identifies, forms and represents the materials of service are key to giving a service its individuality.
8. Forming the materials of service design and service often requires representation, mediation and discourse at the conceptual level.
9. The materials of service design in some situations need to be described in a service performance context and are therefore highly experiential.
10. In many situations the designer is not forming the situation at hand, but forming materials for a future situation. The service designer is therefore not only forming immaterials, but also forming immaterials for a future situation that can be far removed from the forming context.
11. Actors in service situations should also be understood as doing design work, although not the same kind of work as schooled designers are doing in development or transformation processes. Now, start over at 1, and read the statements with the actors as designers in service situations.

Starting the material library

As mentioned earlier, this part of the book is dedicated to service materials. Our intention with this part is to initiate a library of service design materials that hopefully can inspire, challenge and provoke you as a reader. In total, different authors have proposed 18 materials that are important for the design of service. The materials as a whole are by no means intended to be an exhaustive list, but instead have been included to illustrate the richness and complexity of service as a design material. At the same time, the list is a snapshot of current thinking about materials in service design and the starting point for a more complete library. Finally, the list helps us further our own, and hopefully the field's, understanding of materiality, and what it means for service design.

In light of the previous part of the book, we suggest that you consider the definitions of the word material when reading the list, and subsequent chapters about each material. The definitions show how broad the term material is and how much can be included. We also suggest you recall the questions from the representation chapter (Part 1, Chapter 3) and think about how you might come across these materials as various representations during a design project. The questions are:

- Is this material a representation in itself?
- How should this material be externally represented?
- When do the representations of this material occur, and are they internal or external?
- What does this mean for service design competencies?

Another thing to keep in mind is perhaps what materials are missing that you find important. The list of materials gives us an idea about the breadth of materials and associated skills that are relevant in service design. For the purpose of the book, it also provides a way to analyse what it means to work with service as a design material. Furthermore, you might start to find connections and similarities in the texts and form categories or clusters of materials. In the subsequent part of the book we will analyse and show our attempts at categorising the materials. We hope you find this set of materials as exciting as we did, and if you feel like sharing we have a companion website where we collect materials, descriptions or examples of their use and much more (servicedesignmaterials.ep.liu.se).

The materials are presented in random order, with interludes from various service design thinkers and doers. The structure of this part looks like this:

1. Introduction
2. Social structures
3. Touch-points
4. Thinking
5. Culture

2 Social structures

Josina Vink
Institute of Design, The Oslo School of Architecture and Design (AHO)
Josina explores how people intentionally transform service ecosystems, especially as it relates to health and care

Kaisa Koskela-Huotari
Department of Marketing and Strategy, Stockholm School of Economics
Kaisa studies change in social systems and the role of innovation, service design and market shaping in these processes.

Patterns in our social activities provide order and predictability in society. These entrenched patterns, called social structures, guide people in their actions and interactions with each other. For example, the basic unit of the family is made up of many entangled social structures, including shared norms, roles, rules, values and beliefs (shown in Figure 2.2.1). One common role in families is that the adults assume responsibility for the care of children. There are also often rules that regulate who is considered to be family according to ancestry, marriage or adoption.

Social structures are fundamental to service design in two ways. First, these patterns in our actions and interactions are what service design is working to intentionally shape. In other words, social structures are a central material of service design (Vink et al., 2021). This is the case both when the outcome of a service design process reflects a tangible change (e.g., new product or adapted servicescape) or an intangible change (e.g., novel practice or reconfigured service system). Second, the process of service design itself is guided by social structures internalised by the people participating either directly or indirectly (Vink & Koskela-Huotari, 2022).

MAKE THE INVISIBLE VISIBLE

Source: Illustration by Erin McPhee, Creative Commons Public License CC BY 4.0.

Figure 2.2.1   Social structures in a family

Characteristics of social structures as service design materials

Social structures as service design materials have several characteristics that are important for service designers to understand (Vink & Koskela-Huotari, 2022). First, enduring social structures are often highly invisible to people who have internalised them. People perceive them as 'natural' (Voronov & Yorks, 2015) and they easily remain unquestioned (Berger & Luckmann, 1967). For example, the roles of a mother and father are often taken for granted and understood as natural in Western society.

Another characteristic of social structures is their dual nature as both simultaneously intangible and tangible. This means that the more intangible aspects of social structures are brought to life through tangible interactions. In this way, symbols, artefacts, activities and relations are both shaped by the intangible aspects of social structures, such as rules, norms and beliefs, and carriers of them (Scott, 2014). For example, the physical symbol of a family tree that is often used to chart family relationships is an enactment of the entrenched roles and possibly the rules governing who takes what name in family structures.

Social structures are also composed of multiple institutional pillars and, therefore, take many forms, including codified laws, informal social norms and cultural-cognitive meanings (Scott, 2014). Legally enforced structures, such as rules and regulations around marriage, are the most explicit and work to create order and expedience. Less explicit are the normative structures, such as norms and roles around who should do what tasks in a household, that create social expectations about appropriate behaviours in certain situations. And least explicit of them all are the cultural-cognitive structures, such as beliefs and frames about what it means to be a family, that create a shared understanding and meaning.

Service design as shaping social structures

When service design practitioners acknowledge social structures as their design materials, shaping these structures becomes their core activity. Intentionally shaping social structures is not easy due to the above characteristics, but it is possible. As a starting place in this process, in order to avoid simply reproducing social structures in service design, people (both designers and other participants in the process) need reflexivity – an awareness of existing social structures (Vink & Koskela-Huotari, 2022). Building reflexivity in order to intentionally shape these materials is similar to how a carpenter must mill the wood from the tree into usable boards before working with it to build furniture. For example, if people are working to redesign a child welfare service, an awareness of many of the taken-for-granted social structures guiding family interactions is a critical starting place.

While there are methods explicitly aimed at developing reflexivity (Vink et al., 2021), many other service design methods have affordances that enable people to build reflexivity in different ways (Vink & Koskela-Huotari, 2022). For example, people can build awareness of the social structures within families by engaging in bodily experiences like bodystorming or roleplaying a family dinner. These methods can be purposefully used to support three essential processes through which people build reflexivity: revealing hidden structures, noticing structural conflict and appreciating structural malleability. Each of these processes is essential for working with social structures as service design materials.

With some level of reflexivity, people can then engage with the reformation of social structures in service design. Reformation, sometimes referred to as institutional work, involves purposefully creating, disrupting and maintaining social structures (Lawrence & Suddaby, 2006). For example, when redesigning a child welfare service, it may involve creating a new role for a support service worker, challenging narrow, normative ideas of what it means to be family and maintaining meaningful beliefs about what it means to care for children. Although reformation involves changing social structures, it also requires actors to intentionally maintain existing social structures in order to build legitimacy and ensure that the change is not too abrupt.

Reformation occurs by strategically altering the physical enactments of such social structures (Vink et al., 2021). It can include symbolic work that leverages symbols, identities and language to influence social structures; material work that crafts the physical artefacts of environments to advance social outcomes; and relational work that guides interactions to support social ends (Hampel et al., 2017). For example, when redesigning child welfare services, it may include shifting the interactions between the social worker and parents to build trusted norms of support. It is critical to know that this service design process involves a feedback loop and, once something is altered, reflexivity is needed to thoughtfully examine the consequences of such changes to inform further reformation efforts.

Implications

Recognising social structures as service design materials stresses the importance of social structure literacy for service designers, but also for people in general. We argue that a focus on social structures as service design materials directs the focus of service designers toward building the reflexivity of the collectives they work with and within, such as building the awareness of internalised social structures of both people working in a child welfare agency and the families themselves, so that they can more intentionally shape the social structures influencing their lives.

Furthermore, this recognition suggests that service designers have an important role in guiding the messy, often conflictual process of reformation within multiple, overlapping service systems. By leveraging service design methods and other local approaches, service designers can help others to understand and navigate conflicting structures and enable intentional, collective adaptation that is mindful of unintended consequences.

We firmly believe that without recognising social structures as central materials, service design risks reproducing a superficial approach to change that ignores complex and change-resistant contexts. In addition, we believe that there is also a political and ethical imperative for attending to social structures as a focus on designing without mindfully attending to the social and cultural context has great potential to perpetuate harm.

Attending to social structures as service design materials implies both being norm-critical, which involves challenging social norms that contribute to inequity, and being norm-creative, which involves leveraging design to strategically counteract such norms (Nilsson & Jahnke, 2018). Furthermore, it highlights the importance of service design practitioners paying acute attention to intersectionality, which acknowledges the multiple, interlocking axis of power and discrimination across social structures, and focuses efforts on reshaping the arrangements of intersecting social structures to liberate those who are most marginalised (Crenshaw, 1989). The recognition of social structures as materials puts in focus the centrality of power and politics in the process of service design and opens up for more intentional collective action to shift inequitable power dynamics.

Further reading

To support this effort of working with social structures as design materials, we have been working on a collection of academic papers that can be used resources.

For greater depth on social structures as design materials and processes for attending to them, you can read:

Vink, J., & Koskela-Huotari, K. (2021). Social structures as service design materials. International Journal of Design, 15(3), 29–43.

For inspiration on experimental designerly approaches and design principles for supporting reformation and reflexivity, check out:

Vink, J., Wetter-Edman, K., & Koskela-Huotari, K. (2021). Designerly approaches for catalyzing change in social systems: A social structures approach. She Ji: The Journal of Design, Economics, and Innovation, 7(2), 242–261.

To inform how to more purposefully leverage existing service design methods for building reflexivity, look into:

Vink, J., & Koskela-Huotari, K. (2022) Building Reflexivity Using Service Design Methods. Journal of Service Research, 25(3), 371–389

For a more conceptual understanding of how service design relies on shaping social structures within value-creating systems, take a look at:

Vink, J., Koskela-Huotari, K., Tronvoll, B., Edvardsson, B., & Wetter-Edman, K. (2021). Service ecosystem design: Propositions, process model, and future research agenda. Journal of Service Research, 24(2), 168–186.

References

Berger, P. L., & Luckmann, T. (1967). The social construction of reality: A treatise in the sociology of knowledge. New York: Anchor Books.

Crenshaw, K. (1989). Demarginalizing the intersection of race and sex: A Black feminist critique of antidiscrimination doctrine, feminist theory and antiracist politics. University of Chicago Legal Forum, 139–167.

Hampel, C. E., Lawrence, T. B., & Tracey, P. (2017). Institutional work: Taking stock and making it matter. In R. Greenwood, C. Oliver, T. B. Lawrence & R. E. Meyer, eds, The SAGE handbook of organizational institutionalism, 2nd ed. (pp. 558–590). Thousand Oaks, CA: SAGE.

Lawrence, T. B., & Suddaby, R. (2006). Institutions and institutional work. In S. R. Clegg, C. Hardy, T. Lawrence & W. R. Nord, eds, The SAGE handbook of organization studies (pp. 215–254). Thousand Oaks, CA: SAGE.

Nilsson, Å. W., & Jahnke, M. (2018). Tactics for norm-creative innovation. She Ji: The Journal of Design, Economics, and Innovation, 4(4), 375–391.

Scott, W. R. (2014). Institutions and organizations: Ideas, interests, and identities. Thousand Oaks, CA: SAGE.

Vink, J., & Koskela-Huotari, K. (2022) Building Reflexivity Using Service Design Methods. Journal of Service Research, 25(3), 371–389.

Vink, J., Koskela-Huotari, K., Tronvoll, B., Edvardsson, B., & Wetter-Edman, K. (2021). Service ecosystem design: Propositions, process model, and future research agenda. Journal of Service Research, 24(2), 168–186.

Voronov, M., & Yorks, L. (2015). 'Did you notice that?': Theorizing differences in the capacity to apprehend institutional contradictions. Academy of Management Review, 40(4), 563–586.

3   Touch-points as a material

Simon Clatworthy

Oslo School of Architecture and Design (AHO)
Simon works at a design school and tries to understand what makes a service experience memorable and how to design for this.

In the following text I combine touch-points and the journey as an integrated whole. To me, they are inseparable, but I cannot find a good term for this combination.

Touch-points are points of contact between the customer and the service. They occur as interactions along a customer (or user) journey, and the designer works with the choice and design of touch-points to achieve goals of usability, utility and desirability for the customer, and viability and feasibility for the provider.

The service designer works with touch-points at an individual level and with the orchestration of multiple touch-points along the customer journey. The whole service cannot be seen without consideration of the individual touch-points and vice versa. This relates to the commonly used term of touch-point orchestration and how service designers work with the whole and the parts (zooming in and zooming out).

Description and characteristics of the material

Touch-points are usually but not always things the user will interact with (such as a website or app, or a person). They are also things the user might react to, such as an email confirmation, signage in a store or hospital, etc. The degree of dialogue with a touch-point therefore varies.

Touch-points often have physical form, so in many ways they are the constituents of service that are closest to the traditional designer competences (industrial design, graphic design, etc.). Due to their increasingly digital component, interactive design is increasingly important.

Service providers mostly have control over their touch-points during design and delivery. That means the designer can choose to introduce a touch-point and develop its characteristics and behaviours and its position along the customer journey. However, the user may or may not follow this once the service is launched.

There are also touch-points that the company does not control. In airlines, for example, security screening is a touch-point that the airline does not have control over, nor do they have control over the design of the airport itself, the parking/train journey to the airport, etc. Indeed, in such situations, an airline struggles to be able to experientially differentiate itself. There are other

Figure 2.3.1   This example shows a representation of a letter as a touch-point, using the AT-ONE touch-point cards. The choice of this image is to show representations of touch-points, and also that a touch-point can 'go out of fashion' (how many of us receive letters these days?). Utilising a little-used touch-point, such as a letter, can now be a potential source of innovation. During the past United States election, personal letters were sent to swing voters by democrats and had an unexpectedly high response rate compared to emails

touch-points that the company does not control, such as social media, a consumer review or word of mouth. In this case the company can design the service to support these touch-points such that they give a positive outcome, but they cannot control it.

There are again other touch-points, such as natural phenomena – weather, a view, sunshine, etc. – that the designer may take account of. Here the designer is most likely forming a touch-point to create a desirable experiential outcome based on recognition of the natural phenomena, e.g., positioning a room and windows in relation to a particular view.

Touch-points are part of the whole service delivery and can be evaluated in relation to the expected customer experience, the development costs, the logistics of the service, the human resources implications, return on investment, etc. The strength of the touch-point and customer journey combination is that it allows the analysis and evaluation of the service from multiple perspectives, and not just from a design perspective. The designer might be focused on the experiential outcome of a service, but the journey/touch-point combination allows a 360 degree view from all participants of the project team. This makes the touch-point journey combination central to not only service design and co-design but also to service innovation.

Material transformation or forming

Individual touch-points can be categorised as having particular advantages or disadvantages, e.g., a telephone conversation can be characterised as a dialogue material, whilst an SMS might be considered reactive rather than interactive. A person in a shop is often chosen because of their humanness, or put another way, for being human. The designer orchestrates touch-points with an intention to give a particular and desired service experience. So, whilst individual touch-points can be categorised with particular characteristics, I don't think that touch-points as a whole can be identified as having specific characteristics.

Due to the fact that working with touch-points has relevance for all stakeholders in a project, they are ideally suited to co-design, often facilitated by the designer. In this way, the designer also functions as a facilitator, a design manager and an orchestrator.

Touch-points are formed throughout the design process, and also during service provision through interactions in use. The designer's role is mostly at the start of the design process, since service design predominantly works in the first diamond of the double-diamond design process (Almkvist, 2017). The service designer typically has responsibility for touch-point choice and position in the journey, whilst other design disciplines will often (and later in the process) develop the detail.

The process can be seen as a generic service design activity tailored to project context. The inputs are the almost infinite number of touch-points and journey step combinations that may be used for a project. The outputs are a series of touch-points, positioned in time along one or more journey(s). However, this is to simplify what occurs during touch-point orchestration and the touch-point design process is a true design synthesis of multiple factors (user needs, brand strategy, technological possibilities, technical platforms, organisational capabilities, etc.) specific to a project context. In this way, the touch-point synthesises multiple project goals during orchestration.

What does your material represent and how does it represent it?

An interesting thing about touch-points is that the representation of touch-points can form a description of what is, what could be and can also be a key part of a specification (the service blueprint). If we think of a blueprint as being a specification that is detailed enough to allow somebody to make the service, then touch-points are key to this.

Touch-points (and the journey) are also both a representation during design (for example, on a journey map or blueprint) and the final designed objects themselves. Touch-points are central to the customer experience and can be considered a proxy representation of the experience during the design process.

Is it a good representation or does it lack something?
What is the role of the designer?

Existing representations of touch-points are adequate for many projects. These representations are typically pictograms of the touch-point or photographs. However, sometimes they might be generically represented, and their individuality could go missing when placed in context on a journey map or blueprint. The experiential could be developed more in terms of experiential journeys.

Competences needed to work with the material

The service designer needs to have competence in multiple disciplines to be able to design with touch-points. The major competence is that of design synthesis. Connected to this are forming competencies such as product design, visual communication, interaction design, etc. Others relate to organisational design, system architecture and human resources.

Further, the designer needs specific expertise in journey design and visualisation, blueprinting and roadmapping to be able to summarise and specify touch-points in a project. Abilities in facilitation and co-design are key.

It may be that service designers will develop competence in the dramaturgic aspects of a customer journey and experience of time-based media are likely to become important in service design.

The specific competencies mentioned above are a core competence for service design and highly skills-based. I expect in the future that we will see specialisations in touch-point design, ranging on one axis from functional to experiential, and on another from analogue to digital (or tangible to intangible). The type of touch-point focus will most likely be related to the type of service design education being provided.

Reference

Almqvist, F. (2017). The fuzzy front-end and the forgotten back-end: User involvement in later development phases. The Design Journal, 20(sup1), S2524–S2533.

4 Thinking: an underexplored service design material

Rike Neuhoff, Luca Simeone and Lea Holst Laursen
Aalborg University
The authors explore how to foster sustainable and equitable futures through service design.

When reflecting about service design materials, it comes to mind that not all of them are physical materials that you can take into your hands and mould. For our part, we are intrigued by thinking – immaterial, intangible and invisible in its nature; powerful when properly navigated, yet potentially destructive when left unchallenged or going astray.

Background and characteristics of the material

When designing services, our thinking is inevitably confronted with similarly paradoxical questions: How can we find a common denominator between the polarised views of the actors involved in a service? How can we ensure that end-users nestled within their habits and routines will embrace the disruptions envisioned by an innovative service? And, in a broader view: How can we design services that meet our current needs without reducing the chances that future generations can do the same? These questions are paradoxical, tough choices, the space between the rock and the hard place, and no tool can manage away the tension that is underlying them.

Complexity is rooted within paradoxes and tensions (Smith & Lewis, 2011). Service design often engages in contexts characterised by complexity – be it urban, organisational or healthcare systems – and is consequently bound to face paradoxes and tension. Abundant research underscores the importance of our thinking's ability to effectively integrate paradoxical demands and balance the associated tensions in order to thrive in complexity (Gaim & Wåhlin, 2016). That complexity, if not well managed, can be destructive, overwhelming or paralysing (Smith & Lewis, 2011) has not escaped the attention of service design, and a great deal of effort has been put into the exploration of adequate ways to come to terms with it (e.g., Morelli, 2006). However, how our thinking can be supported when confronted with paradoxes or tensions has not yet been at the forefront of service design research. As such, we believe that service design should more deliberately consider thinking as a material to engage with during the design process.

Thinking as a material in design

The meaning-making dimension of design has long been explored (Krippendorff, 2005); the way in which design artefacts are perceived and interpreted unfolds through semiotic plays and meaning-brokering activities. The visual design of a corporate logo invites consumers to think that the company believes in some specific values. The grandiosity of a presidential palace makes the passer-by think about the power held by the dictator of that autocratic country. The flawless user experience of a banking app makes the end-users think that their bank is trustworthy. Yet, it is within service design and, particularly, with regard to the idea that service value is co-created (Lusch & Vargo, 2014) that thinking becomes an essential material to consider. The process through which services come to life – thanks to the coordinated activities of service providers, partners and end-users and thanks to an alignment of their beliefs, dispositions and motivations (Morelli et al., 2021) – is strongly hinged on the way in which all these actors think. Thus, much more so than in other fields, service design has developed an array of methods that can help consider thinking as a material of the design process: lanes dedicated to what the users think while crossing different touch-points are added to user journeys (Stickdorn & Schneider, 2012); motivation matrices foresee desires, interests and incentives of the actors involved in a service (Morelli & Tollestrup, 2007); and service walkthroughs as theatrical representations of services promote embodied and situated knowledge about what actors think and feel while experiencing a service (Blomkvist & Bode, 2012).

Leveraging thinking across paradoxes and tensions

What remains underexplored is the way in which thinking can be conceptualised (and leveraged) in relation to paradoxes and tensions. We believe that design, given its influence on driving change in the world, holds a particularly great responsibility to deliberately reflect on thinking, how it relates to and arises from paradoxes and how it determines what kind of design is being put out into the world. After all, we must acknowledge that design has contributed to a world that, in many ways, is less than ideal (Papanek, 1973). Thinking, though, should not be limited to the idea of actual thinking in the sense of conscious, predominantly rational thinking but just as well to emotional, unconscious and embodied thinking (Kahneman, 2021). It is the combination of both that determines how we perceive and relate to the world around us, and eventually how we plan to reshape it. Common views regard thinking as an abstract concept that goes beyond what is physically observable. Yet, we believe that we can come to experience thinking, that thinking occurs in relation to our feelings, to our emotions, that it is bodily and somatic and that it can therefore be experienced bodily.

Navigating thinking through service design

In terms of methods and approaches, service design may strive at fostering more relational approaches that prioritise reflections about how one's thinking relates to those of others, and to how we intend to shape the world. We can experiment with futuring techniques as a way to think more freely and creatively, imagining futures that integrate competing viewpoints and desires

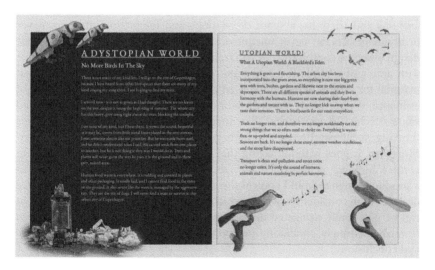

Figure 2.4.1   Juxtaposition of two scenarios that illustrate dystopian and utopian futures scenarios

as to recognise that those demands can and ought to co-exist. Since management theory has long studied paradoxes and tensions, we should draw from these findings and be inspired, for example, by how to make visible paradoxes and tensions using maps as sense-making tools (Johnson, 2014). Service design should strive to resist quick fixes and facilitate the deliberate search for diverse views, support practices to listen attentively and stage activities that challenge our assumptions.

In Figure 2.4.1, we provide an example of futures scenarios created in a service design workshop that depict the participants' thinking in response to a series of design methods. While these scenarios are pure speculation, they are a means to reveal to us the participants' inner world, namely their present fears and desires regarding the future. The scenarios came into being through reflective conversations in which the participants realised that one actor's dystopia may show strong resemblance to another actor's lived reality. In this case, participants reflected that the species extinction addressed in the dystopian scenario is, in fact, already very advanced for some species, thereby exposing them to the concept of contradiction and paradox.

Final thoughts

Working with 'thinking' as a material means to bring into being a space of tensions and frictions, a space of relations and interactions that are never firmly definable and never unequivocally comprehensible. While we cannot design away the complexity, we can train our thinking to become comfortable with ambiguity. While the deliberate consideration of thinking as an actual material for service design implies an expansion of the discipline's sphere of influence, it also points towards the need for an awareness of the increased value attached to approaches that integrate insights from co-design, futures thinking, social psychology and management in an interdisciplinary manner. Moreover, it goes without saying that the service designer does not aim to control thinking – a material that is reactive, complex, animated and alive – as a product designer would control the shape of a piece of wood. Still, service designers can consider the way in which service actors think as a material that can be potentially navigated towards novel directions enabling it to be open towards seemingly conflicting perspectives as to synthesise new knowledge and conclusions.

References

Blomkvist, J., & Bode, A. (2012). Using service walkthroughs to co-create whole service experiences. www.ida.liu.se/~johbl52/WalkthroughFullPaper.pdf.

Gaim, M., & Wåhlin, N. (2016). In search of a creative space: A conceptual framework of synthesizing paradoxical tensions. Scandinavian Journal of Management, 32(1), 33–44.

Johnson, B. (2014). Polarity Management: Identifying and Managing Unsolvable Problems (2nd ed.). H. R. D. Press.

Kahneman, D. (2021). Thinking, Fast and Slow. Penguin.

Krippendorff, K. (2005). The Semantic Turn: A New Foundation for Design. CRC Press.

Lusch, R. F., & Vargo, S. L. (2014). Service Dominant Logic: Premises, Perspectives, Possibilities. Cambridge University Press.

Morelli, N. (2006). Developing new product service systems (PSS): Methodologies and operational tools. Journal of Cleaner Production, 14(17), 1495–1501.

Morelli, N., & Tollestrup, N. (2007). New representation techniques for designing in a systemic perspective. Design Inquiries, Nordes 07 Conference.

Morelli, N., de Götzen, A., & Simeone, L. (2021). Service Design Capabilities (Vol. 10). Springer International Publishing.

Papanek, V. (1973). Design for the Real World. Bantam Books.

Smith, W. K., & Lewis, M. W. (2011). Toward a theory of paradox: A dynamic equilibrium model of organizing. Academy of Management Review, 36(2), 381–403.

Stickdorn, M., & Schneider, J. (2012). This Is Service Design Thinking: Basics, Tools, Cases. John Wiley & Sons.

5   Culture as a material

Claire Dennington and Simon Clatworthy
Oslo School of Architecture and Design (AHO)
Both authors have a design school background and have a shared interest in how
culture influences service experience.

We suggest culture as a material for service design, particularly popular
culture. This is because culture has always influenced design and design has
always influenced culture. However, in service design, the influence of culture
has been missing from the core service design toolbox.

Design historians place designed objects into periods of design styles and these
styles are influenced by the culture from which they have emerged. In 1948,
Raymond Loewy redesigned the Gestetner copy machine, and started what
was to become known as the streamlining style. In the 1980s, Philippe Starck
radically redesigned the citrus juicer for Alessi, and created a product that
is often used to define the post-modern Alessi style. Jonathan Ive designed
the iconic iMac in translucent plastic, and ushered in a period of translucent
plastic products for the home and office, all with a boiled sweet aesthetic. All
of these examples are described as iconic products, icons of their time and a
reflection of the 'zeitgeist'.

We would like this also to be recognised and practised as part of service design.
If you read the core course books within service design, culture is conspicuous
by its absence. This does not mean that culture is absent from service design,
rather that it is not consciously part of it. We think it would be healthy for
service design to be influenced by culture and to influence culture (e.g., see
Figure 2.5.1). We would like to see discussions about style in service design
and trends in service design and to see a recognition for iconic service design
solutions.

In this description we focus on popular culture, since this is often used to
innovate offerings in the market. This is not to ignore broader culture, or
organisational culture, which can also be important materials for service

Source: Conflict Kitchen.

Figure 2.5.1   The Conflict Kitchen in the United States only serves food from countries that the United States is in conflict with. It reflects a culture of conflict and the demonisation of people from the culture that a country is at war with

design. Popular culture has come to be understood as the expression and circulation of shared popular meanings, texts and practices (Barker & Jane, 2016), where meaning construction is interlinked to lifestyle choices and consumption. Storey (2018) notes how we use and interact with the material forms of popular culture, such as books, iPhones, clothes and restaurants, to communicate aspects of our identity. He considers how 'popular culture is not just people acting and interacting, it is people acting and interacting with material objects and material objects interacting with each other' (Storey, 2018, p. 238).

Popular culture is in flux, meaning that trends continually need to be read and translated, offering potential for innovative new services. This has been shown to be successful in services that show alignment to the zeitgeist – an 'interpretation of pulses in the spirit of time' – and that this alignment enhances the emotional connections to the user (Campos & Gomez, 2016). Trends also contribute to an understanding of popular aesthetics and styles that contribute to frame and communicate meaning. By continuously identifying and analysing trends, the service designer can develop an ability to view larger societal, economic, political and ecological movements. This can contribute in developing an understanding of the context of the user and uncover emerging needs and shifting values.

Cultural material can, in a service design perspective, be described as a meaning-laden extract from culture that can be formed into a service. A successful translation of culture into a service could be considered to be a service that customers desire due to its meaning, materiality and social practices. Today, strong cultural themes might be related to the environment, multiculturalism, a move from owning to renting, etc.

How is the material 'formed' by design?

The designer explicitly or implicitly works to identify culture, particularly cultural trends, and the underlying meanings that they represent. These are then translated into a service in some way. This is termed a semantic transformation, and our research shows that the service designer completes a triple semantic transformation during the design process (Dennington, 2018). These three transformations are:

1. translating cultural inputs into concise descriptions of the underlying meaning;
2. translating this meaning into a culturally relevant service offering; and
3. translating the concept into culturally informed touch-points and a journey.

In this way, culture informs service design through both the whole and the parts.

The majority of the semantic transformations occur early in a project, since the cultural influence impacts the service offering and therefore often requires consistency throughout the service. There is also a brand relevance to the semantic transformation. The forming is therefore tailored to the context of each project since the cultural positioning of each organisation is different.

What does your material represent and how does it represent it?

In popular culture, the material of culture is often represented through style. Style is traditionally described in terms of visual form and this can easily be applied to service design through the choice and design of touch-points. However, in service design, style can be described as also encompassing the personality of the service, the behaviours during interactions and the tone of voice. Together, these can be said to describe the style of the service, and these become evident during the customer journey. However, as we have already

Source: Undo Insurance.

Figure 2.5.2   As an example of culturally informed touch-points, the Danish insurance service Undo reflects a culture of youth, smart technology and on-demand insurance (the travel insurance uses location to charge based on destination and time away from Denmark). It does this by, for example, using 'bad' but relatable images and an informal tone of voice

mentioned, culture also influences the offering itself in terms of a culturally relevant value proposition.

The representation of culture during the service design process has not taken a default form within service design. At present, we have been using what we term as the stylistic journey as a way of representing how culture is translated to the service as a whole and in parts (Dennington, 2018). This is in many ways a direct use of a mood board with a focus on the customer experience. The cultural representation has to be inferred from such a mood board in terms of whether it is a good or poor translation of culture into service. The stylistic journey highlights the experiential aspects of the cultural translation using a mix of images and text. However, it is a direct translation of the mood board from other design fields and perhaps misses the behavioural, time-based and tone-of-voice aspects of a service (e.g., see Figure 2.5.2). We would like to explore the stylistic journey in video form as a way of introducing time, sound and transitions. The stylistic journey is a description and a high-level concept description that gives the feel of the service. It does not specify detailed inter-actions, but rather a target experience that should be present in the whole and the parts of the service.

Competencies needed to work with culture as material

These are typical design competencies that are present in most aesthetically oriented design studies. One key aspect is that the designer has to have a cultural lens with which to view the world. This cultural lens needs to be developed.

The translation of popular culture into service requires a good understanding of relevant popular culture, together with the ability to synthesise this, together with organisational history and brand strategy into a strong concept that can be both feasible and viable. So, strong synthesis skills are needed, together with the ability to communicate the resulting culturally driven concepts.

We believe that all service designers should have competence for considering culture in service design, and we would like to see it increasingly become visible within service design processes and tools.

Final thoughts and reflections

One final reflection is the degree to which public services can use culture as a material. There seems to be a pattern that public services do not generally relate to popular culture and we would like to see public services using a cultural lens more often. As an example, public services have been slow to pick up and use the trend towards the environment. We see huge potential for new public services which enable better use and reuse of resources and where the public service takes the initiative for the multi-actor collaboration needed to make them a reality.

References

Barker, C., & Jane, E. A. (2016). Cultural studies: Theory and practice (5th ed.). London: SAGE.

Campos, A. Q., & Gomez, L. S. R. (2016). Memes and symbolic interactionism: A new approach to trend research and design. The Radical Designist.

Dennington, C. (2018). Trendslation: An experiential method for semantic translation in service design. ServDes2018, 18–20 June, Milan (pp. 1049–1063). Milan: Linköping University Electronic Press.

Storey, J. (2018). Cultural theory and popular culture: An introduction (8th ed.). New York: Routledge.

Interlude 1: Materiality in design from a practitioner perspective: interview with Markus Edgar Hormeß, Adam Lawrence and Marc Stickdorn (26 April 2022)

Markus Edgar Hormeß

Partner, WorkPlayExperience

Markus is a leading expert and author on service design and strategic prototyping and co-initiator of Global Service Jam.

Adam Lawrence

Partner, WorkPlayExperience

Adam has worked in psychology to automotives to theatre to design, is a specialist in facilitation, an author and co-initiator of Global Service Jam.

Marc Stickdorn

Co-founder and CEO of Smaply

Marc is a service designer with a background in strategic management and design research and the main author of the This Is Service Design Thinking/Doing/Methods series.

What is the material of service?

Marc: I have a problem with the word material. For me, material is something in the physical world and in service design we often work with immaterial things. But I don't have a better word …

Markus: We are in service design, why do we even have to start with material? And there is still a bias if we look at what is often presented at conferences, there are a lot of visual stuff. Because of what design has traditionally been there is a tendency to make contributions in the form of visualisations. There is a history of that, and that is what a lot of people are good at but looking at the list of materials in this book we can see that service design is much broader than that.

Adam: Materiality can also refer to how important something is, so how physical do things need to be to be material? I often refer to service design as the craft or craftpersonship of emotion. This is what design has in common with theatre or psychology. Design is about organising physical and digital things to make people feel a certain way. So the question is how to arrange the world in order to make people feel safe or motivated or any other emotion, but the emotions that designers work with are immaterial, they are both intangible and implicit.

Why do we need to ask the question about materiality?

Marc: Asking the question about materiality in service design is a sign of maturity. If we compare with other disciplines such as UX [user experience] design, where similar thinking led to the emergence of design systems for instance. This discussion in service design could lead in a similar direction. If we have a clear idea about the things we use to design and what the things we actually design are, then we can also think about libraries of those things. Libraries could be specific to types of organisations, types of industries.

Adam: The idea of patterns and libraries is interesting. Service design is constantly reinventing the wheel and there is not a formal awareness that there are things that repeat, and that we can use again.

Marc: Patterns do exist, such as queuing solutions used at amusement parks and check-out processes in UX design but for service design we need to think about different zoom levels. In service design there is a design system on the level of user interface, for instance what a button should look like. On a larger scale we have patterns for user flows, like the example of the check-out. So in terms of service design we need to add another layer on top of interface on the level of isolated flows of interaction, such as a check-out process. The service layer includes flows as well but on a larger scale. It also includes cross-channel experiences, for instance buying an item online versus in a shop – is it a similar experience?

Especially for large organisations this is a challenge if they want to deliver a consistent experience. Basic standard solutions as a foundation for service design would let designers think about how to really improve the experience and not only how to meet the minimum requirements. As it is now most services frankly don't even fulfil the minimum expectations people have. A potential important skill in the future then is to be able to connect patterns on different levels to create an understanding of the whole service situation.

The craft of service design

Markus: In our work we use prototypes that are both tangible and intangible. We set up a stage, like a store or the home of a user for instance. And then we use props, things to interact with which can lead in specific directions, but the main thing is what people are doing. In that sense we are trying to shape something that is impossible to shape directly. People are making things happen in service and in the real world and they have been long before there was design. There is an interesting gap between prototypes and reality. Often we go lo-fi for very long and then suddenly try to apply it to reality, so there is a gap there.

And there is another gap. People who are responsible for really complex services such as insurance or nuclear power plants – they do amazing stuff in the real world. But they fail at making a simple prototype in-between. So why is that?

Marc: Emotion and trust are not materials we can design but we can aim towards them. When it comes to trust we can use transparency and openness to communicate trust. It used to be that banks were built like fortresses with a clear boundary between the bank and its customers, thus communicating that the customers were not trusted. But they realised this and changed to a more open and transparent layout. The same has happened in restaurants with open kitchens to communicate and create trust. We cannot directly work with these materials.

Adam: The designer can be seen more as the connector in some cases. When we are designing for emotions, we connect the behavioural scientist to the user interface designers for instance. Then the skill becomes connecting people, translating between people and facilitation. And orchestrating.

Markus: A lot of service design is about designing for something that we cannot directly control. We are trying to shape something that is inherently intangible. One material is then figuring out what the leading material is. The material that is most important to work with. There is currently a lack of tools in service design that complement the existing ones and do other things – each challenge needs its own approach. For instance, improvisation is a key skill.

Material translations

Adam: You can't write some things down, like your love for your family. Expressing that requires materials – an artwork or a prototype for instance. If you show Markus with his kids to someone it is immediately clear how he feels about them. But capturing those emotions in another medium is really hard. In service design we often try to grasp things that are immaterial using different materials. Words are insufficient, unless we write a whole novel about what a specific situation makes us experience.

Markus: Words and images do help build trust however but often there is too much talking and too little doing. Also, people are limited by what they are able to understand and simulate in the head. Systems with humans are far too complex for words, they require exploration and experimentation to learn how the system behaves. This is what we do with prototyping, it is not so much about the physical set up but rather the psychological.

Adam: You can think of it as translations between different materials. We use different media to describe the world and the aim is to change the real world. For instance from reality into research data. From research data into visualisations. From visualisations into understanding. Every step of the way we lose some of the in-between, we lose some of what that particular material cannot express. Also we need to use lots of words and images if we want to work together. It is one thing if you are a gardener, working directly on a plot of land. You do not need any in-between then but for many gardeners to work together they need translation media to create a collective understanding.

We have another one of those level situations. On a very basic level we have data, insights, ideas, prototypes, and then there is how is that captured, how is that expressed? How is the idea or the data carried forward (steps of translation here)? And behind that, on the other side of it we have questions like – is imagination a material, is empathy, is clarity? Is the material the post-it, the thing that is written on the post-it or is it the human capacity that leads to the post-it being written? The capacity of imagination for instance. Or persuasion which is so key to success in design, getting people to do things.

Marc: Other such materials include empathy, being able to put yourself in someone else's shoes. And facilitation, connecting the right people to each other. As designers we orchestrate the experience and make sure that the components of the experience meet the minimum expectations and that a few of them exceed the expectations. But a designer also materialises that experience, to give people something to bring home, physically or digitally. That is the designers' job. The process also includes a lot of people. It is a team effort.

Emerging list of materials

Markus: A safe space allows people to suggest things without fear of judgement, it is an abstract space with agreed-upon rules about how to relate to each other during a limited time. Safe space is psychological, not physical. As a material in service design we need to increase knowledge about how to shape safe spaces to allow people to explore freely inside them. Most organisations want to do the right thing but often have problems working in the abstract.

Adam: The in-between is something we talk about a lot. It is an important element of what we are working on. Take online meetings as an example and compare it to a situation where people meet physically. Online – one person speaks, the others listen. There are no ongoing parallel discussions or events that can be important for the conversation. Friction is also part of the in-between, things rub together to generate heat or generate motivation.

Marc: I disagree that only one person can speak in a digital environment. Especially if we have video, there are a lot of side conversations such as reactions and facial expressions and there is chat and so on. It is a different form but still it takes place.

Markus: Technology enables service designers to do so much more and is important to consider as material. AI will allow small teams to do what large teams could, changing how communication looks. Tools is a similar material that enables designers to do things they otherwise could not.

Marc: There is a difference between materials needed to design a service and things needed to run a service. The things we use to design are useless once we have a service up and running. Running a service requires mainly people as a material. However, systems can replace people, such as IT systems.

A service consists of processes – how people do things and what people are allowed to do. And then we have physical materials such as props, interfaces etc. Service design is a huge field.

6   Time, timing, time-ing

Stefan Holmlid

Professor of Design, Linköping University
Stefan has a background in interaction design based on Scandinavian participatory
design with a cognitive science perspective.

Time, and multiple aspects of time, is very material in participation in service
processes. It is also an integral part of design processes, as well as transformation processes that ensue from design. Here the main focus will be on time as a
material of service and in design processes.

Time can be seen with two different lenses: (1) Chronos, as the chronological
understanding of time – the time that passes; and (2) Kairos, the understanding of time as being opportune or right – the qualitative character of a specific
time. These two will be central here.

Although prevalent in many representations of service, it is difficult to provide
a sample of time as a material. Figure 2.6.1 (a and b) is an attempt, a reminder,
of what time can be as a material.

Material transformation or forming

Time in itself is not open for forming, it may seem. Time passes regardless
of what designing we do. In a similar way of reasoning, time would not be
open for transformation. However, this is a limited sense of how time matters in service, mostly rooted in a chronological conceptualisation of time.
Time is also experienced, as well as being part of our cultural assumptions. In
service, actors are using time to do service-y things and achieve intended value
creation.

First, time can be seen as forming, or a mould for, other design materials. A
Chronos approach follows a strict instrumentality, where the passing of time

2.6.1a source: Niklasson (2014).

2.6.1b source: DALL-E generated image. The prompt was 'An outlined photorealistic picture of a person with a newspaper folded under the arm waiting for a bus in a rural setting'.

Figure 2.6.1   Waiting as a material

is a matter of measuring time, and service becomes a trivial sequencing of actions over time. In many senses this is what the service blueprint from service research does. A Kairos approach opens up for deliberately doing design work that aims to position key actions at the appropriate time, at the timing that makes sense. A Kairos approach also shifts the forming initiative from time in itself as a mould to the actions being done and the structure they bring to time. As a consequence time is formed by what actors do; in service as well as in designing. The use of, for example, the dramatic curve to describe the development of experience through a service is a way of forming time. The concept 'suspension of disbelief' also is in a forming discourse with time; without time there would only be disbelief.

Second, when something is done in a service matters, as does the order in which it is done. Most services cannot be fully scripted, so the final design decisions on actual timing and duration will be made in the particular service situation. That is, the embodied and situated aspects of time are there for the actors in the service situation to deal with. This can also be seen in the representations used in design, where many of those aspects are left out, generalised or bluntly hypothesised. This leaves some deliberate design work to the actors in the service situation. This forming of time in context builds on experienced, resourceful and knowledgeable individuals that act within organisational framings.

Third, by using specific language we refer to how time should be formed and used as a material in services. Language connected to ideas, e.g., about efficiency directs attention to time that can be measured, and to how actors use time; without waste, with speed. These senses are then transferred to design processes, design rationale and detailed design decisions.

When introducing time as a material, in relation to service, a couple of abstract concepts can be used to understand time. Lending from music, we can talk about: tempo as the speed at which the service is performed; meter as an overarching segmentation between more or less reoccurring patterns; rhythm as the distribution of initiative, accents and experiences over sequences of actions; and phrasing as the shaping of a sequence of actions to denote a delimited part of a service. Terminology such as accents, pause, synchronicity, counterpoint, syncopation, etc. then also can be translated into service, and possibly find its own service-related terms. Other frames of reference can be used, e.g., from running, with speed, pace, stride, heart rate, etc.

Representations of time

Time as a 'material' is seldom represented, experimented with or crafted. Blueprints and journey maps, although diachron (Diana et al., 2012), are straightforward representations of time as sequence. One action is followed by the next. The extent of manipulation revolves mostly around the order of actions and the kinds of channels used. In many of these, time is taken lightly, which can be seen, for example, in the manner in which pauses or waiting between actions of specific actors is represented. In dynamic representations (Blomkvist & Segelström, 2014), the possibilities to actually unpack and experiment with time as a material are more open.

Chronos is often integrated in representations, at a schematic of sequences level. Straightforward aspects of Chronos are usually represented in a direct manner, such as sequence, parallelism, etc. But the consequences of Chronos are seldom represented, such as tempo, rhythm, pacing, pace change, pausing, etc. Neither are the scaling consequences of chronological time represented. That is, if actions performed by actors in a service are sequenced in a specific way, with specific durations, how would that be affected by an increase in volume?

Let's say there are three actors, and the sequence of their actions looks like Figure 2.6.2.

This is an archetypical service process found in many services, e.g., representing a care process with patient, primary care and specialist care involved. The timing looks like Figure 2.6.3.

This puts tight frames on how this service system will be affected by an increase in volume. A strict instrumental Chronos approach where time is counted is easy to do, while the Kairos approach, where time counts, would require deliberate choices of timing which are dependent on the role of the actors and the actual results of their actions. The representation here is also a good illustration of how time is symbolically, not realistically, represented. Time is often compressed in understanding the current, as well as in enacting possible futures; few prototypes have a realistic three month time span between one service situation and the next.

Figure 2.6.2   A simplified actor process

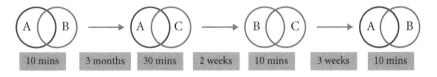

Figure 2.6.3   A simplified actor process with time added

Kairos is seldom directly or consciously represented; however, it occurs in dialogues around representation, and one may sometimes find the opportune time indirectly represented. In its simplest form, questions about what the right sequence of things is has to do with Kairos aspects, but also dialogues about the need to 'wait' for something to sink in, for example, when delivering a severe diagnosis. The representation in Figure 2.6.3 also illustrates that time could be represented with a value perspective. Currently, it uses a value perspective that claims that the value of the different time spans is the same.

If we turn to the service situations and see them as design situations, where the actors in the situation make conscious design decisions, Kairos is more present. In service situations, a service actor can choose when to do what, within limits – within the action spaces that the actors have (Rodrigues et al., 2018). That choice can be directed by Kairos or Chronos aspects. There is a sensitivity in the situation that guides the actors towards leaning more or less on Kairos or Chronos. Such sensitivity is not prevalent in the design process.

In service situations, there are also practices that are capturing the rhythm/pace of the others and adapting to that. That is, being sensitive towards the needs of other actors' sense and use of time, and making in situ design decisions on how to proceed. Some of these aspects may be introduced in representations that are enactments.

Taking a step back and viewing the work with representations as forming and transforming time, designers shift between a chronological way of working and a kairotic way of working. When presenting a customer journey map, or some other representation based on research with the service system, the representation appears as a chronology. But, it is actually a map stitched together from multiple conflicting sources, into a kairotic narrative. This dialectic between Chronos and Kairos materialises in design work.

Developing competence

Understanding time's two natures is central to all service designers, along with the way in which they can be handled in a design process. However, to study them in detail in a specific service may not be for each designer, and may be beyond the design profession in isolation.

As time is multilayered as a material, having its own contexts and meanings in actual service, and other contexts and meanings in design, there is a need to be able to disambiguate and understand the role that time plays in the different contexts. Training to understand time could be done by learning to use enactments as a technique in insight phases of design.

Another aspect is to understand the three kinds of time travel that are involved in design work. Design research is carried out and brought into representations of what is claimed to be what it is like now, while actually these represent something historical in a current setting. Similarly, prototyping is carried out to represent a future, while they are conceived by and in the current. The third kind of time travel is the design of how much time will be used in a potential service, like evidencing designers are engaging in time-ing, that is, a current understanding of a process and its conditions.

Moreover, as the final design is done when the service is happening, designers need to be able to set up involvement and engagement closer to the actual implementation of a service. This could mean, for example, that designers structure and participate in rehearsals of service situations that highlight variations and possibilities, and that give the different actors an understanding of their action space and agency in the situations.

References

Blomkvist, J., & Segelström, F. (2014). Benefits of external representations in service design: A distributed cognition perspective. The Design Journal, 17(3), 331–346.

Diana, C., Pacenti, E., & Tassi, R. (2012, September). Visualtiles: Communication tools for (service) design. ServDes2009, 24–26 November, Oslo (59, pp. 65–76). Linköping University Electronic Press.

Niklasson, M. (2014). Att vänta på cancerbesked: En osynlig aktivitet. Dissertation. http://urn.kb.se/resolve?urn=urn:nbn:se:liu:diva-112442.

Rodrigues, V., Blomkvist, J., & Holmlid, S. (2018). Perceived action potential: A strong concept in development. ServDes2018, 18–20 June, Milan (150, pp. 1162–1174). Linköping University Electronic Press.

7   Organisations as material

Olivia T. Harre
Department of Architecture, Design and Media Technology, Aalborg University

Lene Nielsen
Business IT, Reflect Research Group, IT University Copenhagen
Both authors share an interest in the transformative potential of service design in organisational change.

As a service designer you operate with and within change. In this chapter we consider what it is that changes when service design is introduced into an organisation. We argue that it is not only the product that is transformed, but also the organisation itself. Our definition of material is 'that which is being changed' and in this case, it is the organisation.

Empirically, we draw on the first author's experiences as design researcher in an organisation and combine the experiences with insights from nine semi-structured interviews with professional designers (n = 5) and managers (n = 4). The aim of the interviews was to understand the involvement of a professional designer and the applied design methods in five information technology development projects. At project start the company was new to working with design methods.

Service designers address the context of service encounters, envision new services and business models and engage stakeholders. For these purposes the service designer uses service design methods and tools and produces artefacts that visualise the product as it is and future visions. We argue that the introduction and use of the artefact initiates a change in the material – the organisation. We explore the artefacts produced by service designers and observe how they not only orchestrate a service experience but support a change in mindset and focus that influences the organisation. We show how artefacts simultaneously represent the present 'what is' and propose a future 'what could become'. In our case, the visualisations were formed by designers through three distinct, but interrelated, stages. The three stages are (1) collecting, (2) abstracting,

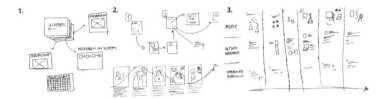

Figure 2.7.1   An illustration of the artefacts at the three stages: (1) a collection of existing artefacts; (2) an as-is user journey; and (3) the to-be user journey

selecting and reframing and (3) anchoring, presenting and awakening. These stages show how service design artefacts change the material (an organisation) and support a strategy shift from a product orientation towards a service orientation (Figure 2.7.1).

Stage 1: Collecting

At the collecting stage, the organisation is pre-set and feature-driven, focusing on functionality with little understanding of users and other stakeholders. The typical artefacts collected at this stage are visualisations from a business and system point of view. The analysis and the questions the service designer asks uncover the present ways of working and the present understanding of the product.

The artefacts used at stage 1 form a bricolage consisting of handwritten meeting notes, PowerPoint slides, screenshots of system functionality, descriptions of system functionality, project timelines, emails, etc. The service designer asks the question: What is known?

In the cases studied, a designer typically collects (and produces) artefacts such as slides with process diagrams, screenshots of the system interface and wire frames. The designer at this stage would describe the collection as being dominated by 'existing wire frames and screen captures mainly focusing on functionality and system capabilities'. The artefacts at this stage present the understanding that the organisation has of being product-focused.

The collecting stage is important, since artefacts are formed by different members of the organisation and the organisation does not have a shared or holistic overview of use situations, the service encounters and the service moments.

As service designer you are not only collecting material, but you are also situating yourself within the organisation and starting the process of showing how a service orientation requires shared knowledge. At this stage, it is important for the designer to ask 'stupid questions' and to be prepared that this new approach might cause friction with colleagues. However, the result pays off in two ways: the designer gains a rapid overview and the organisation takes its first steps towards a service orientation.

Having an overview of the as-is leads to the next stage.

Stage 2: Abstracting, selecting and reframing

In the second stage the designer changes the collection of artefacts gathered at stage 1 through abstracting and organising. The designer looks beyond the existing functionality, beyond what already exists and asks: Who is this for? What does this mean to someone else? What implications can this have for the future use of the service?

The new understanding of the product as service becomes aligned between stakeholders during this stage. This might create tensions in the project group as knowledge gaps and problems are unravelled. The tensions are a first sign of the change of the material – a destabilisation of organisational routines (Rodrigues, 2020).

In a specific case, the designer reshuffled and selected elements from the collection, tied them together and translated them to envision the perspective of the customer. The designer used the collected material from stage 1 and created what he called: 'a coherent narrative and storyboard'. He described the activity of reframing as challenging due to the intense effort of analysing and synthesising the disparate material into a narrative. In the process he kept refining and asking questions of the business expert. For the business expert this provided a new understanding resulting in enthusiasm within the team regarding the broader and more holistic perspective.

This stage not only makes gaps in knowledge clear to all, it also encourages agreement for those aspects that need to be addressed.

At this stage, the change in the material is a move from the individual perspectives to common understandings. The service orientation becomes shared within the project group by framing what a service orientation can be. These two aspects are important when moving to stage 3.

Stage 3: Anchoring, presenting and awakening

The last stage is the most important. Here the artefacts focused on the to-be situation must be disseminated, anchored and integrated within the ongoing project. At stage 3 the designer asks: What is it I can change? How can I change the material? and Who are my stakeholders?

The developed artefacts are anchored within the organisation and often presented to someone external to the organisation, i.e., through a user research interview or user validation session. This is all part of the designer's approach of depicting and envisioning future use concepts. Awakening occurs as a process of inter-reflections of the designer's and the manager's practices. The designer reflects upon what the design practice includes and realises that pushing the organisation, changing the material, is part of the design discipline. The manager reflects upon how interviewing and testing with customers, facilitated by someone without technical knowledge, can initiate a change.

In another case, artefacts that described a service-oriented perspective of being 'in the shoes of the customer' were used with the business expert to ask his opinion. The sketch was refined into a digital version that was used in an interview with a user. Based on the interview insights, the business expert stated that 'the whole business case was changed'. The business expert later used the final user journey map all the time, both internally with managers and his team, but also with customers to support the conversation.

This last stage is the most challenging for the designer. The diverse perspectives and external voices make the involved managers start to reflect. It challenges existing methodological approaches and brings awareness to the organisation's routinised ways of working. Here, the material starts to become fluid and able to change into new forms. The service design artefacts have started a rapid transformation of the material. The ability to enact future concepts with someone else might be obvious to a designer, however, the organisation must absorb this user and customer perspective. Having a service perspective does not only change the product, but also how it is designed and the process of designing. The designer is clearly not only designing the service, but at this stage also actively changing the organisation that is building the service.

Conclusion

Service design artefacts not only form a service, they also prompt a change in the organisation from a fixed state to becoming fluid, service-oriented and able to change. In the cases, we have not yet seen what final form this takes. What we have observed is that the new form (1) includes a perspective that is complex in its human-centred perspective, (2) encompasses an outside-in perspective, (3) provides vision and coherence through narrative components and (4) creates a shared and cemented service orientation.

But what is it exactly that is being changed? We conclude that service design is fuelling organisational change towards a user- and service-centred perspective. The preliminary results shown here emphasise the invisible structures, beliefs, mindsets and routines that service design influences and transforms. We have identified three stages of change that shift the focus of the organisation from the product mindset to the perspective of someone else in a service-oriented way. In this way, the service designer is forming the organisation.

Reference

Rodrigues, V. (2020). Designing for Resilience: Navigating Change in Service Systems (Vol. 2065). Linköping University Electronic Press. https://doi.org/10.3384/diss. diva-165087.

8 Conversations as a service design material

Jonathan Romm

The Oslo School of Architecture and Design (AHO)
Jonathan is a designer engaged with building service design capabilities within complex organisational settings such as healthcare.

Service design facilitates multi-actor value exchanges over time through various touch-points (Clatworthy, 2011). Thus, designing for such exchanges to materialise becomes a collaborative effort involving co-creation through conversation. Throughout a service design process, conversations are carried out to support decision making and the implementation of new service proposals. My main claim is that these conversations are shaped and used as a service design material. Although all design activity is guided by communication (Jones, 2010), the intangible nature of service design makes conversation a core of the discipline.

Service design conversations may take place as part of fieldwork explorations (Segelström et al., 2009), during reflexive conversations among participating stakeholders in co-design events (Aguirre et al., 2017) or during the implementation phase (Shaw et al., 2018). Service designers use these conversations as a material to help them move the process forward and gain influence. Despite all these conversations, little attention has been given to how service designers shape and influence such conversations. This chapter emphasises the importance of conversations and calls for a more deliberate attention to the nature of these conversations. An increased attention to service design conversations may raise the likelihood of more successful service proposals and help to support the implementation process over time.

To explore how designers shape and influence service design conversations, in a real-life setting, two service design labs were embedded inside two large hospitals in Norway. During these interventions, 204 non-exhaustive descriptions of service design conversations were collected using research diaries. The analysis of these collections revealed different types and purposes of conversations taking place, and the ways service designers use conversations to gain influence during the design process (Romm et al., 2020).

Types and purposes of service design conversations

Five different types of service design conversations were found to take place during the service design process: meta-conversations, meaning conversations, approach conversations, plan conversations and practice conversations. Figure 2.8.1 presents the different types of conversation and describes their general purpose. It also provides examples of each conversation type, using healthcare service design for the elderly as an example.

Figure 2.8.2 illustrates how different types of service design conversations are taking place during a design process, using the double diamond as a backdrop (Design Council, 2007). Conversations tend to drift between the different types as illustrated by the overlapping speech bubbles in the figure. For example, they can start off as an approach conversation about overall strategies and

Type of conversations	Description	Purpose	Example
Meta-conversations	Conversations referring to the service design process itself.	Framing process stages and goals, who to include as participants and figure out the means to move forward.	Conversation about what activities should be conducted and who to invite.
Meaning conversations	Conversations about ethics, philosophies, and overal service purpose.	Provide a sense of the 'overall picture' or the meanings behind appearances.	Conversation about what quality of life means for elderly people towards the end of their lives.
Approach conversations	Large-scale strategic conversations on high-order issues.	Clarify and explore possibilities related to long-term issues, such as policies, systems, and outcome.	Conversations on how specialized and primary healthcare may collaborate to provide better homecare.
Plan conversations	Conversation on tactics of service flows and the configuration of service touchpoints.	Understand and develop a service delivery process over time, suportive touchpoints, and resources.	The user journey of an elderly patient experiencing a hip-fracture from paramedics to recovery.
Practice conversations	Operational conversations focusing on short-term matters such as decision making, and detailed procedures related to a specific service stage.	Understand and advance practice related to specific service moments and scenarios that may play out during a service delivery process.	How to meet and inform relatives of elderly patients diagnosed with a chronic disease such as diabetes or dementia.

Figure 2.8.1   Identified types of conversation, their purpose and examples from elderly healthcare service design

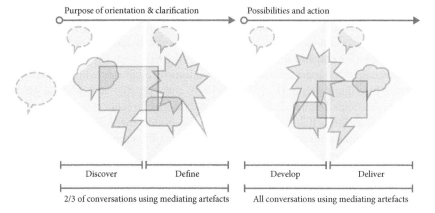

Source: Adapted from Romm (2021) and Romm et al. (2020); illustration by Thiago Freitas.

Figure 2.8.2   Different types of conversation taking place during service design processes

then move to become a plan conversation about tactics of service delivery flows. The arrows on top illustrate the overall purpose of the various conversations. During the early stages the conversations serve the purpose of clarification and orientation, supporting collaborative learning. During later stages, conversations serve the purpose of identifying possibilities and proposing action.

How service designers influence conversations

Service designers were found to shape and influence conversational interactions in six different ways. First, through meta-conversations that influence the process and its outcomes. Meta-conversations help service designers to define and adjust the means of designing, the inclusion of participants and the process steps along the way. Second, through linking conversations to gain propositional leverage. By linking conversational insights, designers can propose directions for further exploration and suggest developments. Third, designers help to reveal ignored fundamental issues through meaning-driven conversations. Service designers raise fundamental questions, mostly in the early stages of the design process. This helps to clarify basic attitudes or, in some cases, uncover important differences between various actors' foundational perspectives. Fourth, designers emphasise the overarching objectives of the design process during conversations. This aids to bridge actors' different interests and viewpoints across organisational divides and helps identify possibilities for collaboration. Fifth, through the influence caused by reframing language. Designers influence conversations through subtle lingual provocations by using metaphors and analogies to conceptualise and describe what they sense. Such lingual disruptions may challenge preconceptions or break schemata, and thus help inspire developments of new mental models. Finally, designers gain significant conversational influence through creating and using mediating artefacts. Mediating artefacts may represent different aspects of the service such as the user journey or specific touch-points (Blomkvist, 2015) and act as co-design facilitation tools (Aguirre et al., 2017). Mediating artefacts make conversations easier to engage with by, for example, offering an overview or illustrating specific proposals.

How to work with conversations as a service design material

While shaping conversations as a material, designers need to first define their intended purpose. Then, the focus should turn towards identifying the types of conversations that are needed taken at different process stages. Finally, ways to support a productive dialogue such as prompts and mediating artefacts may be developed. At the same time, conversations are inherently improvisational and may naturally, and positively, deviate from an envisioned trajectory. Excellent facilitation skills (Rasmussen, 2003) are needed to facilitate fruitful conversations as they unfold. These skills include an open mind and the application of active listening (Weger et al., 2014) alongside techniques for handling group dynamics. In addition, to make use of conversational insights, the ways conversations are documented, collected and linked to one another becomes central for service designers. Service designers should ask themselves how they might capture insights from conversations in an effective way during the process and how they will link and share this insight. Simple routines such as pre- and de-briefing and capturing techniques such as note taking or graphic recordings may help collect, share and reflect on the many conversations that often take place during such processes. Further, to verify sense making across conversations and moderate anchoring bias, service designers may consider including critical feedback loops to challenge their own assumptions while shaping conversations and extracting conversational insights.

Conclusion

Viewing service design conversations as a material emphasises the social and co-creative nature of service design as a practice. Such conversations may be shaped to spark interactions around certain themes and with a specific purpose. Besides helping to push the design process forward, service design conversations support joint learning activities, the identification of possibilities and provide a propositional leverage for designers. To advance service design practice towards working with conversations as a material, we need to become conversational experts. Hence, these issues should be more explicitly included in service design curricula.

References

Aguirre, M., Agudelo, N., & Romm, J. (2017). Design Facilitation as Emerging Practice: Analyzing How Designers Support Multi-Stakeholder Co-Creation. She Ji, 3(3).

Blomkvist, J. (2015). Ways of Seeing Service: Surrogates for a Design Material. Nordes, 6(6), 1–4.

Clatworthy, S. (2011). Service Innovation through Touch-Points: Development of an Innovation Toolkit for the First Stages of New Service Development. International Journal of Design, 5(2), 15–28.

Design Council (2007). Eleven Lessons: Managing Design in Eleven Global Companies. Desk Research Report. www.designcouncil.org.uk/Documents/Documents/Publications/ElevenLessons/ElevenLessons_DeskResearchReport.pdf.

Jones, P. H. (2010). The Language/Action Model of Conversation: Can Conversation Perform Acts of Design? Interactions, 17(1), 70–75.

Rasmussen, L. B. (2003). The Facilitation of Groups and Networks: Capabilities to Shape Creative Cooperation. AI & Society, 17(3–4), 307–321.

Romm, J. (2021). Inside Healthcare Design Labs: Exploring the Practice of Healthcare Service Design in the Context of Embedded Service Design Labs. The Oslo School of Architecture and Design. https://hdl.handle.net/11250/2831969.

Romm, J., Dudani, P., & Prakash, S. (2020). Design Conversations in Healthcare Service Systems. Proceedings from Relating Systems Thinking & Design (RSD9): Systemic Design for Well-Being, 9–17 October, Ahmedabad, 1–28. https://rsdsymposium.org/romm-dudani-prakash/.

Segelström, F., Raijmakers, B., & Holmlid, S. (2009). Thinking and Doing Ethnography in Service Design. International Association of Societies of Design Research, Rigor and Relevance in Design, Seoul, 4349–4358.

Shaw, J., Agarwal, P., Desveaux, L., Palma, D. C., Stamenova, V., Jamieson, T. et al. (2018). Beyond 'Implementation': Digital Health Innovation and Service Design. NPJ Digital Medicine, 1(1), 1–5.

Weger, H., Castle Bell, G., Minei, E. M., & Robinson, M. C. (2014). The Relative Effectiveness of Active Listening in Initial Interactions. International Journal of Listening, 28(1), 13–31.

9   Ritual: meaningful material for service design

Ted Matthews
Oslo School of Architecture and Design (AHO)
Ted has a background in design and explores how rituals, myths and symbols can be utilised in service design for heightened and meaningful experiences.

From minor everyday rituals such as how we greet each other, to more elaborate rituals like birthday parties and grand elaborate rituals like marriage, rituals are a constant and important part of our lives.

Rituals are performative articulations of inner meanings for individuals, groups and society. They have intentional, symbolic purposes following set structures. They create meaningful points of transition through time leading to an emotional shift. Performed together with others they often lead to shared emotional entrainment.

The intentional use of rituals in service provision has been shown to offer value for customers (Liu & Wei, 2020) and to improve consumer experiences (Vohs et al., 2013). In my research, I have used ritual as material and structure for the development of an approach for the design for meaningful service experiences within experience-centric services (see Matthews, 2017, 2021).

Discourses on ritual cover views from sociology, anthropology, behavioural science and theology. The framings here are drawn primarily from sociology and anthropology, teasing out concepts that offer value for service design.

Rituals are not the same as routines. Rituals are symbolic actions which have a real sense of emotional purpose. Routines, whilst repetitive, are more mechanical than meaningful. Setting the alarm and locking the door before leaving home might be seen as a routine. The routine of leaving the home could be elevated to a ritual if a small incantation were to be added before departing, where the ritual intention is about ensuring a good day or keeping the house safe whilst away.

Rituals are informed and learned through a person's culture and are products of their cultural context. Knowing what the ritual of a handshake might mean in different contexts or indeed how long it should last is dependent on a shared cultural agreement. In elaborate and grand rituals the actions are supported with cultural material that act as props and symbols that are meaningful for the culture and for the ritual within which they are used.

The materials of elaborated rituals

Services and rituals have some inherent similarities. Both are time-based structures populated with touch-points that deliver value through the experience. Rituals are, however, populated with meaningful cultural materials and symbolic actions that deliver value by giving meaning to time through the experience. Working with the intersections of these similarities offers opportunities for designers to design meaningful service experiences.

If we were to deconstruct an elaborated ritual we would find that it has an overall intention, a tripartite time structure and is populated with meaningful cultural material acting as props for symbolic action. Rituals are often performed in sequestered places and at specific times. The intention is what the ritual symbolically 'does' and what it means. A graduation ritual is a performative act that will move an individual from student status to professional status. The tripartite structure frames and delivers particular types of emotional engagement to move people through the ritual. The first phase, separation, is about creating a sense of entering the ritual space and leaving the everyday and/or previous status behind. Then, the transition/transformation is where the core of the ritual takes place, and often the experiential high point delivers the core meaning of the ritual. Finally, the reincorporation phase brings the participant back to the everyday emotionally changed. This gives dramaturgy to the ritual but also creates heightened emotional peaks and gives distinct meaning to time. In the case of the graduation, the procession into the graduation hall to music followed by a reflective speech on what it means to grow up is the separation, the calling out of names and receiving a handshake and certificate from the dean is the transition/transformation, leaving the hall and the throwing of mortar board hats in the air is reincorporation. All these phases as exemplified are populated with meaningful cultural material and smaller ritual acts. The graduation takes place at a privileged place like a grand hall and will happen at a specific time at the end of the education. When deconstructing an elaborated ritual we need to be able to understand the meanings and the values expressed in such rituals, the broader sociocultural context from which they emanate as well as the context within which they are used. We also need to be able to read and analyse all the cultural materials and actions that take place during the ritual.

Constructing a new ritual

To construct a ritual that will be meaningful to the participants (as opposed to just adding a series of symbolic actions that look ritualised), then we must decide the overall intention, utilise the tripartite structure to engage participants over time and then populate this with cultural material and actions that might be deemed meaningful for the participants. We also need to consider where and when the ritual should take place.

The designer first engages in a form of cultural aggregation that looks for cultural materials that might appear meaningful and expresses values of the target audience. This is analysed to interpret what the material might say about the target audience and then prioritised and sorted for use in the ritual to be designed. This analysis can also help point to what the intention of the ritual might be. The tripartite structure can help give a dramaturgical structure and a framework for where the material culture might be placed over time.

This is the process that I have utilised (albeit somewhat reductively described here) in the design of ritualised service journeys toward meaningful service experiences.

In a recent service ritual design sprint in spring 2022, master's students from the Oslo School of Architecture and Design set about designing service rituals for fans of women's national football. Students identified the rich cultural material relating to the context through interviews with fans and experts, desk research and a workshop with the Norwegian Football Association. This included meaningful symbols, narratives, actions and values of the team and fans such as actions like the players clapping for fans at the end of games, spending time to write autographs, the meaningful symbols of the team crest the golden star that denotes winning the World Cup and the values expressed through the team's motto 'Stronger Together'. The students also cast their cultural analysis net wider than just the women's football context to include rituals of gifting, Scandinavian domestic rituals, symbols relating to the Ballon d'Or and the collecting of souvenirs to further inform their process. Not all of the material was used in the eventual designs as material was filtered in its value and degree of meaningfulness for the ritual intention of bringing players and fans closer together.

The students then designed a ritual service journey populated with smaller service rituals and touch-points. They imagined the time leading up to the game as a separation phase and the game as the transition and time directly after the final whistle blows as reincorporation. I shall focus on one of these as an example, however, the ritual service journey included ritualised press conferences that utilised some of the symbols and Scandinavian rituals identified. New ticketing was designed with ritual intentional actions and symbols of solidarity in physical keepsakes.

Two students, however, developed a service concept of the 'reverse autograph'. From their cultural analysis, the students understood the unique sense of connectedness between fans and players and how the autograph was a form of ritual contamination of something meaningful through the act of the autographer. Their concept created a ritual where fans won the chance to autograph a banner in a pre-game ceremony with a privileged pen imbued and designed with symbols from the team and football which they could then keep as a souvenir of the experience (Figure 2.9.1). The banner was used by the players before the game as a totem of the stadium's solidarity and then used as a symbol of gratitude during the post-game recognition of the fans and in photos.

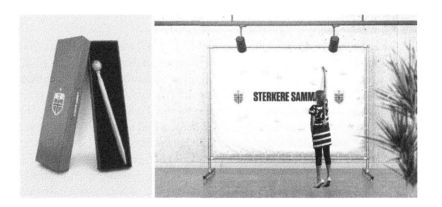

Source: Image by Arindita Dey and Nora Røstø Grøtberg, used with permission.

Figure 2.9.1   'Reverse autograph'

What is being formed in ritualised service design

The materials of ritual are the materials of the meaningful. They are cultural materials that are aggregated, analysed and formed into new arrangements to imbue the ritual with readable meaning for its audience. Within this framework, touch-points are not just tangible interaction points with the service but can be symbolic transitional points that communicate the broader meaning of the whole.

For the service designer it requires the development of skills in broader cultural analysis and draws from the traditional role of the designer as cultural intermediary and interpreter. While this material might be identified through engagement with a target audience, its final assembly into an eventual ritual must happen behind the mystical curtain of the designer's own interpretation. Designing these kinds of rituals for people I believe is not a co-designed process as seeing the making of the ritual can destroy the sense of authenticity by the user. This, I must emphasise, must be done in a careful and respectful way as one works with material that matters to people. However, for the ritual to work it has to fit and indeed work for the culture and target audience you are designing for. If the ritual feels inauthentic then it will be rejected. It is upon the ritual designer to be a servant for the community they are designing for.

Rituals are such an important aspect of our human experience that to not include them in the design of services is to not fully engage in human-centred design.

References

Liu, Q., & Wei, H. (2020). Rituals in service: A literature review. Journal of Service Science and Management, 13(1), 178–187.

Matthews, T. (2017). Sacred service: The use of 'sacred theory' in service design. Journal of Design, Business & Society, 3(1), 67–97.

Matthews, T. (2021). Exploring sacred service design. PhD thesis, Oslo School of Architecture and Design.

Vohs, K. D., Wang, Y., Gino, F., & Norton, M. I. (2013). Rituals enhance consumption. Psychological Science, 24(9), 1714–1721.

10   Certainty and its artefacts

Thea Snow
Director of the Centre for Public Impact Australia and Aotearoa New Zealand
Thea supports governments around the world to embrace service design

Stefan Holmlid
Professor of Design at Linköping University
Stefan is a service designer with a background as an interaction designer based in
Scandinavian participatory design with a cognitive science perspective.

In the often complicated and complex contexts that service systems offer, uncertainty is common. In order to cope with this and create security and predictability, *certainty artefacts* become a material in service design.

Certainty artefacts are the constructs we create to achieve a sense of control, despite the fact that in the environments in which we find ourselves operating there is, in fact, very little certainty at all. Used well, certainty artefacts render structure and scaffolding without seeking to resolve the underlying uncertainty. Used poorly, certainty artefacts become confused with the truth and seek to conceal the inherent uncertainty that characterises so much of our lives and the world we live in.

Different types of certainty artefacts

There are four different types of certainty artefacts:

1. **Personal certainty artefacts**. These are the artefacts which we create in our own lives every day. For example, a weekly calendar.
2. **Procedural certainty artefacts**. These are artefacts that are often used at the level of an organisation or entity. Examples are organisational five-year plans, or even annual budgets.
3. **Institutional certainty artefacts**. These are artefacts created and enforced by our institutions. For example, *probability-based economic models*.

4. **Paradigmatic certainty artefacts**. There are also certainty artefacts which exist at the level of societal beliefs. These artefacts are invisible; embedded in our *deepest set of beliefs about how the world works*. For example, property is something which can be owned by individuals.

Institutional and paradigmatic certainty artefacts are integrated into our belief systems and deeper institutionalised patterns. While they may not be directly formed in service design, they have influence over service design processes and results.

In addition, while paradigmatic and institutional artefacts might be outside the realm of our control much of the time, even knowing they exist is important in the way that it then enables us to interrogate how they influence design work. For example, if a service is constrained by a law or regulation (an institutional certainty artefact), recognising the constructed nature of that constraint opens a new sense of possibility for change and reform at the level of procedural artefacts.

Certainty artefacts as a design material

Certainty artefacts are a material that designers work with and manipulate – they play a role in both service design and service provision. Some certainty artefacts are the product of deliberate design processes (for example, a customer journey map), while other certainty artefacts may emerge more organically through the process of service provision (for example, a project Gannt chart).

Certainty artefacts are an important tool to help us navigate complex environments. They create a basis and a space for rational arguments, keeping some of the complexity at bay. However, what is important when working with certainty artefacts is to make them visible, and help them be understood as a construct. This is true both in respect of those artefacts which are actively designed and those which are more emergent. Making certainty artefacts visible enables those working with them to be aware of their existence, and the need to critically engage with them. The trap with certainty artefacts is forgetting that they are a representation of reality, rather than reality itself. By forming and reforming certainty artefacts, and by interrogating and disrupting them, they become a material that encourages those working with them to engage with our complex realities, without denying the uncertainty that sits behind it.

Certainty artefacts in service design processes

In the service design process context, certainty artefacts are crafted by multiple actors, sometimes in collaborative processes. As a design team, certainty artefacts are created to make sense of aspects of the service system. As a leader, certainty artefacts are made and picked up, to make sense of progression and relationships of a development process.

The character of certainty artefacts, to give stability in complexity, can be thought of as a means to create a 'secondary belief' within which rational decisions can be made, regardless of whether they can be interpreted as rational based on the underlying complexity. When this secondary belief, and its system of rationality, is mistaken for reality, the means becomes a false end.

Deliberate forming of the artefacts acknowledges that they are temporary representations to create certainty. Therefore, using multiple, maybe competing or complementing, artefacts is part of good forming practice. Moreover, deliberate reforming of the certainty artefacts in use, through interrogation and disruption, is critical to ensure that the certainty artefacts are not confused with reality in itself, but as a tool which enables us to navigate complex environments.

For example, a customer journey map can be made, or used, as a certainty artefact, carving out a shared sense of certainty from the underlying irregularities and uncertainties, rather than being used as a representation of a customer journey in the service.

Certainty artefacts in service provision

In the service provision context, certainty artefacts are also formed by multiple actors and in multiple settings.

Some certainty artefacts are created by staff as personal or process artefacts for themselves. Examples include to-do lists, or notes of the topic order for a client meeting. Other certainty artefacts are formed in interaction between actors from different parts of the service system, and emerge in and from those interactions, either as temporary process artefacts to support specific steps to be taken or formed as an integrated part of the values co-created. Examples include a note by the lab technician about what blood tests the medical team need, or an agenda for a meeting with the football club sent out to members of the club.

Yet other artefacts are formed by other actors, who engage with services in different ways such as patients and their next of kin, as personal or process artefacts. Some of these are embodied, while others may merely be ways of thinking. Examples include a schedule for getting back into jogging, or a list of requirements for purchasing a product. Because these artefacts are often more incidental in their nature, rather than deliberately designed, there is a greater risk that they will not be understood as being constructs which can – and should – be interrogated.

Many of these artefacts can be made part of processes of designing, because they are integral to the co-creation of value, and some could be made part of suggested design solutions. More important, though, is to recognise the necessity of understanding that actors will create their own certainty artefacts, and therefore to make space for those who engage with services to create the necessary certainty artefacts to navigate the situation at hand. Put differently, there is a responsibility on service designers and managers to deliberately make room for the forming of 'certainty artefacts' as an aspect of good service.

Design work and certainty artefacts

This added materiality, an additional role, of artefacts in designing, links the aesthetic and constructivist design practice with process management and the joint relational work in development processes. Documenting the design work behind and around certainty artefacts requires its own attention and careful documentation of its design rationale.

Consequences for education and research

Taking a step back, certainty artefacts point to the multiple roles of artefacts in design. This highlights the need, in education, to introduce these multiple roles and techniques to work with them in those different roles. More specifically, introducing certainty artefacts as a design material, and learning how these are formed and what it means to form them, by designers and others, is necessary knowledge for service design practitioners. It may be of help to make comparisons with boundary objects and infrastructuring.

To continue systematic knowledge development, there is a need to perform research on the multiple roles of artefacts for service design. One aspect of this is the role of certainty artefacts in processes that professional designers are engaging in. Another aspect is the in situ design of certainty artefacts in service provision, seen as improvisation as well as professional expertise. Finally, increasing the understanding of the use of certainty artefacts in service provision can be explored.

Further reading

Blomkvist, J., & Holmlid, S. (2012, September). Exemplars in service design. ServDes2009, 24–26 November, Oslo (59, pp. 19–30). Linköping University Electronic Press.

Bødker, S., Dindler, C., & Iversen, O. S. (2017). Tying knots: Participatory infrastructuring at work. *Computer Supported Cooperative Work, 26*(1), 245–273.

Snow, T. (2021). Certainty artefacts: The constructs we create to make sense of the world. Centre for Public Impact. https://medium.com/centre-for-public-impact/certainty-artefacts-the-constructs-we-create-to-make-sense-of-the-world-607e95f6cc33.

Star, S. L., & Griesemer, J. R. (1989). Institutional ecology, translations and boundary objects: Amateurs and professionals in Berkeley's Museum of Vertebrate Zoology, 1907–39. *Social Studies of Science, 19*(3), 387–420.

Interlude 2: Expertise as material of service design: interview with Lavrans Løvlie (2 December 2021)

Lavrans Løvlie

Partner, PWC, Norway
Lavrans heads up the service design
team with the formal title Service
Innovation and Service Design.

Description and characteristics of the material

My first thoughts about a key material in service design was the designer's ability to identify and utilise knowledge, skills and expertise from people who know about things that designers do not know about. To be more direct, it is a designer's expertise to identify the necessary expertise needed for a project. Services are complex because they involve artefacts, digital interfaces, humans, technology organisation, and it's pretty impossible for one person or even a design team to recognise all relevant opportunities and consequences.

First, I need to give a bit of history and context. In our service design practice, we found that designers had really good ideas and were presenting them in a materially suitable form. This is design using materiality in process, concept and idea, and then communicating them well. However, it wasn't enough. We were not able to support clients long enough to support them in their further journey with these. Normally these ideas take a long time to bear fruit, and we often find that a concept designed five years ago is only now something that an organisation can make real. We have found that the right expertise in a project can accelerate this, and make things real, much more quickly. Forming the expertise by bringing in the right knowledge accelerates the project towards a delivered outcome. The usual service design aspects are still there, but now they are better grounded together with other disciplines.

At first, the 'new' material was the organisation. The structure of the organisation, politics, etc. became a material to form. Technology was a material to make this necessary, but it also required expertise at system level. We kept returning to the question, 'How do you architect a service?'. To do this we found we needed organisational people and technologists to play ball with. We were working with business models and needed economists on board. The nitty gritty of business models. In public service the relationship between investment and effect upon society needed to be made explicit, and that required new competences. Over time this has led to us understanding that having the right expertise involved in a project is not only important, it is the designer's responsibility. This makes it a design material because the expertise that a project has is what gets transformed into a solution.

Working with this material does not put the designer at the top of the food chain. It is ordinary practice in lots of fields but the point here is to do smarter design in service design projects. The driver is a quest for better design and utilises a responsibility that the designer has and an ability that the designer has. What is specific to design is the way it is done. The other experts are not used to working using diamond-shaped processes and they find it exciting and motivating to work in a team that works this way, facilitated through design. Not only this, the designer also facilitates how specialists can utilise expertise from others. This is where the design ability to visualise comes in. The designer has both models to craft a project co-design process and the models needed to create a shared understanding. In our current work, that's how we consider the designer's role. A project is immensely powerful with a great team, and we have found that the designer identifies the knowledge needed, brings it in and has the ability to integrate this into the project. In this way, the designer forms the expertise needed, continually adapting this as the project progresses.

As an example, we had a project with the new Munch museum in Oslo about how to get children into the museum. We recognised that personal data would be an issue if we were to involve children in the way we wanted to, and the way the museum wanted to. So we integrated a personal data lawyer into the project and identified that this was actually an opportunity to develop something for the client that they could reuse again and again. Instead of using a long dry legal document, we created a simple, visual solution that was easy to understand and that gave real informed consent [Figure 2.12.1].

Models are key to this, and perhaps models would be my second material, linked to expertise, since models are used to understand, communicate and detail. Models are very deeply connected to how designers think and require principles, simplicity and visualisation, and it turns out that they are useful in co-design processes. This is because core to design is the ability to identify the essence of something. Identifying the essence is both a way to think and, together with visualisation skills, a way to express that thought. This is often described as the designer 'nailing it', and being able to draw this essence is a

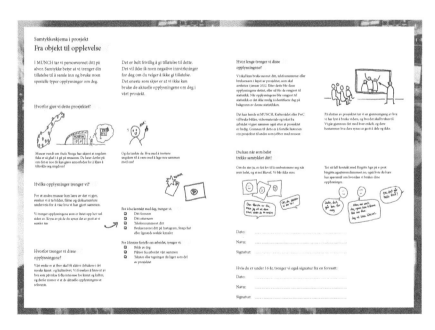

Source: Lavrans Løvlie

Figure 2.I2.1   The simplified consent form designed for the Munch museum in Oslo

skill that the designer has that others do not possess. The journey is an example of how models create shared understanding.

In many ways what I see here is the designer's abductive approach meeting the university deductive approach. For example, an economist has different views of knowledge formation, and it can be challenging when they meet the abductive approach. In the university non-abductive approach, a large part of the double-diamond process is missing, and solutions suffer because of it. Likewise, results can suffer from the opposite – quite often a deductive approach is the right medicine. Understanding these different modes of thinking and how they sometimes collide helps explain why things turn out the way they do. The abductive approach is old knowledge within design but is slowly becoming mainstream elsewhere. It is still considered something that is used only in a workshop or considered to be something that happens in pockets. There are also some who have the ability to transcend these ways of thinking – Elon Musk is maybe an archetype of such a naturally creative person. Someone who can unify these approaches. It is the unification that is important, but that is also difficult.

How is the material 'formed' by design, and does this occur with others?

A good question. I think it is formed by a culture, a culture of collaboration, informed by process. Design informs the process, in which expertise can be formed creatively during the process. Visual models help form the material. A process of insight, understanding, idea and hypothesis is something enabling it to happen. The ability to craft something as real, through evidencing, supports the process. The ability to craft the end experience is key. The journey map or blueprint is a good example of the manifestation of expertise in a project. Different parts of the journey or blueprint represent different areas of expertise but the visualisation encapsulated the knowledge in an integrated way.

Knowledge that is needed is identified as the project is set up. Sometimes things appear during a project, where a special expert is needed. An example of a project we just won – a new hospital and how can they reshape the administrative model for a hospital. Can we put this together in one team to serve the medical teams across their silos? This would be a huge transformation. To proceed with this direction we thought that we needed to bring in system-oriented design (SOD) and we found an expert in simulation of hospital operations. SOD and simulation allowed prototyping at system level rather than at data level. So here, the material (expertise) was formed during the process and during the forming (co-design) it changed with the addition of SOD. It's in the forming. The material is formed during the process, in the same way that clay is formed. The forming occurs mostly during the first part of a project. It is collective and formed across disciplines. However, it is a design-led forming, but requires others to work together. A contributing factor to this is that the appetite for uncertainty is high with designers, which makes the designer well suited for working with the material.

Materials and representations of service

When you work in a cross-disciplinary way, you represent a service in different ways. An economist will represent in a spreadsheet as flows of money or values going in and coming out. A personal data lawyer will represent it as a legal document and adhere to the standards of the law. The designers will represent it in multiple ways – a digital app, scripts, invitations, t-shirts, hoodies and all are representations of what the service might do. The client needs all of these different types of representations and they are usually there, but not integrated. Now, when considering expertise as material, the different facets are integrated.

Competences needed to work with the material

A designer needs process competency in order to know where we are and where we are going. There is also a need for competency in curiosity, of knowing beyond one's own expertise. There is also a need for competency in visualising a number of things. Knowledge of design process is core, and then design tools help and enable people that know different things to work together. Workshop techniques using the tools and visualising under way help integrate all types of expertise. Attitude and humility are important. A lot of the craft in design thinking is useful in creating the right design atmosphere.

We should not forget the designer's 'synthesis muscle'. Design tends to overemphasise its ability at empathy and sometimes hide behind it. We tend to be a bit cautious when brought in and asked to justify a design approach. In this case we can clutch at empathy and this can underplay the skills the designer has in co-design and forming expertise. Curiosity is a term that designers rarely use, but is descriptive of this ability to explore and synthesise and is highly relevant to this material.

In our team we have been conscious of, and worked very hard to, remove barriers for people to work together. An issue with design is one of conceiving its identity as being a minority. This breeds tribal language and a defensive attitude. We have actively tried to break this down. The design office is not different to the others. We actively work to try to avoid tribal language and do not try to 'look cool'. We consciously try to use words that others understand, we try to be sharing and open and curious and interested. Added to this we consciously try to develop friendships with other competences.

Final thoughts and reflections

These are not thought through, but some reflections on consequences this might have for service design.

Firstly, I am not sure if there is a tool available that can be used to teach how to form this material.

For education, I think there is a tendency to create a safe bubble for students, but this can also create a prejudice towards other disciplines and this costs in terms of the sharing of knowledge. Education needs to remove the barriers that somehow appear due to feeling different, and also remove the feeling some design students have of being privileged.

For practice, I am not sure I can add to what we spoke about earlier and the focus upon curiosity, synthesis and a genuine interest in what other people know and how people work. Designers need to remember to ask if they do not understand something. Curiosity is a muscle too.

11 Collaborations

Per Linde
Assistant Professor of Interaction Design and Head of the Design Unit at Malmö University

Anna Seravalli
Associate Professor of Design at Malmö University
Per and Anna are participatory design researchers interested in questions of democracy in the public sector and in public services design and delivery.

Services rely on the interaction between different people and organisations to be delivered. These interactions can have different intensity and require different levels of coordination.

In this chapter, the focus is on specific kind of interactions and collaborations, where two or multiple parts mutually engage with each other to make and decide upon something (Wood & Gray, 1991). Pure collaborative services (Jégou & Manzini, 2008) are not that common, but elements of collaboration are increasingly found in many services. Concepts like prosumption (Bruns, 2008) and co-production (Voorberg, 2017) are describing, and inspiring, services in which users and professionals collaboratively shape and deliver solutions. For example, in the treatment of diabetes, patients and professionals are increasingly collaborating in formulating and evaluating treatment plans.

Collaborations can vary in relation to who is involved (professionals and users, only users or only professionals), how decisions are taken in the collaboration and if there is or is not consensus among the people involved.

Collaborations as a sociomaterial phenomenon

Social interactions depend on contextual and individual aspects, but also on pre-existing social relationships. While a service might engage people who have never met before, their interactions are heavily shaped by existing views and practices within different communities, and organisations they belong to. Returning to the diabetes treatment example, the interactions between patients, nurses, doctors and patients' families are often shaped by specific views about patients and healthcare systems, different professional cultures, the organisational culture in which healthcare professionals are embedded and values and habits of the patients and their families. Social norms and values are collectively and continuously produced and reproduced through social interactions and, in some cases, they are challenged and transformed. Often, changes tend to emerge at the margins of a specific community or in the collaborations between different groups (Wegner, 2011). These changes are both intentional and contingent processes, meaning that intentionality, broader contextual factors as well as serendipity are at play (Callon, 1984; Czarniawska & Joerges, 1996).

However, collaborations are not only social. As the participatory design tradition and science and technology studies have highlighted, material aspects also play a crucial role. Materiality does not only support and organise interactions, but actually shapes them. This rhymes with a relational ontology that recognises how people and artefacts are defined through the relationships that entangle them. When it comes to interaction between the nurse and the patient, it unfolds very differently if their meetings take place in an office, at a patient's home or online. Their interactions are also influenced by the different artefacts that are part of the service (paper and pen, digital platforms, etc.). Material elements can thus either support or disrupt collaboration between participants and, in some cases, even allow for collaborations without consensus among different parties. These so-called boundary objects are plastic enough to allow for local appropriations by different groups while still retaining a general shared meaning (Star & Grisemer, 1989; Leigh Star, 2010). A diabetes treatment plan can become a boundary object between the nurses, doctors and patient if it can support a shared and holistic approach to the disease, while also enabling different views on and specialised ways to engage with this chronic condition.

Changes in the way diabetes is treated have been opening up for reconsidering social norms and values about this condition and about the relationships among the different involved actors. However, one should be careful with associating these openings to broader societal changes. Social norms are extremely difficult to transform, since they tend to be so embedded in our ways of living and thinking that they are hard to pinpoint in the first place (Gramsci, 2011). Moreover, by shaping relationships among groups and communities, norms and values have a central role in reproducing power relationships and conditions of oppression and privilege, which are particularly difficult to challenge and transform (Pease, 2010; Gramsci, 2011).

Co-designing collaborations: foreseeing use and mutual learning

Co-design is a preferrable approach when it comes to services that rely heavily on collaborations, since it allows to engage with the practical and political aspects of collaboration. The involvement of the people who will collaborate in the service in the design process allows to anticipate possible challenges and opportunities that can emerge at use time (Ehn, 2008), like possible frictions among the groups who are supposed to collaborate. In doing so, co-design is a process that focuses not only on creating solutions, but also support mutual learning among participants (Simonsen & Robertson, 2012). Co-design can foster participants' reciprocal understanding of each other's positions and views, as well as make visible norms and values regulating interactions among different groups, thus having a social transformative potential that is often related to the people who are part of the process. In order for learnings to spread from single processes to organisations and communities, a further dedicated effort of translation is necessary – an effort that engages with finding ways of introducing and fostering appropriation of these new perspectives, through negotiations and mobilisations of possible allies (Seravalli et al., 2022).

Approaching collaborations as (co-)designers: navigating political concerns

Collaborations challenge the understanding of design materials and of the relationship between the designer and these materials. By defining design 'as a conversation with the materials of a situation', Schön (1992) highlighted the tight relationship between the designer and the materials they engage with. Embracing the political nature of collaboration, it entails to recognise how designers are also part of the situation, since they are deeply entangled with the context they are trying to engage with. This means that designers are not neutral in the process and, as a consequence, they cannot expect to get a full and objective overview of the situation, nor to be just facilitators (Suchman, 1987). This calls for critically considering the designer's position in the process and who they are siding with (Simonsen & Robertson, 2012). It also opens up for enhancing mutual learning among participants, and to foster critical collaborative reflection on action in the process (Seravalli et al., 2022). By weaving together their partial perspectives and understandings, participants can recognise and name existing conditions of privilege and oppression and decide how to engage with them.

Co-designing for collaborative and political affordance

However, the possibility to foresee use is always limited (Ehn, 2008), likewise the possibility to grasp the dynamics of power relationships. For this reason, when designing services, it might make more sense to focus on creating pre-conditions for collaboration rather than trying to shape it directly. We cannot design for complete accuracy, but maybe we can design for a performative use and for the possibility, for the people involved in the service, to reshape it during use time (Fischer et al., 2004; Ehn, 2008; Binder et al., 2011).

In doing so, we need artefacts with a collaborative and political affordance. Returning to the diabetes example, this could mean designing a journal that can afford different uses – and thus ways to relate to each other – for example, allowing only healthcare professionals or both healthcare professionals and users to be able to write in it. In this way, the people involved can shape the collaboration, as they want or are able to, given contextual conditions during use time. Given the political nature of collaboration, it is important also to think about how to support collaborative reflection on action at use time, by for example shaping service elements that allow for dialogue and critical reflection among the people involved.

In this perspective, the (co-)design of services becomes a way to deliver not fixed solutions, but rather artefacts that can afford different kinds of collaborations, and processes that can help people in engaging with the political dimension of the collaboration as it unfolds.

References

Binder, T., De Michelis, G., Ehn, P., Jacucci, G., & Linde, P. (2011). Design things. MIT Press.

Bruns, A. (2008). Blogs, Wikipedia, Second Life, and beyond: From production to produsage (Vol. 45). Peter Lang.

Callon, M. (1984). Some elements of a sociology of translation: Domestication of the scallops and the fishermen of St Brieuc Bay. The Sociological Review, 32(1_suppl), 196–233.

Czarniawska, B., & Joerges, B. (1996). Travels of ideas. In B. Czarniawska & G. Sevón (eds), Translating organizational change (pp. 13–48). Gothenburg: Gothenburg University.

Ehn, P. (2008). Participation in design things. Participatory Design Conference, Bloomington, IN, 92–101.

Fischer, G., Giaccardi, E., Ye, Y., Sutcliffe, A. G., & Mehandjiev, N. (2004). Meta-design: A manifesto for end-user development. Communications of the ACM, 47(9), 33–37.

Gramsci, A. (2011). Prison notebooks, Vols 1–3. New York: Columbia University Press.

Jégou, F., & Manzini, E. (2008). Collaborative services: Social innovation and design for sustainability, Vol. 1. Milan: POLI.design.

Leigh Star, S. (2010). This is not a boundary object: Reflections on the origin of a concept. Science, Technology, & Human Values, 35(5), 601–617.

Pease, B. (2010). Undoing privilege: Unearned advantage in a divided world. London: Bloomsbury Publishing.

Schön, D. A. (1992). Designing as reflective conversation with the materials of a design situation. Knowledge-Based Systems, 5(1), 3–14.

Seravalli, A., Upadhyaya, S., & Ernits, H. (2022). Design in the public sector: Nurturing reflexivity and learning. The Design Journal, 25(2), 225–242.

Simonsen, J., & Robertson, T. (eds). (2012). Routledge international handbook of participatory design. New York: Routledge.

Star, S. L., & Griesemer, J. R. (1989). Institutional ecology, translations and boundary objects: Amateurs and professionals in Berkeley's Museum of Vertebrate Zoology, 1907–39. Social Studies of Science, 19(3), 387–420.

Suchman, L. A. (1987). Plans and situated actions: The problem of human-machine communication. Cambridge University Press.

Voorberg, W. (2017). Co-creation and co-production as a strategy for public service innovation: A study to their appropriateness in a public sector context. Thesis, Erasmus University Rotterdam.

Wenger, E. (2011). Communities of practice: A brief introduction. STEP Leadership Workshop, University of Oregon, October.

Wood, D. J., & Gray, B. (1991). Toward a comprehensive theory of collaboration. Journal of Applied Behavioral Science, 27(2), 139–162.

12   Behaviour as service design material

Johan Blomkvist

Senior Lecturer of Service Design at Linköping University
Johan is a service design researcher with an academic background in cognitive science and interaction design.

This chapter concerns the behaviours that occur in service, how they come about and how they can be, to some extent, shaped as part of design efforts. Behaviours are naturally occurring based on both deliberate choices and subconscious cognitive processes. Understanding behaviours, both current and future, is central to design. Design is about changing a situation into a preferred one but for change to occur behaviours also need to change. New service elements can fail or lead to other unintended consequences if behaviours are not properly understood. A deep understanding of the underlying meaning of behaviours, on the other hand, can reveal opportunities for services that greatly improve elements of service co-creation. An underlying challenge for design is that many behaviours are not planned in the way we might often assume. A choice to not eat meat, for instance, comes not from carefully weighing the pros and cons but often more from our friends, life experiences, our ability to cook vegetarian food, the perceived impact on the environment or animal welfare, etc. Of course, whether or not to eat meat might be a big decision with many behavioural implications and we 'behave' all the time as a result of more or less conscious cognitive processes. To be able to change behaviours, then, it might be necessary to consider the origin of behaviours. Several reasons why behaviours occur in the first place have been put forth. Recurring explanations for why behaviours manifest include motivation, opportunity and capability (Figure 2.12.1).

Motivation, opportunity and capability

Michie et al. (2011) have suggested that behaviour occurs based on variations in a system of factors. Their system has been organised as a framework consisting of motivation, opportunity and capability, termed COM-B. The

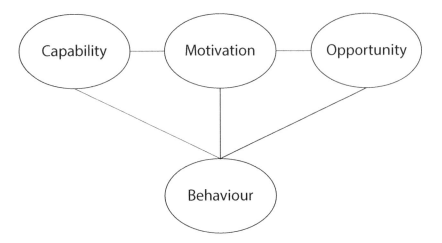

Source: Adapted from Michie et al. (2011).

Figure 2.12.1 The COM-B model of human behaviour

authors operate in a healthcare context where interventions are designed specifically to change behaviours. Hence, the underlying purpose of the system and understanding behaviour are closely tied to an ability to design efficient interventions so that people can reach target behaviours.

For a behaviour to change, at least one of those three factors needs to change. Motivation as a source of behaviour has both reflected and automatic origins. We can be motivated to start eating healthier but at the same time be motivated to eat that tasty piece of chocolate in front of us. Similarly, many of our behaviours are automatic in the sense that they are routines or patterns that are largely unconsidered during our everyday activities.

The theory of planned behaviour (TPB, see Ajzen, 1991) is a model of behaviour from a rational and conscious standpoint. The model has its roots in the theory of reasoned action and at the core it explains behaviours based on people's intention to carry out certain behaviours. The theory has been used in service design to inquire about people's intention to use a meal planning and delivery service (Blomkvist et al., 2014). However, TPB assumes that people make active and informed choices about what actions to take and neglects some aspects, such as the physical context.

For a behaviour to occur, the person that behaves also needs to be able to perform the behaviour, i.e., the capability. Capabilities can be both psychological and physical. For instance, you might need the required nutritional knowledge to start eating healthier and you need mental facilities to stick to a diet. There can also be physical constraints that hinder certain behaviours.

Opportunity as a source of behaviour means there must be external or contextual factors that allow for the behaviour, both from a social and a physical standpoint. Healthy eating must be a socially accepted behaviour, and there must be feasible ways to acquire and prepare healthy food to be able to perform the behaviour.

All these factors contribute and have different weight depending on the behaviour of interest. The system of sources of behaviour can also be placed within a larger context of interventions and policies that influence the ability to change behaviour. For design there are important lessons about how to work with behaviours as material. From a design standpoint it is less important to have a specific target behaviour, but rather to understand behaviours in a specific context and explore how changes in that context might influence behaviour.

Strategies

So, armed with some more knowledge about what aspects need to change for behaviours to change, we should also take a look at some ways to influence those aspects. The COM-B framework already has a set of intervention categories: education, persuasion, incentivisation, coercion, training, restriction, environmental restructuring, modelling and enablement. These can serve as inspiration for design but are probably best suited to the specific healthcare context in which they were conceived.

One approach that goes hand in hand with COM-B is nudging. Nudging was suggested by Thaler and Sunstein (2008) and it is about making it easy for people to behave in certain ways, sometimes described as helping them behave in accordance with their own values or intentions. Like the COM-B framework, this approach emphasises that much of behaviour is not reflected, or the result of optimisation. It is rather emergent and based on conflicting factors. Returning to the healthy-eating behaviour example, we might know that too much fat is not good for us, but still be unable to change our eating habits. Nudging in this example means creating physical and immaterial preconditions for behaviours in the world that make it easier to choose healthier food.

Thaler and Sunstein's thinking and philosophy around nudging extends further than the concept of nudging itself, which is actually quite limited as a design object. Nudges are not incentivised by any other source than alignment of behaviour with your own intentions, meaning, it is not a nudge if you are penalised for not performing a behaviour, or if you are paid money to perform it. With behaviour as a design material we have at our disposal many different tools or strategies for changing behaviour through design. A concept that is valuable, and that is also taken from Thaler and Sunstein's work, is choice architecture. Choice architecture is a construct consisting of the many influencing factors that lead to behaviour. If they are picked apart, it can be possible to indirectly shape the material by directly manipulating aspects of the architecture. I suggest that there are two overarching approaches here: concealing the unwanted options or highlighting the wanted ones. For a more comprehensive list of patterns for influencing behaviours through design, see Lockton, Harrison and Stanton (2010).

Gamification is another way to change behaviours but often with less noble purposes. Gamification does not necessarily mean helping people act in accordance with their beliefs, but rather make them spend more time (and/ or money) by appealing to people's innate reward system. Games appeal to people in experiential ways that we naturally gravitate towards. This is a powerful way to capture people's attention that builds on a thorough understanding of human cognition, with perception and biases being the most easily exploitable. Understanding the choice architecture also means understanding some basic functions of cognition. This understanding can be used for good, but also for perpetuating dark patterns or otherwise mislead people.

The fun theory was a marketing project by DDB Stockholm for Volkswagen (D&AD, 2010). Their idea was that the easiest way to change people's behaviour was to make it fun. The organisation set up three experiments to see if fun could make people make sustainable choices. One experiment was targeted towards making people use the stairs instead of escalators. To achieve this they turned a set of stairs next to an escalator into a giant piano. According to their own calculations this made 66 per cent more people choose the stairs. All experiments can be seen on their webpage, but the piano example is the most clear example of how the choice architecture was changed in a very playful way.

Designing for behaviours

Healthier eating can be addressed many different ways. It is probably too late once unhealthy food has been brought home and the person trying to eat healthier is standing in front of the fridge. One way to change the behaviour is to make sure the person does not get up from the sofa and walk to the fridge. Another way is to make sure there are plenty of healthier alternatives closer to hand. Yet another way is to make sure that there is no unhealthy food in the fridge, or in the house. For this to work the nudge needs to happen in relation to shopping. A good understanding of choice architecture and specific individuals enables appropriately designed options at opportune times (see also Part 2, Chapter 6). Of course, many more nudging situations that encourage healthier eating can be imagined but many behaviours in actual service are not isolated events that can be easily manipulated or designed. Behaviours are situational, contextual and social and whether we perform a behaviour or not depends on our individual motivation. Service is composed of multiple actors, sometimes with conflicting but ultimately joint co-creation goals, and with interdependent behaviours mediated by sociotechnical systems. Furthermore, each situation has its own properties and individuals are different from each other, but it is here where most of the current research can help, through COM-B or TPB and other design strategies. On the contextual level much less is known about how behaviours change and how to approach designing. Examples that take a wider perspective, considering contextual and social factors, include Vink et al. (2021) and Stuart (1998).

References

Ajzen, I. (1991). The Theory of Planned Behavior. Organizational Behavior and Human Decision Processes, 50, 179–211.

Blomkvist, J., Åberg, J., & Holmlid, S. (2014). Formative Evaluation of IT-Based Services: A Case Study of a Meal Planning Service. Interacting with Computers, 26(6), 540–556.

D&AD. (2010). dandad.org. Retrieved 10.21, 2022, from The Fun Theory: https://www.dandad.org/awards/professional/2010/digital-advertising/18245/the-fun-theory.

Lockton, D., Harrison, D., & Stanton, N.A. (2010). Design with Intent: 101 Patterns for Influencing Behaviour Through Design. Equifine.

Michie, S., van Stral, M. M., & West, R. (2011). The Behaviour Change Wheel: A New Method for Characterising and Designing Behaviour Change Interventions. Implementation Science, 6, 42.

Stuart, I. F. (1998). The Influence of Organizational Culture and Internal Politics on New Service Design and Introduction. International Journal of Service Industry Management, 9(5), 469–485.

Thaler, R. H., & Sunstein, C. R. (2008). Nudge: Improving Decisions about Health, Wealth, and Happiness. New Haven, CT: Yale University Press.

Vink, J., Koskela-Huotari, K., Tronvoll, B., Edvardsson, B., & Wetter-Edman, K. (2021). Service Ecosystem Design: Propositions, Process Model, and Future Research Agenda. Journal of Service Research, 24(2), 168–186.

13 Experience as a material

Simon Clatworthy
The Oslo School of Architecture and Design (AHO)
Simon is interested in the facets of designing for experience.

Choosing to describe experience as a material is an easy choice, since the majority of service designers are designing for experience in one way or another. On the other hand, it is an elusive material for the service designer. Elusive because the experience gained by users, employees and others occurs much later from when the designing occurs. Not only this, the experience is subjective, and only the user experiences the user experience. We can also question if the designer is forming experience as a material at all, or whether the forming actually occurs at the time that users experience the service. The designer is therefore designing to enable a specific experience, in a time far, far away.

A dictionary definition of experience describes it as an incident, occurrence or event that leaves an impression on someone. In other words, something that happens that we somehow remember in an emotional way. If we dig a little deeper, then we find that the impression might not last. Indeed, the impression might not even register unless we actively try to remember it. We will also find that the experience that we remember is different to the one we had.

Experience is central to value creation. Vargo and Lusch state that value is 'uniquely and phenomenologically determined by the beneficiary' (2008, p. 7). Pine and Gilmore (1999) describe experience as a separate economic category, a distinct sort of offering. It has a strong relationship to brand, and brand experience is described as 'the customer's interpretation of the meanings communicated through the branded offerings over their multiple interactions – i.e. the product of their relationship' (da Motta Filho, 2012). Further, collective experiences are different to individual experiences, and Durkheim describes collective effervescence as an ecstatic group state (Olaveson, 2001). I describe experience as the core focus for any service organisation (Clatworthy, 2019). Experience, often described as the customer experience, is important for business, and Wladawsky-Berger (2018) stated that 'customer experience is the key competitive differentiator in the digital age'.

Recent research into neurocognition shows how our expectations influence our experience. Lisa Feldman Barrett blurs the distinction between expectation and experience, stating:

> Through prediction, your brain constructs the world you experience. It combines bits and pieces of your past to estimate how likely each bit applies in your current situation … In short, your experience right now was predicted by your brain a moment ago. Prediction is such a fundamental activity of the human brain that some scientists consider it the brain's primary mode of operation. (Barrett, 2017, p. 59)

This is important when considering the design of our material, since as designers we are taking account of the user context and expectations, but we are also designing to form them. So, as a material, the designer is working with forming the expected experience, the lived experience (what actually happens in use) and the remembered experience (how we would describe it to others).

Material transformation or forming

The designer works in two ways when forming the material. Firstly in terms of forming a description of the experience that it is hoped that the user will have. Secondly in terms of forming multiple other materials in an attempt to make that experience occur.

When describing the experience that is wished or desired, the designer uses representations and describes the experience as if it were happening. This is a mix of representations that can conjure up experiences as a means of experience prototyping. This uses our ability to empathise and imagine the experience. The final experience will be elusive and only had by the user at a later date (see, e.g., Figure 2.13.1).

When forming the materials that are a part of making the experience happen, the designer will form multiple materials. The most common are the offering, the touch-points and the journey. However, all service design materials will in one way or another have an impact upon the experience. This part of the forming can be described as an orchestration of the multiple service materials needed to support the desired experience. The degree of forming the other

Figure 2.13.1   It is not possible to show an experience in an image, although it is possible to show someone having an experience, from which we can infer what experience it is (but only the person having it will know). Designers therefore represent experience by using mood boards (left), using experience words and graphic experiential evidencing (right)

materials depends on the focus given to the experience in a project. If the project is experience-centric, then everything will be formed around making that experience happen. If, however, the experience is not in focus, the experience will be a consequence of other decisions, and deliberate forming will be minimal.

The forming occurs in a designerly way utilising the designer's abilities of abduction, synthesis and representation, and the complexity in achieving this cannot be underestimated. Seemingly simple experiential aspects of a service can require significant and sometimes costly development for the organisation. The experience is therefore a holistic endeavour, yet it is also in the detail. It is not enough to conceive of a relevant experience without also being able to consistently support its occurrence. Even small breakdowns in a service can have a large impact on the experience that a user has.

The experience is 'formed' by being described and specified (I use the term 'specify' loosely here) at an early stage of the project, in connection to the service concept. It is here that the partnership of offering and experience are described. This is generally formalised as a blueprint or journey description together with some form of roadmap to make this occur. Other deliverables might be a brand experience handbook (da Motta Filho, 2012), evidencing of the expected service, stylistic or culturally expressed experience (Dennington, 2017) or graphical experiential evidencing (Matthews, 2017). Elements of the experience are formed during development by design, for example, specific interactions with touch-points. The experience itself is formed by the customer or user during use.

The forming occurs both alone and as a co-design process and is tailored to the specific project and organisation in question. Co-design is central to ensuring that any design for experience can actually be developed and implemented, since each project participant is an actor with relevance to enable the experience.

The designer chooses elements of the service to create a unique combination dependent on the project and its context. The designer does not directly form each of the sliders in the image, but rather can form elements of the service such that the slider can be increased or decreased. The synthesis of elements creates the unique 'mix' for each service.

Competences needed to work with the material

I would suggest two competences are needed, and they are clearly linked. The first is the ability to imagine an experience and, as part of this, rapid experiential prototyping of parts or the whole are needed. Experience of experiences and experience with describing an experience are central. These are typical design school skills developed through practice. Further, the role of aesthetics is important, since experiences are aesthetic. However, the aesthetics of service experience are poorly described and understood at present.

The second set of competences needed by the service designer is the ability to orchestrate a service (primarily touch-points and journey) to create the supporting features for the experience to occur in use.

Final thoughts and reflections

Experiences are increasingly becoming the focus of the organisation that provides the service. This has relevance not only to commercial services but also to public service, and although often questioned by public service as being a form of commercial manipulation, the terms 'patient experience' and 'citizen experience' are increasingly being used in projects. This is because the experience of a highly functional, reliable and easy-to-use service is itself an experience of value.

References

Clatworthy, S. D. (2019). The experience-centric organization: How to win through customer experience. O'Reilly Media.

da Motta Filho, M. A. (2012). The brand experience manual: Addressing the gap between brand strategy and new service development. Leading through Design, 667.

Dennington, C. (2017). Service design as a cultural intermediary: Translating cultural phenomena into services. The Design Journal, 20(sup1), 600–613.

Feldman Barrett, L. (2017). How emotions are made, Macmillan.

Matthews, T. (2017). Sacred service: The use of 'sacred theory' in service design. Journal of Design, Business & Society, 3(1), 67–97.

Olaveson, T. (2001). Collective effervescence and communitas: Processual models of ritual and society in Emile Durkheim and Victor Turner. Dialectical Anthropology, 26(2), 89–124.

Pine, B. J., Pine, J., & Gilmore, J. H. (1999). The experience economy: Work is theatre and every business a stage. Harvard Business Press.

Vargo, S. L., & Lusch, R. F. (2008). Service-dominant logic: Continuing the evolution. Journal of the Academy of Marketing Science, 36(1), 1–10.

Wladawsky-Berger, I. (2018). Customer experience is the key competitive differentiator in the digital age. Wall Street Journal, 20 April.

14 Data matter: as data become matter, design matters

Petter Falk
Adjunct Lecturer at Karlstad University
Petter is a political scientist with a focus on critical data studies, democracy and design.

Three reflexive questions on data, design and materiality in the age of datafication

Data are a material produced by abstracting our life and our world. As more and more aspects of life and society depend on data-driven processes, more and more scholars argue that we live in an era of datafication (Mejias & Couldry, 2019). Being a human in a datafied society means operating in context where measurements and categories turn more and more aspects of

Source: Picture by Petter Falk.

Figure 2.14.1 Exploratory data workshop with public-sector stakeholder

your life into data (Cukier & Mayer-Schönberger, 2014). And working with design means enabling, reforming or potentially resisting that process.

What we mean by data in this era of datafication, and who gets to define it, is often subject to a technocratic order of power (Ruppert, 2017). In a conventional computational understanding, data are often seen as a set of symbols represented in sequence within a given computer system (Nelson et al., 2009). That is usually how data are viewed through the lens of organisational digitalisation – taking something analogue and turning it into multipurposed informational building blocks, funnelled through practices such as production, processing, storage and utilisation (Russell & Norvig, 2006). Here, in logics and language, data are an asset, equivalent to an economic value or to a promise of latent knowledge (Fussell, 2022). Hence, any design processes related to data-driven systems and services easily become motivated by maximising value based on these technocratic logics and language (Kitchin, 2014).

But when dealing with humans, using the narrow and instrumental definitions and narratives of contemporary discourse will not automatically represent and serve for the subjects whose daily lives, social interactions and work are being translated into data. It might be suitable from a machine-readable point of view, but not from the point of view of the people and society. So, in this text, I wish to highlight how design can approach a material understanding of data within the ongoing process of datafication. I do this to underline that anyone in a position with leverage over design aspects in a data-driven process – be it interface, user experience, information technology infrastructure, service design, database or analysis – also has leverage over how data as artefacts represent the needs, wishes and hopes of those subjected to datafication. Building on the idea of information as material (Dourish, 2017) and what Schön defined as a reflexive conversation with the material (1987), I here wish to outline questions related to data, datafication and material properties and settings that should be asked in the research, design and iteration of data-driven processes.

How does design affect this moment that is translated into data?

The material arena that translates human and non-human bodies into numbers, statistics, text, etc. is the epicentre for data creation. The rooms, the framings, the service design; you are not only designing the technical systems but also the social system that is the spatial-temporal locality for data creation.

When you design these spaces and settings, you affect the structured digital information created there.

The design of the sociometrical context involves the arrangement and moderation of a vast gallery of actors, decisions, relationships and dynamics (Kitchin, 2014; Bates et al., 2016). The technical design can be understood as both the alignments of multitude of materials, such as wires and circuits, but also the shared digital boundaries, i.e., interfaces, that create and facilitate digital data points (Brady, 2019). In this course of work, designers can never assume that the digital reading of a designed space can encapsulate a moment in time in its entirety. It will never represent or grasp the totality of social complexity – it is just a matter of how we acknowledge this failure and make something useful out of it (see Box, 1976).

So know this: organisations, institutions and services collect data in a particular way, use specific datasets to explain things or phenomena or need specific data in order to make decisions. This has to do with traditions, politics and, to some extent, what data can be accessed in the moment (Breit et al., 2019; Loukissas, 2019). And those reasons need to be clarified and examined in design – be it in the doctor's office, a smartphone interface or in the backend of a database. Asking how design affects this moment is one way of opening that discussion.

Why do we need this?

Design, in a more grand sense, matters as it can alter the premises of what datafication is. It can do so by institutionalising methods and avenues for individuals and communities to decide by themselves how they wish to be represented, or if they want to be represented at all in data. Technology is not a force of nature. It is a sociotechnical process. Here, the designer should keep in mind that datafication is driven by a logic of creating and consuming an increasing amount of data, it constantly adds to a narrative of techno-determinism where more is always more (Mejias & Couldry, 2019). Speaking to this, not measuring something is a very contra-intuitive idea in datafication. It is a missed opportunity, even unethical (Baym, 2013). But good design that creates both purpose and value sometimes mean doing less of something. Sometimes, it even means doing nothing at all. Less is sometimes more.

It is also a question of who needs data. Questioning how a particular data point, dataset or data-driven system is deemed necessary means questioning everything from the service interaction to the political agenda the systems serve. In this investigation, trying to expose the politics of a particular data-driven service means the functions and properties of specific datasets or data points will follow. For example: is the use of data meant to serve or/and control?

Designing avenues of resistance can help the subject, be it individuals or organisations, to reclaim the power of definition over data to better serve their needs and purposes (Fussell, 2022). To this effect, it has been said that the strangeness of data is their strength (Ruppert, 2017; Loukissas, 2019). In a reflexive conversation, one should embrace this fact and incorporate it into a more inclusive and adaptive logic. This can include elaborating on a multitude of methods and practices – digital and analogue – that apprehend and acknowledge tacit information like language, gender and power dynamics, and can serve both to nuance the digital data-driven system but also challenge its impact and intentions. In doing this, designing in an increasingly datafied era does not mean that data as material in design need to be understood as only digital-structured measurements. They can be physical artefacts, art or stories from the lives of people. What is important is how they represent the subjects they interpret, and how insight is gained in their favour.

References

Bates, J., Lin, Y.-W., & Goodale, P. (2016). Data journeys: Capturing the socio-material constitution of data objects and flows. Big Data & Society, 3(2).

Baym, N. K. (2013). Data not seen: The uses and shortcomings of social media metrics. Florida Marine Research Institute Technical Reports. https://doi.org/10.5210/fm.v18i10.4873.

Box, George E. P. (1976). Science and statistics. Journal of the American Statistical Association, 71(356), 791–799.

Brady, H. E. (2019). The challenge of big data and data science. Annual Review of Political Science, 22(1), 297–323.

Breit, E., Egeland, C., & Løberg, I. B. (2019). Cyborg bureaucracy: Frontline work in digitalized labor and welfare services. In J. S. Pedersen & A. Wilkinson (eds), Big Data. Edward Elgar Publishing.

Cukier, K., & Mayer-Schönberger, V. (2014). The rise of big data: How it's changing the way we think about the world. In M. Pitici (ed.), The Best Writing on Mathematics 2014 (pp. 20–32). Princeton University Press.

Dourish, P. (2017). The Stuff of Bits: An Essay on the Materialities of Information. MIT Press.

Fussell, C. (2022). Four data discourses and assemblage forms: A methodological framework. https://osf.io/jvcqw/download.

Kitchin, R. (2014). The Data Revolution: Big Data, Open Data, Data Infrastructures and Their Consequences. SAGE.

Loukissas, Y. A. (2019). All Data Are Local: Thinking Critically in a Data-Driven Society. MIT Press.

Mejias, U. A., & Couldry, N. (2019). Datafication. Internet Policy Review, 8(4).

Nelson, D. E., Bradford, W. H., & Croyle, R. T. (2009). Making Data Talk: The Science and Practice of Translating Public Health Research and Surveillance Findings to Policy Makers, the Public, and the Press. Oxford University Press.

Ruppert, E. (2017). Where are data citizens? In R. Kitchin (ed.), Data and the City (pp. 201–212). Routledge.

Russell, S., & Norvig, P. (2016). Artificial Intelligence: A Modern Approach, Global Edition. Pearson Education.

Schön, D. A. (1987). Educating the Reflective Practitioner: Toward a New Design for Teaching and Learning in the Professions. Jossey-Bass.

15 Clay: a tangible catalyst

Matilda Legeby
Designer at Experio Lab and Samhällsnytta, Design MFA from Konstfack
Matilda has a background in product design, focusing on just social transition with
participatory methods and aesthetic knowledge.

Tangible catalysts are a wide and gaudy range of materials that give the manipulator the possibility to embody experiences through an aesthetic process. Preferably the material has a sensory spectrum that can be formed by the hand and body. It can be fabric, scraps found outside, wood or building materials. The properties of these materials vary and therefore you need different approaches and skills when shaping them. But the most important property is that you can manipulate the material and give it an expression, and that the process of the embodied creation gives room for your embodied reflection. The practice of using tangible catalysts is the communication of experiences that are difficult to put into words.

In my practice I have explored the embodied experiences of being in relation with the public sector, its services and policies. How does it feel to be in these processes, and how does your body correspond to this situation? As a tangible catalyst, clay has played an important role in this practice (Figure 2.15.1).

Clay is a material to use when embodying thoughts when thinking with your hands. A material that directly gives your thoughts shape. Or gives shape to your thoughts.

It can be warm, or cold, wet, or dry or drying. It can want to be shaped, or be in a shape. It responds and bends with your thoughts in your hands. No tools needed. It can break.

It is a set volume and colour. It creates warm feelings for some, referencing a creative process with a tangible result. It creates fear within others referencing that same process, and anticipatory joy, or stress, of performance due to anxiety of creating something that is visible in the room for everyone to see.

149

Source: Matilda Legeby.

Figure 2.15.1   (a) Clay; (b) clay shaped by participants in a workshop; and (c, d) 'Whose water?', inspired by the empty riverbed at the water powerplant Harsprånget, formerly used by the Sámi as a pasture for reindeer

It can help you think.

And help you think with others.

Using clay is one way of building on the artistic knowledge within all for exploring the experiences of oneself and others. Doing so requires an open mind, with an emphasis on the explanation by the creator of the meaning of the object. The material is aiding to give shape, and giving words to explain bodily experiences. These subjective feelings can then travel, as a part of the service design process in creating collective understanding for a situation.

By making visible the experience of the body it might be possible also to talk about what yet has no words or is best given gestalt through bodily expressions. How is it to be entangled in a process with the public sector? In the process of asylum? How is it to meet people who are applying for asylum? This type of artistic material can be used for different purposes during a service design process: early, as a way of allowing for embodied reflection; in the middle, as a way of communicating; and at the end, as a reminder or trigger for continued dialogue.

Exploration of lived experiences

My colleagues and I had arranged a small workshop for a woman from Syria applying for asylum. As a part of the workshop, we asked how it felt to be in Sweden in an asylum process. She was to describe it in clay. The woman created a body, without legs, without head and an arm cut in half (Figure 2.15.2). 'It feels like you are here with your body, but only with the ability to be and act like you have half an arm. It is in this part of the body; the stomach and the heart, this is where it feels.'

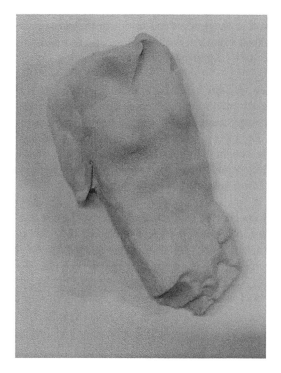

Source: Matilda Legeby.

Figure 2.15.2   A body with half an arm in clay, created by a woman from Syria applying for asylum in Sweden, 2016

Here the designer is not the creator but the one who gives room for reflection through creation. A type of collective design for the purpose of getting hold of and being able, with more than words, to share something that is difficult to grasp. Although you can never understand what another person is going through, I got a glimpse of a bodily experience of being in a Swedish asylum process. This piece of clay was also used later in the project to communicate with other actors involved in the process.

Participatory workshops with lived experiences present in the room

Clay can also be used as a tool for communicating findings between different groups of actors in a service design process. Objects created in clay, or other artistic representations, can be used to make the stories of the participants' experiences travel in the process and minds of the participants. One purpose of embodying lived experiences through artistic representations is to create emotional relations to experiences of others.

We used it when we were exploring how we could improve the reception of children and youth migrating to Sweden without parents or caretakers. The gestalts in clay were created based on the lived experiences of the children in the process. The pieces were used as triggers in workshops with the actors representing the system – the border police, the Red Cross and representatives from the Migration Office. The embodied experiences were considered a required extra dimension to consider by the actors.

One of the objects created was based on the experience of a girl who came alone to Sweden in 2014 at the age of 15 years old. Her story was represented by a gestalt (Figure 2.15.3) and through this quote: 'My lawyer was only focusing on my breasts, saying that they were so big that I could easily be over 18'. This was based on the experience told by the girl when she met her public counsel as he was supposed to assist her in an age assessment case.

Objects as a result and trigger for continued dialogue

Artistic representations can also be used at the end of a project to leave something behind that becomes an advocate for a continuation of the dialogue.

Source: Matilda Legeby.

Figure 2.15.3   Breasts in white clay, created based on the story of a
15-year-old girl and her public counsel

The example below was created as a summary of findings of unknown
unknowns in the relation between parents with experience of migration and
preschool teachers. The objects created were meant to be reminders for per-
sonnel to try to see what is not evident. Reminding them that a small effort
in trying to understand why something is happening can mean a lot for the
individuals. For example, when the children do not have appropriate clothes
despite frequent reminders.

The preschool teachers in the project were talking about the difficulties for
parents to adapt to the Swedish weather, the school system and culture. In
a discussion this was exemplified with a mother of a 3-year-old when arriv-
ing with her child at the preschool in the middle of the winter. One of the
preschool teachers told us that, instead of telling the mother again that her
daughter needs proper shoes, she curiously asked why the daughter was wear-
ing sandals. The mother answered: 'If she can't have her sandals she screams,
and if she screams the social welfare will come and take her away from me'
(Figure 2.15.4).

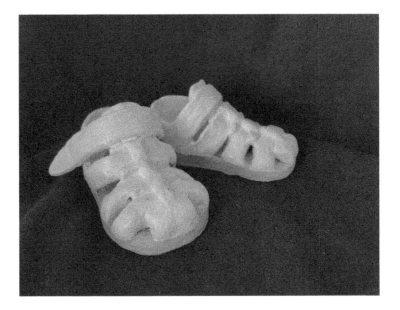

Source: Matilda Legeby.

Figure 2.15.4   Sandals in ceramics, created based on the story of a
preschool teacher and her dialogue with a mother

The objects created in artistic material can manifest the embodied experiences
that the design process at hand aims to explore. Often, the mental models of
participants, the target group or the practitioners meeting the target group
surface when a reflection around the experience is made room for. Mental
models and norms often need to be explored in order to create understanding
of what is needed to create actual change.

Clay is good for self-reflection and the creation of an object allowing for
reflection. But it has its shortcomings when used in groups. The creation of
one's own piece to reflect together with others adds a layer of communication. But clay offers space for self-reflection and the material qualities are best
brought forth in a setting when exploring your own perspective. In my role
as a designer, it is my responsibility to create a co-creative process where the
experiences from the individuals who are involved are at the centre. When the
individuals themselves can't bring their full embodied knowledge into a room
with the stakeholders in the process, the creation of material that represents
the individuals' experiences is crucial for that experience to travel. And that
experience is critical for a service design process.

The skill needed is not in shaping a piece of clay, it is in the design and the facilitation of a process; to understand what is beneficial to bring from events of exploration, how that can be done, including how to represent the richness and complexity of a lived experience of a person. This includes the intention of why this material is collected, both physical and in stories. The design competence here rather lies in how to structure a service design process, and the ability to plan and carry out that process, with artistic material as one of several enablers. To collaborate with another designer or artist with a competence in a suitable practice is another way of using artistic material in co-design processes. Then, the competence of a co-creative inclusive service design process is the designer's, and the competence of using an artistic expression lies within a collaboration expert, when using drama, fabric or clay as tangible catalysts in a service design process.

The artistic skill of using different media should be included in the training to become a service designer. Both for training the artistic qualities of design and as a tool for reflection and expression in the designer's own process. It is also important for the knowledge of what can be used in a design process when collaborating with others, even though the focus should be the process around and the intention of using artistic material.

Further reading

Agger-Eriksen, M. (2012). Materials matter in co-designing: Formatting and staging with participating materials in co-design projects, events and situations. PhD dissertation, Malmö University.

Markussen, T. (2013). The disruptive aesthetics of design activism: Enacting design between art and politics. Design Issues, 29(1), 38–50.

Pettersson, K. (n.d.). Welcome back. www.katjapettersson.com/WELCOME-BACK.

Schön, D. (1992). Designing as reflective conversation with the materials of a design situation. Knowledge-Based Systems. doi:10.1016/0950-7051(92)90020-G.

Seravalli, A. (2014). Making commons: Attempts at composing prospects in the opening of production. Malmö University, School of Arts and Communication.

Vink, J. (2019). In/visible: Conceptualizing service eco system design. PhD dissertation, Karlstad University.

Interlude 3: Data as material of services

Amalia de Götzen, Nicola Morelli and Luca Simeone
Service Design Lab, Aalborg University
Amalia, Nicola and Luca work to make service design useful to build a better society

With an interview with Chris Downs
Partner at Normally.com.

Introduction

Data are a numerical translation of reality; they describe almost all the phenomena that characterise people's lives. Even emotions, attention, interest and opinions can be quantified and translated into data. We use and produce data when we want to go shopping, when we need to take public transport to go from A to B, when we go to the doctor or share pictures of our holidays in our preferred social network. Data are a material emerging from services, but at the same time, the relation between data and people's lives makes data the most effective material to manipulate when generating services for people. In reality, before being a material for designers, data are used by data scientists or by statisticians, but the questions they ask to their datasets are of a very different nature than those a designer would explore. If we want to imagine designers as manipulators of this material, we must notice that the designer's toolbox is unequipped when it comes to utilise our intangible, numerical and quantifiable data traces. Competences and attitudes on data literacy are, at present, very much lacking in the service design culture.

From a designer point of view there is often a view that data can be difficult to interpret and to play with. Data are a very plastic material, despite their digital nature. They are a material that can continuously change and naturally allow for an iterative design process. Data can represent the user the designer is working with but can also represent the complex system the service is part of. Kun et al. (2019) explore the possible data work that could inform the beginning of a design process, when the designer is exploring the context and framing of the design problem. The data material can be datasets, text (e.g., tweets), Instagram images and posts or other numerical data. The material may then be transformed into different visual representations such as heat maps, word clouds and alluvial diagrams and can be explored from different perspectives and answer different questions, providing numerous insights.

However, data as a material is rarely creatively used in the design process, where, especially in the context of design for service, it often comes into play in the latter phases of the process. Here, its use is about customisation of a given service offering, recommendation systems and the like, with all the ethical implications that an extractive paradigm implies. A design strategy, where data-driven inquiry happens along the whole design process, would likely change the outcome of the design process quite substantially. This approach would also change the way data are represented or even aggregated, shaping such representations around the stakeholders that are involved in the process.

In the following section of the chapter we present an interview with Chris Downs, Design Leader and Founder at Normally. He has been working with data as a material for 20 years and enthusiastically shares his knowledge

Figure 2.I3.1   All the thinking in our conversation comes from the team here at Normally

and experience. In the interview, we explore data as a material for service design and we investigate how data sources complement the classical design inquiry. Chris would like to stress that the views he gives in the interview are developed by Normally as a whole company, and not just himself (Figure 2. 13.1).

Interview with Chris Downs (20 October 2021)

Describe your material, and say a little about what it is and is not

Data. To be more precise it is data and related technologies – things we use to handle the data: databases, machine learning, algorithms. I cannot think of any services that are not dependent upon data. In fact we, at Normally, would say that data is 'the' material of service.

At present, we can see three types of service design occurring: the first is the more traditional strategic service design approach, and is about being architectural and master-planning a service. This approaches services as green fields and develops new service concepts. We view this as taking a top-down, or god-like view.

The second type works on improving existing services with multiple platforms and the service designer tries to stitch disparate things together. It is more tactical and operational and often boils down to screen design and touch-point optimisation. Here there is a crossover with UX [user experience] and UI [user interface] designers. This is a middle-out perspective.

The third level is relatively new. It is more of a material view and works with the data itself to explore new opportunities based upon what the data affords. From this approach a new understanding is emerging of the material of data, one that strategy and traditional user research do not identify using conventional methodologies. In many ways, this can be described as a move from data-driven design to design-driven data. This uses design to change the properties, meaning, value and impact of the data (on a user's experience).

When designing with data we recognise four components of it. Maybe we could call them organs rather than components:

1. Collection strategy and mechanisms (Collect).
2. Do something with it (Model).
3. Once modelled, make it somehow available to the user (Render).
4. The rendered data is then controlled (Control).

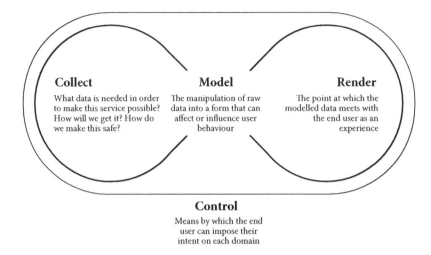

Figure 2.13.2   The four components (or organs) used when forming data

These organs are analogous to the stages of design process, although they are not necessarily carried out sequentially. We usually draw it as more of a loop and each part is interrelated. The four organs are important and it took us a long time to clearly articulate them. We struggled to identify the four parts, but realise now that they are really strong (Figure 2.13.2). We are very aware of these stages and we use them internally in all of our projects. We cannot overstate the power they have when working as a team since different people with different skills might be brought into the team at different stages of forming the material.

Collection

We devise a collection strategy and identify the rules and politics around it. What we need to collect, where to get it, and how to get it. Then lots of other more detailed and contextual considerations are made. At this stage safety and ethics are key aspects to consider.

Modelling

Here, we start thinking about what happens if we bring the collected datasets together. Can we see a correlation over time, can we extrapolate a future from it, for example, to use it for prediction? Can we interrogate it so it tells us something that we did not know before? A lot of effort has gone into our own R+D [research and development] to find effective ways to model data. Collection is a well-known space, but modelling has potential for new and novel ways of thinking using AI [artificial intelligence] and machine learning. It is difficult to look at something modelled that hasn't also been rendered with some intentionality. For example, with Spotify the modelling is deliberately agnostic. They do not care about what you listen to and they are not trying to get you to listen to any particular music. They just want you to continue listening. There is no editorial voice. But if you go to a goal-based service it has a final goal and tries to get you to achieve this. For example, Apple Health on the watch has a desired end state built in and it has goals for what you should do each day or week. The intentionality is a key question here for the designer – what do we want the data to do?

Rendering

Rendering is the point at which the user and the modelled data meet. We have to admit that this is not a great term but it is one of the most exciting topics at the moment. So, in Spotify, if say you have listened to three tracks, the fourth track is suggested by Spotify as a continuation of your listening. Your data is rendered as the next song or as a recommended playlist. As a designer you are creating a platform for the user to form the experience themselves and in forming the experience they are directly and indirectly manipulating the data. In the Spotify example, after playing three songs and having a fourth suggested, then the user is indirectly manipulating the data, just by listening to that fourth song. By giving a song a like, the user is directly manipulating the data. As designers we are looking for the best way to enable users to manipulate data so that we can support them in performing tasks and achieving their goals. In this way, the designer is enabling capabilities and this is core to enabling experience. With Apple Health it is rendered as a data visualisation and it is up to the user to act upon this.

Rendered data is often used to reflect on the past and we experience that 95 per cent of rendering is here. For example, analysis does this and visualisation does this too. However, we can also use it to influence the future. Data is then being used as a material to reflect and affect, and we can use it to, for example, to automate. As a studio we are particularly interested in affect – influencing the future. Rendering experience is a term we have started to use, and we can say that as designers we are rendering data for an experience.

Control

Rendering can be a way of influencing experience or behaviour and this is where the final stage comes in – the locus of control. This is where the end-user can influence any of the other three organs. This influence can vary from being able to prevent data collection to influencing how it is modelled and rendered. For example, Netflix will model your data and suggest films based on your previous viewing and inferences based upon this. However, a user can give a star rating to a film, which is a way of influencing the modelling by saying you don't have to infer what I think, I am giving you a clear and strong signal. The star rating is a control input that influences the modelling and the subsequent rendering.

Earlier we worked for utilities and we developed data visualisations showing usage of, for example, gas, and comparing it with historical data and the data of your neighbours. That renders people's usage data as a visualisation of the past in a hope that it will influence them to change behaviour in the future. The Nest thermostat goes further than this and uses data to influence our experience of the temperature (Figure 2.13.3). Nest uses the rendered data and uses it to automate temperature regulation. It does not produce data visualisations to stimulate users to change settings, but instead it renders it as an experience. You experience the data through the warmth or cooling. The data effectively disappears and is rendered as a comfortable experience rather

Figure 2.I3.3   The Nest learning thermostat

than being historical data to aid decision making. These are two examples of how design decisions about rendering and control of data can give different experiential outcomes.

As designers, we can render for control on a spectrum from interaction to automation. Recommendation engines such as Spotify and Netflix render automatically as part of the attention economy. They use the ability to use data to form experiences so that our attention is maintained. We think there is an opportunity to move away from the attention economy to put that power in the hands of the user and increasingly support the intent of the user. This is where data helps users better achieve what they want to achieve, instead of what the company wants as an outcome. This shifts the power back to the user and is enabled by users controlling the data for their own intent. We describe this as a move from the attention economy to the intention economy. In the intention economy the rendering is controlled by the end-user.

Can you provide a sample of your material in context?

If you go to 'download my data' on Google, you can see examples of what is collected as data. But we can get trapped by trying to define data in too much detail as a material. In the product design world, material is not discussed in the same way. If we make a comparison to physical materials, we talk about plastic as the material of a product and we rarely talk about the chemical composition of specific polymers. As designers we form plastic, and rarely go into the chemical composition. The same is true of data as a material.

Further, in product design we talk about a product's external case, its components, its interface as separate parts. The materials of each part influence the experience of using the product. As product designers we have the language for this. We do not confuse the case and the interface when we are discussing design, and we can have specialists for different parts. With data, the same is true but we found that we lacked a language to deconstruct these components and that made collaboration difficult. So, we created our own language and a description of how they relate to each other. This formed the collect, model, render and control organs described earlier.

How is the material 'formed' by design, and does this occur with others?

Data is continuously formed, is forming and never stops. Clay gets fixed, metal gets milled. We can say that in these contexts that a material has an end point.

Data continues to be formed all the time. Data is one of the few materials that creates more of itself – its use creates more of it. In other words we are, as users, continually manipulating data and creating data.

As designers we are looking for the best way to enable users to manipulate data so that we can support them in performing tasks and achieving their goals. In this way, the designer is enabling capabilities and this is core to enabling experience.

When does the forming occur?

It is continuous and never stops. A continuous flow of material. The designer is a part of a number of people forming the material. The data might have been formed in some way by engineers or data scientists, and the designer might come in and influence this. Designers can ask questions about how the data is rendered, could be rendered or should be rendered. The user still has autonomy through user control to influence or ignore this. The forming happens continuously and is influenced by different actors. Designers have influence during a part of this, and of course the end-user may render the data themselves. Things are changing in terms of how it is formed and we are moving away from a period where it was not 'designed' at all. Now designers are finding ways to contribute and are in many ways fixing broken parts and gradually being brought in from the start. The designer's contribution has until now happened by accident and to some degree luck.

What competencies are needed to work with your material?

The basic designer skills of collaboration, empathy, user research and prototyping are all core competences. However, we need a shared language, and need to use that as the basis for collaboration. You can be a non-technical designer as long as you have many of these competences and are able to communicate with specialists.

How should service designers develop competence in your suggested material?

First of all, at the moment, there are few places to develop this competence. Instead, the most important competence is that of curiosity, experimentation and the confidence to take risks and to point that curiosity in the following four directions. Firstly, you need to take on board that data is a material, understand the four organs we have described and actively use this terminology. Secondly, identify examples of where you see data collection, modelling, rendering and control in the world and ask yourself to what extent design decisions have been made in each of the four areas and what could happen if those decisions were altered. Thirdly, understand the work of a data analyst or software engineer and be curious about the issues and challenges of AI and machine learning. Finally, engage in the issues and debates around data and ethics.

Are these competences something that all service designers should have, or are they more of a specialisation?

This is absolutely a core part of service design. We cannot think of any service that does not run on data. Almost all services have similar journeys in terms of data. Understanding these steps and the intricacies of data design is important. The underlying data is the same. Whether delivered by a human intermediary or directly digitally there is a pattern that is built into this through data and data usage patterns. So, every designer needs to have an understanding of it and its opportunities.

Further reading

Several artists and engineers are joining forces to find new artistic expressions that can impact on the general perception of data. Among them we can mention the work of Salvatore Iaconesi and Oriana Persico at www.he-r.it/a-datapoietic-way-of-dealing-with-the-unexpected/.

Reference

Kun, P., Mulder, I., de Götzen, A., & Kortuem, G. (2019). Creative Data Work in the Design Process. Proceedings of the 2019 ACM SIGCHI Conference on Creativity and Cognition (pp. 346–358). Association for Computing Machinery. https://doi.org/10.1145/3325480.3325500.

16 Human bodies

Fernando Secomandi

Assistant Professor at Delft University of Technology
Fernando is an academic researcher specialising in the intersection of design and philosophy of technology

Frederick van Amstel

Assistant Professor at Universidade Tecnológica Federal do Paraná
Frederick is a design educator and researcher with the mission of raising critical consciousness in service design and nearby fields.

Human bodies as service interface

Whereas designing with any kind of material necessitates a body, service design approaches the bodies of humans as one of its primary materials. Services are often materialised in human-to-human exchange; that is true both for 'high-touch' services traditionally associated with low-status occupations, such as domestic care, waitressing, sex work, etc., as well as for 'high-tech' services that privilege intellectual capacities, such as management consulting, lawyering and designing. In all these activities, humans use their bodies to mediate exchanges, in the way they present themselves to others, in the way they talk and gesticulate, in the way they move around space and in several other bodily ways for enacting services.

In this chapter, we discuss how certain aspects of human bodies can be approached as materials for service design. Building on the perspective of postphenomenology, an experience-centric approach to the philosophy of technology, we frame the human body as a key service interface (Secomandi & Snelders, 2013; Figure 2.16.1). Service interfaces can include anything that mediates service experiences, such as built environments and connected digital devices, but also human and animal bodies. We hold that human bodies, like any other form of technology, can be enacted and designed as artefacts. For instance, clerks' interactions through chat or email can be enacted and designed in several artefactual ways. Even in the case of face-to-face interaction,

Figure 2.16.1   Human bodies as service interface

services are always encounters with an interface, in which bodily artefacts occupy a mediating position.

Postphenomenology and bodily artefacts

Our conception of bodily artefact is elaborated below with reference to a few cases spanning across various service settings.

From a postphenomenological perspective, every human body has a two-fold constitution, sometimes described as our ability both to 'be' and to 'have' a body. In services, as in all other domains, human experiencing depends on an interplay between these two dimensions, which can be more precisely defined as *body schema*, or the perceiving body, and *body image*, or the perceived body (Secomandi, 2015, 2017). The body schema is associated with our bodily capacities to act, but is largely implicit in all perceptual acts. Body images are more explicit representations of one's own body and can include perceptions, attitudes and beliefs pertaining to it. Although the body image is always perceived 'in relation to' the body schema, it is not 'external' nor derived as an exact representation of it. The body schema, in turn, is not invariant and can be to some extent influenced or shaped by the body image. Body schema and body image are mutually constitutive of one's position in the world. As argued further below, designers often give form to services by manipulating or at least influencing the body images of the humans involved in their co-creation, so that these humans can act in concert by design and not just by chance.

Body schemata and body images are not necessarily co-extensive with the boundaries set by the human skin. The body schema of a dentist, for example, can be extended through the incorporation of technologies, so that she is able to experience a damaged tooth by 'touching' it through the tip of the probing instrument. The body schema can be extended 'inwards', too, through techno-logical implants, such as when the new dental crown from the patient of the above example transforms the experience of chewing food.

Also entangled in technologically mediated service relations are body images. The visual display of physical activity in self-tracking devices can influence users' body images by quantifying their bodies, monitoring them around the clock, classifying them as active or sedentary and so forth. The body images of other humans can also be experienced through mediating technologies, an example being the gesture of courtesy of a cleaning worker manifested through the fold of the toilet paper in a hotel bathroom.

These examples show how human bodies are never just natural and obtained by birth. They are always *artificial*, in the sense of developing and acquir-ing meaning in accordance with humans' own intentions in social contexts. Furthermore, they are *artefactual*, too, in the sense of retaining a material dimension in lived experience that cannot be entirely reduced to the 'natu-ral world' nor to the 'human inner-self'. Because human bodies live in this dual role of shaping and being shaped, they can be considered designerly; in other words, human bodies are always design bodies (Angelon & van Amstel, 2021). The design and enactment of bodily artefacts in services is best evidenced when design bodies use body images to attain ends in inter-personal relations.

Physical skills, utterances, gestures, hair styles, etc. are common types of body images that can mediate the exchange of services, often in association with other technological artefacts. An example relating to physical skills is when a beginner skier starts to practice getting to the bottom of a slope by following a ski instructor. While imitating the instructor, the beginner can initially become aware of his own body as dangerously clumsy in negotiating turns and stops along the track. As learning progresses, the skier is then able to deliberately apply a more skilled body to tackle difficult slopes and experience them as tamed and exciting. In this example, we hold that the body image of the skier is extending the original body schema in association with other incorporable artefacts (skis, clothes, poles, etc.) as means for experiencing the world.

Before concluding this section, we observe that body images can not only be constituted through social interaction, as in the example above, but can also be shared with others and change across cultures. A customer may note how the gestures of cashiers vary in shops in The Netherlands or Brazil. While in The Netherlands cashiers will keep staring at buyers, apparently indefinitely, until all items are bagged and pocketed, Brazilian cashiers will quickly redirect their gaze to the next in line after the last item is handed over.

Human bodies in service design practice

In the previous section, we showed how human bodies can constitute services. Essentially, all service exchanges involve bodywork, insofar as human bodies are necessary for their co-creation and delivery. In this section, we argue that approaching these bodies as a material for service design primarily entails co-creating body images in service interfaces.

In principle, designing human bodies should be a concern for anyone who, in one way or another, influences the participation of people during actual service encounters. Because discourses about design are generally lacking regarding service activities whose outcomes traditionally depend on bodywork (e.g., hairdressers, doctors, actors, waitresses, athletes, etc.), we focus here on the work of service designers.

In service design practice, human bodies are often enacted as materials through various tools and techniques (e.g., visualisations, prototypes, etc.) that can offer alternative perspectives on human bodies. A toy figurine that is used to enact intended actions for client-facing workers can highlight bodily artefacts in particular ways, for example, how they should move in space, gesticulate and talk and so forth. Similarly, but in a different direction, an arrow crossing down the service blueprint invisibility line dismisses the bodily artefacts used to interact with clients and requires other artefacts to interact with colleagues and suppliers. Underlying these enactments is a necessary reference of the tool or technique to body images of the humans intended by service designers. That is what allows the thematisation of servicing and serviced bodies as an artefact in the design process to be communicated about, tinkered with and eventually prescribed. To be sure, bodies do not just become an artefact through design, for they are already artefacts in any service interface. What design tools and techniques add is the enhanced ability to grasp, handle and shape bodily artefacts in service interfaces.

As with any other design material, human bodies hold the potential to express intentions along many interesting dimensions, such as aesthetic, symbolic, affective, etc. As with other materials, the ethics of designing human bodies must be approached with care and discernment, especially when the intentions of service designers are to be expressed by the bodies of others with whom or for whom they design. When human bodies are treated solely as artificial and artefactual without considering them as designerly, their capacity to design themselves can be disregarded together with their intentions. The result of that is an oppressed design body, eager to revolt and take back its design freedom.

Consider the case of managing the emotions of client-facing service workers for a profit. In many service settings, workers can feel pressured to assume bodily artefacts that sit at odds with their own feelings and intentions, for example, when flight attendants are instructed to always have a smile on their faces. In such cases, workers may feel a discrepancy between externally imposed body images they are expected to manifest and their actual bodies. This type of conflict can be amplified when gendered, sexualised, racialised and deskilled versions of body images are stipulated by external design bodies, such as managers and design consultants, who may not know or care for those bodies. The dilemma between designing body images for their own self and for others can stay in place, even if workers are included as design bodies and participate in the design of the service.

Ethical challenges like those should not turn designers away from approaching human bodies as service materials. It is obvious that serious conflicts can emerge within and among human bodies when these are designed without consideration for questions like who is doing the designing and for what purpose. However, these conflicts also point to the deeper phenomenological reality of both being and having a (design) body, which is an inescapable if somewhat ambiguous human condition in the first place. We invite service designers to embrace this ambiguity with critical imagination and consider body images as an artefact that can be projected 'ahead' of the present condition, mediating between the bodies that we are and those that we can become.

References

Angelon, Rafaela, & Frederick van Amstel. 2021. 'Monster Aesthetics as an Expression of Decolonizing the Design Body'. Art, Design & Communication in Higher Education 20 (1): 83–102.

Secomandi, Fernando. 2015. 'Bodies as Technology: How Can Postphenomenologist Deal with the Matter of Human Technique'. In Postphenomenological Investigations: Essays on Human–Technology Relations, edited by Robert Rosenberger and Peter-Paul Verbeek. Lanham: Lexington Books.

Secomandi, Fernando. 2017. 'Service Interfaces in Human–Technology Relations: A Case Study of Self-Tracking Technologies'. In Postphenomenological Methodologies: New Ways in Studying Mediating Techno-Human Relationships, edited by Jesper Aagaard, Cathrine Hasse, Jan Kyrre Berg Olsen Friis and Oliver Tafdrup. Lanham: Lexington Books.

Secomandi, Fernando, & Dirk Snelders. 2013. 'Interface Design in Services: A Postphenomenological Approach'. Design Issues 29 (1): 3–13.

17   Sound

Ana Kuštrak Korper
Postdoc at Linköping University with a background in musicology

Vanessa Rodrigues
Assistant Professor at Linköping University, Service Designer at Expedition Mondial
Ana and Vanessa have a shared interest in sound as a complementary modality in designing for service.

Sound is an essential part of every servicescape, providing cues for action and influencing how we interact with the environment. Through visual representations, service design tools and methods have been rendering the intangible aspects of the service visible and making the complexity of intertwined network of actors' processes and artefacts more accessible. Although visual understanding is elementary in human perception, other sensory information (auditory, olfactory, tactile) can extend, change and complement the visual element (Schifferstein & Wastiels, 2014). Sound has a unique temporal dimension that emerges in use and/or through interaction of various sound-producing artefacts. Thus, sound can be used as a complementary material for representing movements, dynamics and temporality inherent to service contexts. Also, sound can facilitate performative forms of representation that have inclusive potential and influence creative experimentation. Auditory cues can therefore not only be used to explore temporality in service but also generate distinctive insights in relation to predominantly visual service design tools and techniques. For example, in our experimental workshop, participants sounded out different heartbeat rhythms of a young and elderly person to showcase their simultaneous progression through the day. This chapter explores the use of sound as a material for representation to facilitate aesthetic disruption and spur reflexivity in the service design process (Vink, Wetter-Edman & Aguirre, 2017).

The characters of sound

Sound is often described in terms of its physical properties as an acoustic wave, produced when an object vibrates, that varies in frequency, amplitude, speed and direction (Berg, 2020). The scientific study of sound in physics is vast and includes those below the threshold of what the human ear can hear. However, in this chapter we will focus on defining and understanding sounds that humans can perceive and are thus an inseparable part of their auditory experience. These sounds entail both natural and artificial sounds that are intentionally or consequentially produced and altered in an acoustic environment, for example, a busy street. In considering sound as material, it can be described as having the following characteristics: loudness (intensity), pitch (height or ordering dimension) timbre (sound quality or 'colour' related to the sound source) and duration (Taylor & Campbell, 2001). These characteristics can help qualify a single sound, but more importantly they can also enable qualification of the organisation and movement of a single or multiple sounds as they occur in a given environment over time. For example, we can characterise the sound of an alarm as soft or loud (loudness), short or long (duration), high/low (pitch) and tinkling or beeping (timbre). But we can also discern a rhythmic pattern and pace of an alarm (related to duration), its ascending, stationary or descending movements (related to pitch), potential changes in intensity (related to loudness) or changes in texture and colour (related to timbre) if the number of alarm sounds changes over time. Sound characteristics enable us to recognise, analyse and categorise different sounds in the service context and point to understated aspects of a servicescape. But they also offer a shared vocabulary to consider the aesthetic and affective influence sounds might play in co-creating the service experience. These characteristics thus become essential in creating, using and making sense of sound as material for representation.

Sound in design representations

Representations are used during the service design process for articulating, learning, collaborating, communicating and maintaining empathy, and are most often focused on the visual modality (Blomkvist & Segelström, 2014). On the other hand, sounds are temporal, and the auditory experience is inseparable from its performance, much like the service experience. As this chapter focuses more narrowly on understanding sound as a material for representation in the design process, based on our previous work (Kuštrak Korper et al., 2020), we maintain that sound as a material is represented through performance. This can include audio recording of a hospital wait-ing area (to capture the acoustic environment) and complement articulating insights about the patients' waiting experience; or it can include a collabora-tive sonification of multiple user journeys in that same context that can more vividly juxtapose differences in experiencing the time component and thus facilitate learning and empathy. This also implies there is a spectrum of engagement and intervention that service designers can resort to when working with sound for representational purposes, depending on their goals and competences. Sonification[1] of a visual representation can be done indi-vidually and collaboratively and service designers can act as solo creators of a sound representation or as a participant/facilitator in a collaborative sonification. Awareness that service designers and other potential partici-pants bring their own competences, experiences and cultural background into working with sounds should be acknowledged. Sounds bring a different dimension to the experience of space (proximity, density) and time (flow, beat); a component that is often out of focus in visual representations of service contexts. It can tap both into the aesthetic aspect through experi-mentation and playfulness as well as the physical, embodied aspect through its production and listening. Sounds can also expand ways users express their experience, emotions, thoughts and environments and use sound as a modality to elicit empathy.

Design competence and sound

It might seem that working with sound requires musical expertise. While we acknowledge that some basic knowledge is welcome, we would also like to point out that the level of expertise depends on the type of sound representation ser-vice designers wish to work with as well as the role that designers assume in the design process. From our experience in working with sound representations, understanding the material in terms of its characteristics and building shared vocabulary is important. However, the lack of it does not exclude people from engaging with sound as a material, as sound making is such an essential part of our everyday life and people's own perception of their 'musical skill' is usually culturally generated (Marcus, 2012). In one of our workshops, our participants had varying degrees of knowledge and experience of music. They described the process as fun, co-creative, powerful, new and interactive. However, experi-menting with a novel medium of representation also had them reflecting on

---

1   In this chapter we refer to sonification as a layperson term for any act or process of producing sounds. We do not refer to the meaning it has in sound design and related fields.

the intimacy, confusion, discomfort, unsettlement and difficulties of working with sonification. From participant feedback, we understand that developing competences to work with sound as a material requires a well-planned facilitation, a beginner's mindset, time, practice, shared vocabulary, confidence to experiment and embracing scrappiness. Finally, using sound as a material would also require the development of critical listening skills that are not only subject to understanding the characteristics of the sounds but also reflect on the sociocultural meanings of the soundscapes they inhabit.

Some consequences for education, practice and research

Sounds and music can offer tools for the exploration of temporal and spatial elements of service that service design tackles through visualisations. As noted by our workshop participants, auditory forms of expression are lacking in service design beyond a presentation and the occasional video. In practice, we see opportunities for creating empathy, communicating insights and extending the meaning of narrative and flows represented through service design tools and methods. Sound and listening are an underused sense in how we do design work. Introducing sound as a modality for expression in the service design process presents novel ways of expressing experience and presenting data and can act as a 'circuit-breaker' that pushes one out of patterned thinking. For service designers to use sound to their advantage as an aesthetic and reflective disruptor, they need to develop their critical listening skills and sound-related vocabulary to both absorb and express sonic information and to facilitate the process of sonic representation. Educators can draw on extant methods and research from the fields of sound design and landscape design to support listening and sonic exploration. For example, Schafer's (1992) exercises in listening and sound making can serve as an excellent starting point for budding and expert service designers. Exploration of sound as representation in service design creates more space for multidisciplinary collaboration between service designers and sound designers. There is an extensive body of knowledge in sound design that service design researchers can draw on to support their empirical investigation. One example is the Listening Across Disciplines research project that positions listening as an emerging investigative approach and aims to generate insights about how sound can reveal hidden potentialities and contribute to our understanding of culture and daily life. Thus, we see sonic representation as an important addition to the service designer's repertoire that can help generate insights and knowledge about service through reflection and aesthetic disruption.

Further reading

Here are some of the useful sources you can consider for exploring, experimenting and playing with sounds:

Chrome Music lab: Excellent sensitising with different sound elements. We especially like the shared piano option. https://musiclab.chromeexperiments. com/Experiments.

LangoRhythm: A text-to-music converter starting with the idea that music is a language. There is an accompanying TedX talk to check how this software was made. https://kickthejetengine.com/langorhythm/.

Musitude: An application that allows playing various instruments through your keyboard controls. No previous musical experience required. https:// musitude.com/.

References

Berg, R. E. (2020, November 5). Sound. Encyclopedia Britannica. www.britannica.com/ science/sound-physics.
Blomkvist, J., & Segelström, F. (2014). Benefits of external representations in service design: A distributed cognition perspective. The Design Journal, 17(3), 331–346.
Kuštrak Korper, A., Blomkvist, J., Rodrigues, V., & Holmlid, S. (2020). Hear hear! Why sound in service design should matter. ServDes2020, 6–9 July, Melbourne (pp. 6–9). Linköping University Electronic Press.
Marcus, G. F. (2012). Musicality: Instinct or acquired skill? Topics in Cognitive Science, 4(4), 498–512.
Schafer, R. M. (1992). A sound education: 100 exercises in listening and sound-making. Indian River: Arcana Editions.
Schifferstein, H. N., & Wastiels, L. (2014). Sensing materials: Exploring the building blocks for experiential design. In E. Karana, O. Pedgley & V. Rognoli (eds), Materials experience (pp. 15–26). Butterworth-Heinemann.
Taylor, C., & Campbell, M. (2001). Sound. Grove Music Online. www.oxfordmusi conline.com/grovemusic/display/10.1093/gmo/9781561592630.001.0001/omo-9781561592630-e-0000026289.
Vink, J., Wetter-Edman, K., & Aguirre, M. (2017). Designing for Aesthetic Disruption: Altering Mental Models in Social Systems through Designerly Practices. The Design Journal, 20(sup1), S2168–S2177.

18 The service offering as a material

Oslo School of Architecture and Design (AHO)
Simon works at a design school and is trying to understand what makes a service experience memorable and how to design for this.

I propose the service offering as a material for service design. The offering is something that all designers form (in part or whole), which all customers (or users) relate to, and is the core of service value, since it is key to value in use. However, it is something that is difficult to describe and represent directly.

By service offering I mean: an offering describes the functional, usable, emotional, social, idealistic and self-identity benefits that are promised, expected and/or gained from a service.

I use the term offering rather than value proposition because it uses everyday language (what did they offer you?) rather than a business term. It is therefore a user-centric term, but is generally interchangeable with value proposition.

Description and characteristics of the material

The offering is a multifaceted construct related to the value that lies in use of the service:

1. The projected offering is what the service provider thinks their service offers.
2. The perceived offering is what the customer or user imagines the service to offer, before use.
3. The experienced offering is what the user or customer experiences in use.

4.   The remembered offering is what the user or customer describes after using the service.

It is one of the few materials that brings together the three spheres of service:

1.   The projected offering is part of the provider sphere.
2.   The experienced offering (the value in use of the offering) is part of the joint sphere.
3.   The perceived offering and remembered offering are part of the user sphere.

It is the perception and experience that a customer or user has of the service offering before, during and after use that is key to value, although without a projected offering, the customer cannot perceive any offering at all, and therefore cannot co-produce value.

There is a high degree of cultural negotiation in how the offering is perceived by the customer. It also changes over time and in context. The offering is clearly related to, and perhaps a proxy for, an expected customer (user) experience. Since we know that experiences are as much predictions created in our minds (Barrett, 2018) ahead of the bodily experience, then the projected offering could be described as a promise of experience.

The designer, through the service design process, has a strong influence on the projected offering. The designer forms elements that suggest functional, usable, emotional, social, idealistic and self-identity benefits that together are synthesised into the projected offering. The synthesis is the conversation that the designer has with the materials. The designer can only design the projected offering, although during the design process, the cultural awareness of the designer allows them to make assumptions about how an offering will be perceived.

The composite image in Figure 2.18.1 describes the core of the projected offering from Airbnb. Airbnb doesn't describe the functional element of its service, rather, it focuses on the experiential aspects. The key offering is the experiential difference between going to a destination (as an outsider) and the feeling of being part of a destination (as a local). This experiential offering can be deconstructed into perceived functional, usable, emotional, social, idealistic and self-identity benefits. The converse is also true, and the designer can construct an offering that combines functional, usable, emotional, social, idealistic and self-identity benefits as part of the synthesis that occurs during co-designing and the forming of the offering.

Source: Image composition: (left) Wikimedia Commons (https://commons. wikimedia.org/wiki/File:Hotel_room_in_Berlin_1.jpg); (right) the author.

Figure 2.18.1 The difference between visiting a hotel and the feeling of being a part of a city is the core of the Airbnb offering

The projected offering is present in Airbnb imagery in such a way that the expected offering can be imagined, almost experienced, beforehand, and such images are culturally interpreted by the viewer.

Material transformation or forming

Developing the projected offering is a classic design synthesis in which multiple aspects are combined in a unique way to craft an offering that is considered appealing to the market/users. The designing and forming of the projected offering occurs through a co-design process and is synthesised at the end of the first double diamond as a concept description. This is where the service designer's role typically ends, with a specification or a roadmap for the implementation of a projected offering.

Is the forming activity tailored to the context of each project? If so, how? What are the inputs and outputs of the forming activity?

The synthesis used to form the offering is unique to the context of each project, since each organisation is unique. Elements synthesised may include user needs, brand strategy, company strategy, competitive climate, popular culture, technical possibilities, etc. (inputs). The offering is the output and the transformation occurs in the synthesis of the multiple aspects of service.

I believe that the offering is the key material that is co-designed during the first phase of the double diamond and key for success of the service. This is because the offering allows decisions about service viability, desirability and feasibility, and is ultimately related to user perceptions of value in a service, and therefore its success.

Representations of service

We have no explicit representations of the offering simply because it is a fuzzy notion. The combination of the following representations all describe parts of an offering:

1. Customer journeys, blueprints and roadmaps, although these do not explicitly represent the offering. The reader has to extrapolate from them.
2. Expected quotes from future users.
3. Advertising and marketing materials for the future service.
4. Analytical descriptions describing the benefits or value proposition.
5. Evidencing (examples of the future service in use and in context).

The offering is indirectly described in all of the above representations, and has to be synthesised to be understood.

The target users for the offering description are the design team, leadership and potentially others (e.g., media). It is also the customer/user and the employees since the projected offering is commonly part of evaluations and testing before development and launch.

Competences needed to work with the material

The competencies needed by the designer to work with the material are typical design school competences, especially those of concept design. A strong understanding of users and culture is a part of this. The design competences of synthesis, visualisation and co-design are core competences used in the development of the offering. In addition, competencies from marketing, business, technology and organisation are important. These specialist competences are usually present in a project team.

Service design needs to focus more on explicitly describing the offering as a key part of their deliverables. At present, it seems that the designer is happy for the offering to be implicit within their representations. I believe that the offering needs to be clearly articulated in service design as a separate element of a service concept.

In reality, I believe that all of service design relates to the design of the offering, either through the development of service concepts, journeys, blueprints, etc., or through implementation of the offering, its provision as a service and its evaluation and redesign.

Are these competences something that all service designers should have, or are they more of a specialisation?

The offering is described in all service design projects, but in different ways for different clients/teams. It is therefore a core competence that should receive more attention. All service designers should have greater competences in offering design and representation. In public service, there may be a greater focus on the functional and usable aspects, the service ecosystem, actor network and organisational and technical implications that enable it. In commercial services, the marketing and experiential aspects may be more in focus, in addition to the aforementioned aspects.

Final reflections

Firstly, the service offering and the customer (user) experience are becoming inseparable and use similar representations. This is increasingly becoming relevant due to our understanding of experience as being strongly influenced by our expectations and how these expectations are strongly influenced by the projected offering (see Barrett, 2018). In this way the projected offering informs the expected offering and influences the experience that will be had when used. But I believe it is more than this. The offering therefore creates expectation in the user/customer and guides them in terms of what experience they should expect to experience. In this way, the offering is an experiential promise, of value that can be co-produced in use. This makes it difficult to differentiate between the offering and the experience, and the two blur into each other. The more we understand about how our experiences are strongly influenced by internal scenarios, the more that the offering becomes inseparable and a core part of the customer experience.

Secondly, I just want to underline the importance that the offering has for service and service provider success. The service offering is linked to perceived value in use and real value in use and this is equally relevant for commercial and non-commercial services. This highlights its importance for service design.

Reference

Barrett, L. F. (2018). How Emotions Are Made. Mariner Books.

19   Policy, governance

Stefan Holmlid
Professor of Design at Linköping University
Stefan is an interaction designer based in Scandinavian participatory design with a cognitive science perspective.

There are multiple understandings of 'policy'; sometimes watered down into any decision made by some body of actor/s that creates a frame or direction for the actions of that, or another, body of actor/s. This creates an imprecise term, where more precise terms would be beneficial, for example terms such as rule, regulation, procedure, principle, heuristic, routine, decision and others.

Here the focus will be on policy in the sense of governmental policies and policy development. However, a lot of what is developed here can probably be translated into other types of policy terminologies.

It is common to view policy in two different ways. First, it can be seen as those things that are written down in laws and regulations. This is policy in its institutionalised form. It's an obvious material that can, and is, formed, although not always with design in mind. Second, it can be seen as those things that actors in policy-related contexts do. This is policy seen as enactments. These enactments are socio-material practices of policy (Figure 2.19.1). Both senses are part of different policy development processes.

Material transformation or forming

One sense to understand policy in the context of service design is that it works as an input to, or frame for, design work. Policy is then a material that is formed in some other context and process, probably in something depicted as a policy development process. This is a convenient position, a rationalistic and static understanding of policy as well as of service design's

Source: Antrop, Naturvårdsverket, Vinnova, Maria Klint, Martina Thyberg, Johanna Celion och Erik Hammarström.

Figure 2.19.1 Examples of policy enactments in a shop environment

role in forming policy. Policy is set outside the scope of service design, and hence whether it's a material or not is an uninteresting question for service design.

A variation of this is that services are direct representations of policy, as defined by policy makers. This may be the case sometimes. This understanding is also hinged on a rationalistic understanding. Moreover, it poses a major challenge to service design, in the form of whether policy and service then is the same material, and whether by reforming a service the service designer should assume that they have the mandate to also reform the corresponding policy.

However, most of the time a written policy is interpreted by a governance system into regulations, that are translated by organisations into rules and procedures, that in turn are applied by management structures, employees and computer systems. The latter are often developed by external organisations based on public procurement. Hence, policies have multiple materialisations through contextual and situated interpretations throughout such a system. Service designers may be part of any or several of those contexts, then contribute to the network of interpretations.

A second sense is to understand policy as being expressed through what services are developed, how these services are designed and through the actions performed in the services. This sense resonates directly with policy as being enacted.

A simple example would be the design decision to utilise a straightforward queue system (first-in, first-out or first-come, first-served), or a system with a VIP bypass, in let's say admitting children to public daycare centres (pre-school, kindergarten or even primary school). Both are possible but express two different sets of policy. The latter may be prohibited through policy.

Another example would be public park caretaking. Design decisions are often made as the balance between operant and operand resources. A decision can be made on the amount of wastepaper bins defined per square metre and a service schedule. That is, the available waste volume is decided by the maximum empty waste bin volume at any given time, and all waste volume above this will litter the park until someone removes it. Another design decision could be to calculate the amount of wastepaper bins to how many people are visiting the park doing high-littering activities, and adapt a service and governance schedule accordingly.

In all of these cases policy is enacted in the service; policy is constantly formed in these enactments. Policy as a material is thus formed through interactions in service situations, through resource and action space integration between actors. Sometimes the design space in the situation is large, and sometimes it is more narrow. Hence, policy and policy enactment are part of the designerly work of forming a service.

A consequence of thinking of policy as being formed through enactments is that the experiences from such enactments can be made part of more formalised policy development processes, aiming to change, e.g., written policy. That is, deliberate experiments and prototyping of policy enactments also are part of redesigning, or rather reforming, policy.

A third sense that is important to have in mind is that services can be seen as the system of resources that make human (and beyond-human) rights available to citizens (and other human and non-human rights holders). Policy then can be seen as part of the infrastructure that makes this possible. That is, one of the manipulable material of rights is policy and associated services, across the public, private and third sectors.

Materials and representations

The representation question when it comes to policy as a material has a couple of turns.

First of all, policy is seldom directly articulated in representations of service, and is therefore not directly open for deliberate manipulation through the representation itself. However, it is not difficult to add a reflexive layer to the use of any of those representations, on how they represent certain policies and on how policy could be altered.

Second, the service in itself can be seen as an indirect representation of policy, where routines, information technology systems, relations, etc. are a collage of interpretations of policy. Mapping and sense-making practices in service design, with their associated representations, therefore also represent policy.

Competences needed to work with the material

As governance systems are not necessarily trivial, but often layered and full of goal conflicts as well as being different in different countries, there is a need for a service designer to be well read up on, or experienced in, the system of governance they operate within. It matters whether the governance system is social democratic or market liberal. Alternatively, service designers need to work together with professions and practices that can take on a role to be the bridge between design and designing and policy development and governance systems. Nonetheless, designers need to have a decent overview of the rights and belief systems that are the reason for making policy at all.

Moreover, a service designer that wants to work with policy needs at least a basic understanding of different styles and philosophies around policy and policy development.

Most probably, being a service designer that works with policy as the main material will be a specialised area of practice, while the basic relational understanding should be introduced in university programmes.

Further reading

Kimbell, L. (2015). Applying design approaches to policy making: Discovering policy lab. University of Brighton.

Kimbell, L., & Vesnić-Alujević, L. (2020). After the toolkit: Anticipatory logics and the future of government. Policy Design and Practice, 3(2), 95–108.

Legeby, M., McAleenan, P., Andersson, H., & Holmlid, S. (2018, July). Guiding the welfare state towards a co-creative and explorative mindset: When a crisis is an opportunity. ServDes2018, 18–20 June, Milan (150, pp. 612–628). Linköping University Electronic Press.

PART 3

QUALITIES BY WHICH SOMETHING MAY BE CATEGORISED

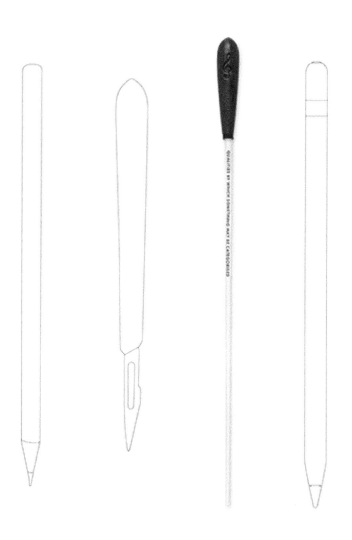

Introduction to Part 3

Part 3 of the book is dedicated to an examination and analysis of the materials suggested in Part 2. The first chapter is an initial reaction to the broad mix of materials, and some thoughts that emerged about materiality as a word and concept. Second, we examine the properties of the materials by comparing them and also by looking at them as a whole. This is followed by three attempts at categorising the materials using different strategies. In the following chapter we suggest service can be seen as hypermaterial and bring up some consequences of designing for and with a broad mix of materials. Another character of the materials is layeredness – across, within and conceptually. We discuss what material layeredness means for design. Finally, we propose a framework where materials can be sorted, and an associated model for exploring materials of service.

1   Making sense of a material mix

In this part of the book, we dive into the suggested materials in Part 2 and try to make sense of them. In total, 18 materials were suggested, and it can be a little overwhelming to make sense of them all and to find ways to think about what each material means for service and design. To help with that we will go through different perspectives and features of the materials. For instance, what does it mean that there is such a mix of tangible and intangible materials? What assumptions do we make about materials and what does this mean for design? What happens when designers cannot directly influence their materials, and what does it mean for the tools designers use?

We open up with some general first impressions or reflections on the materials. After that, we facilitate an overview of the materials by offering a few options for how the materials can be categorised. We also discuss what different categorisations mean for how we understand design in relation to materiality. Without going too far from the material descriptions in Part 2, we then continue to extrapolate from the materials how they influence our understanding of service design. By the end we land in a simplified model of materials that we find helpful when thinking about both the materials in this book but also other materials that might be considered.

Reacting to the material mix

It has been refreshing to accept that some of the materials suggested are indeed materials, and that in itself can open up for new materials as being embraced as part of design. We would like to see this develop into a material library, and on the companion website to the book we will develop a living library that we can co-produce, so that everyone can discuss and develop this understanding further.

The suggested materials are redefining what a design material is, and the range from tangible to intangible is notable. When we say redefining, we do not refer to a dictionary definition but more to the traditional view of materials in design being material and directly formable. Many of the materials, even the intangible ones, are indeed formable, but indirectly. This indirectness has material implications. Forming many of the materials in this book lacks the immediacy of forming for example metal, wood or clay. In the Heidegger sense, crafting 'traditional' materials physically gives a direct feedback, evident in the crafted object. You hammer a sheet of metal and it bends, hopefully to a desired shape, through constant direct interaction. With service design, the feedback is not immediate. Indeed, the feedback can come months or years afterwards, and that means that the designer often needs to add a representation/prototyping layer to simulate and/or stimulate the result of an action. This means we are forming materials for future situations. The immediate bodily reactions to forming are not there and become replaced by an intellectual interpretation of a future, even when these explorations are directly made through visualisations.

Indirect materials can also mean that they depend on an intermediary. This intermediary can be a person, a group of people or even whole organisations that need to implement and adjust to change. This opens up a new category of materials where design skills no longer have to do exclusively with craft or aesthetics, but also with, for example, people skills, politics and communication. A similar challenge exists in interaction design, where designers create interface solutions that are then implemented by programmers. Architects create solutions but rely on engineers, contractors and other stakeholders to build houses. The main difference here is that designers and other involved parties know what should be built because there is a model or blueprint to follow. However, the negotiations with other stakeholders about how and what to design are considered circumstantial in most fields. A notable difference from other (design) fields, judging by the materials presented in this book, is that these elements can be considered part of the design material itself! One important consequence is that evaluation of the material forming cannot always be done by the designer(s) but rather the project teams, or even front-line employees or customers.

The materials clearly highlight differences between service design and traditional forming disciplines, yet at the same time, some core aspects remain the same. By this, we mean that individual materials may have different characteristics and affordances, but the synthetic integrating approach of design remains similar. This is reassuring, since there is a long heritage and evolution of design approaches, and it would be challenging to replace these.

One question that this has raised is: Does this redefine designing as a process, design as a specification or design as an ambition? We consider that these materials redefine design as a specification and design as an ambition, due to their nature, but perhaps they have less of an impact on the process. The number of materials relevant to design are increasing, but we would argue that the core processes are the same – exploration, prototyping, ideation, synthesis, etc. However, it must be mentioned that the process that is implied as part of almost every material is one of co-design – the designer forming directly and indirectly aspects of shared exploration, understanding, ideation and decision making. We return to this in Part 3, Chapter 5.

Inherited assumptions about materiality

The underlying presumption of the book is that service can be seen as a material. The word material in itself has been questioned (see for instance Part 2, Interlude 1) for various reasons. One is of course that materials have negative connotations for sustainability. Service, and the design field engaged in designing it, has distanced itself from materiality and offered an alternative way to enjoyable experiences, one that does not rely exclusively on new products. However, this book very clearly does not consider material to mean physical, but rather seeks to emphasise the point that designers seek to create something new, and that that something is traditionally thought of as (a) design material. Simply asking about the domain, context or field would not get to the designerly heart of what service is.

By focusing on materiality we inherit some assumptions, for good and for bad. Some assumptions about materiality that are close at hand is that materials can be seen, touched, have weight, firmness, malleability, buoyancy and so on. Framing service as material gives access to such qualities, and we can start to ask what weight, firmness or malleability means for the materials of service (which we will do in Part 3, Chapter 2). Service as material can also have more meanings, as seen in the dictionary definitions in the Prologue. The library of materials in Part 2 expands the possible meanings of the term material even further. However, since we are using the word material, and most people already have a relation to that word, we should say something about where the analogy does not help.

There is a risk that too much is inferred from the dichotomy of goods and service, material and immaterial. For instance, being non-physical does not mean that a material is endless: creativity, imagination, patience, trust and emotion can all be depleted. One way of understanding what designers do in relation to intangible materials is keeping house or economising (in Swedish: *hushålla*) with human resources.[1] Keeping house with human emotions by encouraging creativity and imagination, instilling both trust and curiosity to shape and move change in a specific direction, requires a very specific sensitivity to metaphysical elements. Knowing where and with what to push and pull, when to be gentle or stern and how to convince people and make them prepared for change are some of the skills involved in shaping service. A concept in service design that has gained widespread attention is the touch-point, and an associated tool is the customer journey map. Seen from traditional design, or from the perspective of related disciplines, customer journey mapping lacks validity. Often it shows one idealised customer's interactions within a service, one journey out of an endless range of possible journeys, with one customer that might not even represent a customer segment or otherwise be based on quantitative design research. So why is it so iconic? One interpretation is that, like many service design tools and techniques, it is not meant as a model of actual service, but rather as a way of keeping house with human intangible and metaphysical resources.

One interpretation of the word material is something that is important. Something material is something that exists, and we have a tendency to trust what we can see and feel more than things we cannot. These assumptions can be found also in literature about service, which partially explains why service logic theories (see Part 2, Chapter 4) have been so revelatory and paradigmatic. Service logic theories have had severe impact on businesses, with servitisation processes leading to things like X as service (travelling as service, games as service, food as service, etc.) and new ways of thinking about the relationship that firms have with their customers. Service logic also puts the immaterial at centre stage. Our hope is that the number of materials keeps growing and enriches our understanding of service as material for design. Theories of service logic have been helpful, but the materials in this book show another story, one where the properties are more in tune with design as a field and practice.

---

1 This definition of (service) design was originally suggested by Tomas Edman, Experio Lab, Region Värmland.

2 Categorisation of materials as a way of understanding their characteristics

If you as a reader expected to find a single, straightforward and objectively true categorisation of the materials in this book, then unfortunately you will be disappointed. We have found no single way to arrange the materials that we all (the authors) can get behind. As you will notice, each categorisation has its drawbacks, and many more sorting strategies can potentially be imagined. However, attempting to categorise gives new insights into the nature of the materials and the nature of service design itself. If you as a reader want to add your own, or just discuss existing categorisations, you can do so on the companion website.

In the following we will share our attempts and associated insights. But before we get to that, we examine the materials from Part 2 again to refresh our memories and abstract some knowledge about them.

As a reminder, these are the materials from Part 2:

Social structures	Time	Collaborations	Clay
Touch-points	Organisations	Behaviour	Human bodies
Thinking	Conversations	Experience	Sound
Culture	Ritual	Data	Offering
	Certainty		Policy

Using material properties as a lens to examine the materials

Let us look at the materials through a lens of their properties. We mentioned earlier how weight, buoyancy or malleability can be qualities or properties of a material. An earlier attempt to identify properties of material in service design, in comparison with interaction design and industrial design, suggested joint and differentiating categories; tangible and virtual material, visual, experiential and active aesthetics, and social, temporal and spatial dimensionality (Holmlid, 2007). Here we examine and explore the breadth of material properties, based on the material descriptions themselves, with the hope of creating a space where all the materials fit. This step hopefully also helps the reader in the next step, where we try to identify meaningful categories.

We find materials in the full spectrum from intangible to tangible, from visible to invisible. Some materials stand out and warrant mentioning. Since much has been said about tangibility and service, we start there. Some of the materials are material in the traditional or typical sense of the word material. Clay can be warm or cold, wet or dry or drying. Sound has loudness (intensity), pitch (height or ordering dimension), timbre (sound quality or 'colour' related to the sound source) and duration. Thinking on the other hand is described as being immaterial, intangible and invisible. The authors (Part 2, Chapter 4) also acknowledge the challenge of designing (in any traditional sense of the word) thinking in service. Sound is invisible but still perceivable, and can be seen as another complementing dimension to tangibility. Fully tangible and perceivable is clay, and much of its role as material in design comes specifically from the ability to touch and shape it. Service offering is also largely a tangible material. For both of these materials, clay and offering, the authors mention an effort required of humans to make sense or extrapolate from the materials. So despite being physical and tangible, the materials are not standalone. They require interpretation to make sense of.

As part of the space of properties that is emerging, we should also note symbolic actions, values and culture as part of rituals. Culture (at least the specific niche of culture in this book) itself is a consequence of shared meaning, meaning construction and lifestyle choices. Routines, user and customer perspectives and practices are included as properties of organisations.

For behaviours to occur, there needs to be motivation, opportunity and capability, but for this material we can also see that behaviours are situational, contextual and social. For design, this creates a list of aspects to work with, but at the same time there is no easy way to shape motivation or capability. Similarly, human bodies are described as a key service interface that can be further broken down into two interconnected aspects of human experiencing: body schema and body image. Body schema is implicit bodily perceptions, and includes augmenting technologies with which perception is enhanced. Body image relates to explicit perceptions, attitudes and beliefs about one's body, which are most commonly the object of design but which are difficult to shape. Perhaps counterintuitively, shaping time seems easier since it includes timing, and time-ing. Time is also one of the materials with highest firmness, since it influences and changes other materials.

The tangible to intangible spectrum raises the question of how materials influence each other, and which materials can be used to shape other materials. In the physical world, harder materials can shape softer ones. A hard material like metal, when it comes into contact with a softer material like wood, will leave an impression. Perhaps there is an analogous relationship between some of the materials. A material that changes another material is often considered a tool, like using a chisel to shape a piece of wood. No material in the book is directly described as tools in themselves, but to a degree clay, for example, can be seen as a tool. It has the ability to shape how participants think based on how it is shaped; the material can leave an impression (see also Part 3, Chapter 3: Tool making). Some materials, like organisation and ritual, are also described as materials that are influenced by material components, like symbols and artefacts (more specifically by artefacts). Certainty and conversations are also described as being tightly coupled with, and influenced by, physical artefacts.

Many materials have both physical and non-physical constituents: rituals, collaborations, experience and touch-points. Some materials even encompass many other materials, such as organisations and social structures. Materials that contain other materials, and/or physical and non-physical elements, have natural internal conflicts within them. We can theoretically examine these conflicts further. For instance, it is easy to make the assumption that physical materials have more of an impact on non-physical, but that is not always true. For instance, social structures are described as both intangible (rules, norms, beliefs) and tangible (symbols, artefacts, activities, relations). The authors of the chapter Part 2, Chapter 2, however, argue that tangible aspects are shaped by intangible aspects. It is reasonable to assume that the rules, norms and beliefs held by a group will be reflected in the physical world around them. On an individual level, norms and beliefs are part of the social context that influences behaviours, that in turn is part of conversations and collaborations. Another very straightforward example of intangible materials influencing tangible materials is when clay is used to express elements of a participant's internal world. So being physical in the context of service does not necessarily imply harder, as in a material that will leave an impression on the other. For service we might be better off thinking about a word such as resistance.

Resistance in service

Anyone who has tried chiselling wood knows that different wood types have different hardness, which changes how much force you need to apply to shape it. Softer wood requires more delicate moves, while harder wood is more forgiving since the chisel only leaves small marks. Also, within the same piece of wood there are differences in hardness. Areas around knots can be really difficult to shape. There is a difference in resistance across a single piece of wood, and between different wood types. Similarly, when attempting to change service there will be resistance. The resistance can take many shapes. It can come in the form of boundaries discovered during design processes. For instance, rules, regulation and laws that limit the kinds of available solutions. If we take governmental agencies in Sweden as an example, boundary-setting resistance comes mainly in the form of issues related to security, laws and legal matters and legacy systems. If you are trying to create a new purchase experience in a government agency in Sweden, you are restricted to using the same solution as other government bodies based on a collective procurement process.

The resistance of service is not always directly observable or noticeable but can be made perceivable. Boundaries can also be softer, such as needing approval from the right authority, internally in organisations or outside of the organisation. In bigger organisations there are often divisions or groups that set boundaries, but there can be individual, relational issues that are hard to notice: in-built systems might not function well together, or with a new feature of a service the service might not work well with service delivery staff or customers because behavioural patterns conflict with the new service. Some of the materials in the library of materials in Part 2 specifically help with identifying resistance. Through conversations, rituals, behaviours and bodies (Part 2, Chapters 8, 9, 12 and 16), the pliability of service can start to become visible. Conversations are a big part of negotiating change, and certainty arte-facts help in transitioning from a current mindset to a future (certainty) – how people think around what they do as part of service (thinking).

Aggregate level of material properties

If we take a step back and consider the materials, we find that each material contributes a number of properties that, on the aggregate level, can be seen as properties of service. Some of the properties that stand out are:

1. Service has cognition.
2. Service has behaviour.
3. Service has mood.

Service has cognition

Thinking has already been suggested and outlined as a material of service, and on the aggregate level, there is also an emergent type of cognition.

The people and artefacts in a service possess both situated and distributed knowledge. The cognition of a service comes into play through materials such as thinking, conversations, collaborations and certainty. Also, the rituals and cultures present in service influence cognitive processes. For instance, signs and symbols will have different meanings in different services depending on the people within them. The signs and symbols embody cultural aspects, and are expressed for example through actual bodies. By examining the physical expressions within services it becomes possible to understand the cognition. In a similar way, cognitive processes in a service can be observed in the behaviours.

Service has behaviour

Social structures and cognitive processes give service a specific behaviour. A restaurant service in Sweden behaves differently from restaurants in Portugal. Figuring out how to behave as an individual in a service requires observation and collaboration with locals. As a designer, a service's behaviour can be difficult to notice and requires reflexivity as well as norm criticality (see Part 2, Chapter 2). Another way to conceptualise behaviour is to consider service personality (Aaker, 1997). For instance, while personality is useful when deciding how an organisation wants people to experience or perceive their service, behaviours are how the personality is manifested. Ideally, the behaviour across all touch-points should communicate the same personality. However, since service also consists of humans, behaviours change over time. These changes can be indicative of the mood of a service at any point in time.

Service has mood

This aspect is not directly observable from the materials but is more of an emergent side effect. The mood of a service also interacts with the cognition and behaviour. For example, if the workforce is under threat (from lay-offs, restructuring, etc.) that will influence the willingness to change, trust, accommodation, openness and so on. Collaborations and conversations will take on a new shape and individual behaviour will change as a consequence. If threats or conflicts persist between parts of services it can start to affect how a service is perceived. For instance, it might lead to a mismatch between the offering and perceived service, and it might ruin the experience altogether for customers. This will in turn influence the service mood since customers talk to other customers. Another mismatch might occur in the digital and human sides of a service, since the digital expression of a service might not change as a result of changed worker attitudes.

On smaller time scales, mood can also change based on sudden or foreseen contextual changes. One example is what happens at an emergency ward after a recent traffic accident – the mood is calm but anticipating before and hectic and reactive after. At an emergency ward, people are trained and prepared for situations like that. People act quickly but methodically. But if accidents occur at a hotel or elsewhere the mood might be less controlled, even panicked. In restaurants there are many mood changes during the day but most are predictable, such as the lunch hour rush or slower periods in the mornings.

A New Service Development categorisation

One way to understand the material mix is to connect the materials to an existing categorisation. In this case we look at the categories used in Blomkvist (2015). The categorisation used a framework from New Service Development (NSD), suggested by Edvardsson and Olsson (1996) as a way to connect material aspects of service to an existing conceptualisation. In their framework, Edvardsson and Olsson proposed that there are three elements of service development, from a quality perspective: system, process and concept. *The system* consists of resources needed for processes to take place, such as people, technology, physical spaces and organisation. *The process* is a chain of activities that make up service. The process can be divided into two types, a service process that is the template for what and how a process should unfold and customer processes, which are actual processes that take place during a service. The aim of the service process is to manifest the service concept. *The concept* is described as the value provided by service to customers and consists of both what should be done for the customer as well as how it should be done. As an element of service development, the concept needs to be based on a good understanding of customers' needs and expectations. Together, the system, process and concept form the prerequisites for service, i.e., what is developed. Based on this understanding we made the categorisation in Table 3.2.1.

This is a top-down categorisation with pre-existing categories that the materials are grouped according to, which leads to a categorisation that fits the perspective rather than the materials themselves. Overall, the guiding principle for the categorisation was that the categories should be understood in their own context. This means that the materials should be seen as elements that are developed (or part of development) as prerequisites of service. Of course, this forces us to use some creative freedom in how the materials are understood.

Table 3.2.1   Categories and design elements found in Blomkvist (2015) compared to the materials suggested in Part 2

System (components, things, locations)	Process (actions, procedures, interactions)	Concept (experiences)
Time	Social structures	Offering
Culture	Touch-points	Thinking
Sound	Ritual	Clay
Organisations	Experience	Collaborations
Data	Human bodies	Conversations
Policy		Behaviour
		Certainty

System

The system contains time, culture, sound, organisations, data and policy. These materials are all resources for the processes that are going to take place in services. There are material properties that can be influenced by design, but also some that are more difficult. For instance, time is a factor but also something that can be used consciously to design elements of service. Similarly, some sounds can be designed, while others are emergent and/or unintentional. Culture is more difficult to place but should be seen here also as something that exists irrespectively of design but that can be used as a tool while designing. Organisation can be easily placed here since it was mentioned by the authors as a component, but based on the material description (Part 2, Chapter 7) it is not as clear. However, this is the best fit for the material. Policy is also indirectly mentioned in the original framework and can be placed in the system category. Data are part of making sense of a system, and are generated by the processes in systems. We choose to focus on data as a resource available for decisions about the service.

Process

Overall, the distinction between process and concept is difficult to make in relation to many of the materials. The process contains both materials for the service and the customer process. Touch-points have many different roles and meanings and can be both the archetypical interaction (as a visual representation of an instance of a customer journey map) and the actual physical interaction between service provider and customer. The aim behind a touch-point representation in a customer journey map is often to capture or illustrate some value, and as such it fits better in the concept category. In this categorisation, however, we focus on the touch-point as the actual interactions that make up the processes of service. It is within the conceptual space of such touch-points that human bodies shape interactions and take part in the performance of rituals. Experiences are in turn shaped partly by those interactions, which is why experiences are not part of the concept in this categorisation but rather the process. Social structures stand out here because they have less in common with the concept and more with the system. Also in this case we decided to focus on the processual aspects of social structures, emphasising the social above the structures.

Concept

The concept category can to some extent be understood as the offering, as a way to capture an understanding about what the value of a service could be for a specific target group. One group of materials that is difficult to place contains materials that are mostly relevant during design time; materials that are not present when actual service interactions take place. For instance, certainty (artefacts) are mostly relevant during design. The same can be said for clay, and perhaps for most of the materials in the concept category. Clay is in concept because of the way it is described, it serves as a tool for empathy and tangible catalyst during design time with external stakeholders. At the same time, thinking, collaborations and conversations take place throughout the development and actual process of service, but here we focus on how such materials shape a service concept. Through collaborations and conversations it becomes possible to identify values and desirable outcomes for customers. This in turn depends on data and an understanding of systems, but mainly helps create an understanding of what a service should do for its customers. The same reasoning lies behind the inclusion of behaviour in this category, since from a development perspective it is vital that behaviour is understood in order to provide meaningful value.

What we learned from the New Service Development categorisation

It is important to consider the time and context in which the NSD elements were proposed. In 1996 there were no service logic theories, even though similar thoughts were developing. In Edvardsson and Olsson (1996), system, process and concept were developed in parallel and the result was a set of prerequisites for a service. A service process as a whole consisted also of customer process and customer outcome – the prerequisites were developed from the perspective of a service company. The conceptualisation is focused on a service delivery idea rather than a resource integration one.

Moreover, it is not intended for design. Design was seen as a phase of service development, often as a stage where a concept was developed. Hence, the materials in each category do not make sense from the perspective of NSD, especially since the materials are not exclusively relevant as part of service prerequisites.

From a design perspective, this categorisation conveniently compartmentalises the materials and breaks down elements of service. Adopting this view means service can be divided into three categories where design effort can be directed and suggests what the relevant materials could be. The categorisation might be useful for high-level management of large design projects or strategic work. Also, designers specialised in system, process or concept design could be imagined, but if one were to study the material descriptions in Part 2 more closely, there would be conflicts in both their placement per se but also in how the materials relate to each other. This is a challenge for this view.

A bottom-up categorisation

Another, perhaps more appropriate way to organise the materials is to consider *how they relate to each other in design*. This can be done using a bottom-up approach, looking at the materials in themselves without using any predetermined categories. Hence, we started by grouping the materials without any specific goal or category in mind. We then examined the groups more carefully and started to make sense of why specific materials were placed together. After a few different attempts over the course of several meetings we found a categorisation reflecting four elements of design. These were renamed several times and could continue to be so. One factor that separates this categorisation into two parts is how the materials relate to designers' activities. Is there a direct impact on the material, i.e., do designers directly manipulate or influence the materials or are more people or processes required to change the material? The result can be seen in Table 3.2.2.

In the following text we will refer to designer(s) as people involved in design activities during development of service (e.g., schooled designers), not the front-line staff that interact with customers and 'design' the service encounters. We will now take a closer look at each category and the materials therein.

Table 3.2.2   The resulting categories from the bottom-up approach

Design context	Hands-on design		Hands-off design	
	Experiential	Context	Indirect	Societal
	Touch-points	Clay	Experience	Certainty
	Sound	Conversations	Organisations	Policy
	Offering	Data	Behaviour	Culture
		Collaborations	Social structures	Thinking
			Human bodies	Time
			Ritual	

Experiential

This category contains materials that designers can manipulate directly and that are related to experiential aspects of service. This includes materials related to what it feels, sounds or looks like to take part in service. The materials are not necessarily part of service but relate directly to elements of service and specifically perceivable aspects. Changes to the material occur instantly and can be directly observed by the designer.

1. Touch-points – material that span across many different domains of service, from quick sketches of interaction between a service organisation and a customer to actual physical interactions as a service is taking place in the world. However, as a hands-on design material they are often part of the creation of customer journey maps, and focused on how a service is, or should be, perceived by its customers. Hence, as a material it relates to how people experience service and that can be manipulated directly by designers.
2. Sound – this is in itself an experience, and sounds can be designed, both intentional sounds and unintentional sounds.
3. Offering – unlike the experience, the offering is designed hands-on and has an intended experience. It is one of the materials that indirectly shape experiences. One aspect of the offering is the remembered experience, which is out of reach for design but can be indirectly influenced.

Contextual

Here we find materials that are directly manipulated but that create possibilities or space for design activities. These materials pave the way for human- (or customer, or user) and service-centred perspectives to take place.

1. Clay – used as a stand-in for materials that help designers generate insights and understand humans in various ways. They help express and share otherwise invisible aspects of life and as such help designers understand contexts.
2. Conversations – designers are part of conversations, and the author argues that conversations should be more consciously shaped by design. Some conversations relate specifically to services but the conversations are not developing or transforming services. Conversations are also impacting the service delivery staff when they are involved in design, and the material is thus very close to being in the experiential category. The conversations aid in making design more impactful on many levels and thus fall into the context category.
3. Data – the author uses data in the broadest sense of the word and illustrates how design can influence, quite directly, how people share their data. Data also fit the hands-off categories since the influence normally is limited in a specific design project. However, as a material it is something that creates objectives for design and can be created as part of design activities.
4. Collaborations – to a very large extent, collaborations are not directly impacted by design. However, the authors describe ways in which designers directly create or change collaborations through social and material practices. The material fits the hands-on category because designers take part in collaborations, and the materials and social practices become tools with which collaborations are changed and given form.

Indirect

Materials that are described as being impacted by (hands-on) design but in an indirect way. The material changes based on design activities but in a somewhat unpredictable way and often at a later time. The material changes with society and over time as well. These materials require both hands-on design skills but also more strategic thinking and planning. They also tend to require actively working to understand design in a larger, cultural and social context, with perspectives that are not readily apparent.

1. Experience – indirect and asynchronous change to the material based on design activities.
2. Organisations – design produces artefacts that in turn influence organisations. The relation is indirect and to some extent 'out of the hands' of design.

3. Behaviour – described as something that can be influenced by hands-on design but only indirect.

4. Social structures – the authors mention structures both as something that happens in the world and partly as something that exists internally within the minds of humans. Social structures can be consciously changed through reflexivity, but the material needs intermediaries. The authors describe it as carpenters needing to mill wood into boards before it can be used to build furniture. There is a level of hands-on design, but the material is always a step or more removed.

5. Human bodies – while a designer can work on designing a piece of clothing or work attire for a group of workers, the authors consider a much wider definition of human bodies, much of which is out of the hands of individual design teams.

6. Ritual – rituals are described as time-based structures that have meaning to the people involved. They can be created through the development of touch-point and cultural (or symbolic) material. Design works closely with participants to create rituals, but the influence is indirect.

7. Time – the material is in one sense a hands-off material when viewed as the passing of time and time as something that is measured. In another sense it is a hands-on experiential material when viewed from a Kairos perspective. Design is forming the material indirectly, or is including it as one quality in a design.

Societal

Societal materials are those that are more than one material away from hands-on design and where changes in the material are unpredictable. Many of the other materials are impacted by these materials. The intention might not even be to change the materials in this category, but rather for design to take them into account.

1. Certainty – this and its artefact are discussed by the authors with examples of different artefacts. Some are made to support design (context category) and some are produced by other functions, and some are beliefs held by people. In the end, certainty is not the same as the artefact but more of a perspective that influences, and is influenced by, artefacts. Certainty as a material is not directly worked with, but rather is a concept to consider.

2. Policy – described as the societal institutions that often are in the form of laws and regulations, but also as the actual action in society that enacts

policy. Design works with both aspects as materials, and ties together across the micro and macro system levels.

3. Culture – the authors talk specifically about popular culture, but mention, e.g., organisational culture as well as even broader notions of culture. However, pop culture is an expression of societal movements.

4. Thinking – we can train our own thinking but mainly the authors talk about thinking that goes on in the world, and how design can attempt to gain insights about how and what people think.

What we learned

This categorisation illustrates the different scales at which service design operates. On the left side, design is limited to a specific aspect of service, with hands-on crafting of materials. The next step, context, is about creating preconditions for design, making design impactful and increasing awareness about design perspectives. The indirect category contains materials that require design to operate on a more strategic level and at the scale of organisations and management. Finally, the categories reach all the way to the societal level with materials that are out of reach for design change but that can be influenced by it, and is influenced by it in return.

As a way to categorise materials it is closer to a design view than the NSD categorisation and reflects largely the role of design in relation to the materials. By that we mean that the categories relate to how design is able to change materials, and to some extent explores the boundaries and reach of design. Materials on the left are more easily changed than the ones on the right. More hands-off materials means larger groups of people are involved in/with the material. This requires a different set of skills than the hands-on materials.

An ontological structure can be noticed with this categorisation where some materials are building blocks for other materials. The hands-on categories work in tandem: touch-point mapping relies on data and is anchored in the organisation through collaborations and conversations. Clay helps build the empathy needed to design a service offering. The hands-off materials can benefit from these aforementioned materials: the goal of the offering and the touch-points are to create experiences that suit organisations and customers. However, to design for behaviours and rituals, and to some extent social structures, many design techniques with material components are required but those materials are not present in the materials in Part 2.

In some descriptions of service design authors include things among the materials. This list, however, is quite devoid of things, with a few exceptions. Most materials are not worked hands-on into something that customers experience, but rather experiences, organisations, social structures, etc. in themselves. This illustrates that there are different types of service design and, as such, this categorisation can be useful in identifying those types, and for creating service design education with different scopes or focus areas.

The four orders of design categorisation

After trying to categorise the materials according to Service Dominant Logic (Vargo & Lush, 2004, 2008) (everything kind of goes everywhere) and looking at the stages of a typical design process (everything can almost go everywhere there, too), we viewed the materials through the lens of Buchanan's (2001) four orders of design (here we have updated Buchanan's third-order term 'action' to be 'interaction', as is common practice today). What is interesting when looking at the four orders is that we have materials in all four orders. These range from traditional design materials (e.g., clay, sound) through interaction materials (e.g., touch-points) to thought materials (conversations, thinking, etc.). However, what is interesting is that the 'lower'-level materials do not stand alone. Instead, they are used primarily to achieve tactical or strategic goals in the higher orders. These can be tactical or strategic for the service in question or for the organisation itself. This is best exemplified in the material description about the organisation as a material, where it shows how service design artefacts function as organisational change agents.

There seems to be a material migration from the symbolic towards the strategic/tactical and structural/systemic from the lower orders (see Figure 3.2.1). The more traditional materials are utilised as part of tactical or strategic goals and are employed to give a tactical and strategic contribution. For example, the materials culture and ritual are strongly based on symbols and meaning, yet can transform a service offering the journey and touch-points and thereby become both tactical and/or strategic. Touch-points can be seen as 'things' and use symbols in their design, yet become interactive in a service context. However, all of these lower-level materials are used, or leveraged (you could say), by the service designer to work at the interaction thought level. In other words, the symbology of a logo on a business card has little service value unless meaning and symbology are also utilised in other touch-points and integrated into the systemic structure of the service. This is another way of saying the alignment of elements is needed at the systemic level to deliver meaningful

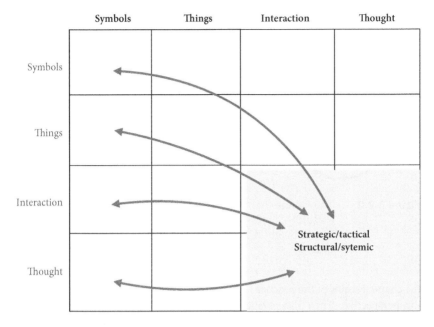

Note: It is important to note that it seems like all materials have a strategic/tactical and structural/systemic consequence.

Figure 3.2.1   The four orders of design adapted to show the interrelation between materials at all levels

experiences. This goes the other way, too. The core systemic (and thought) elements need to be translated and made visible through touch-points (things) and logos (symbols). This happens both during the design process and during service delivery. A logo or SMS confirmation needs to be an experiential reflection of the offering, the structure of the service and what the service aims to achieve. Therefore, there is a leverage or migration both ways (see Figure 3.2.1).

This leverage and interconnectedness is not new and have been described in design management (Cooper & Press, 1995). However, what is evident is that we can conclude that service design is, at its core, a tactical and strategic design field. This implies the need for more strategic competences as part of education and practice. Further, within service design, the traditional materials of design have migrated to the interaction/thought level and vice versa. As such, this reinforces the visualisation by Wetter Edman (2011; see Figure 3.2.2) of an interconnectedness. She writes about how practice and perspectives are related: 'At some point

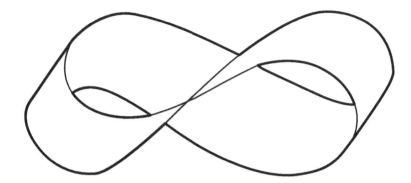

Figure 3.2.2   The infinite loop visualisation by Wetter Edman that is
a useful visualisation for how materials interrelate and
interact with each other across all levels of the Buchanan
orders

the characteristics of the practice – the inside – turns and becomes the outside –
the perspective. Then the perspective, in due course, when implementation
demands specific tools and competences, organizes the specific practice – the
inside – to realize the desired context for value creation' (p. 105).

References

Aaker, J. L. (1997). Dimensions of brand personality. *Journal of Marketing Research*,
34(3), 347–356.

Blomkvist, J. (2015). Ways of seeing service: Surrogates for a design material.
Proceedings of the Nordic Design Research Conference, 1–4.

Buchanan, R. (2001). Design research and the new learning. *Design Issues*, *17*(4), 3–23.

Cooper, R., & Press, M. (1995). *The design agenda: A guide to successful design management*. John Wiley and Sons.

Edvardsson, B., & Olsson, J. (1996). Key concepts for New Service Development. *The
Service Industries Journal*, *16*(2), 140–164.

Holmlid, S. (2007). Interaction design and service design: Expanding a comparison of
design disciplines. Nordes Conference, Stockholm.

Vargo, S., & Lusch, R. (2004). Evolving to a new dominant logic for marketing. *Journal
of Marketing*, *68*, 1–17.

Vargo, S., & Lusch, R. (2008). Service-dominant logic: Continuing the evolution.
Journal of the Academy of Marketing Science, *36*, 1–10.

Wetter Edman, K. (2011). *Service design: A conceptualization of an emerging practice*.
ArtMonitor.

3   Addressing the material mix: service as hypermaterial

We have seen a large variety of materials that constitute service. They vary in scope, from simple clay manifestations of emotions, to large societal phenomena like organisations, social structures and culture. We have also discussed how different the materials are in terms of tangibility. With such a mix, one view is that service is not material, but rather *hypermaterial* – matter and form melt together with ever changing immaterial elements. Hence, the properties of the material depend on what aspect of the material you look at. Starting from the assumption that service is hypermaterial we continue our examination of the materials and we zoom out a little to discuss the implications of hypermateriality and the specific mix of materials in this book.

What about design?

One immediate issue when considering the mix of materials is how many are indirectly manipulated. This was discussed previously (Part 3, Chapter 1), where we also stated that a mix like this makes evaluation difficult. Design might lead to actual change in service years after an intervention or project takes place. At the same time, all design is about the future, a situation that is made better than the current through some intervention. This means that design changes situations, sometimes through new products or interfaces and sometimes through less perceivable changes. Service is also in a constant flux, since it involves humans. However, designers are trying to shape service in specific ways, and as any design material it will react. Applying a force to a material reveals its reaction and, through practice, the designer can learn to change a material in a desired way. For service, the reaction is difficult to predict and the level of resistance to change is not constant across different service contexts. What happens with forming and shaping in design?

Looking at the suggested materials in this book, very few can be considered mainly/mostly physical. The amount of intangible, abstract or non-physical elements are more common. These are elements of service, but also of everyday realities of human beings. To be able to understand and work with immaterial aspects of reality, designers need to make representations, both for their own sake and for the sake of coordination and collaboration (Part 1, Chapter 3), simply because service is too complex to keep track of and understand in the head with the help of internal representations. In the chapter about organisations (Part 2, Chapter 7) as a material we see different versions of how service is externally represented. There also seems to be a difference in how designers represent service compared to other disciplines. Either way, service development work is partly work with an emergent, human-made external representation of service.

Herbert Simon referred to design as a science of the artificial (Simon, 1996), meaning that design works in-between the outer environment and our inner world of imaginations and thoughts, to create an artificial (i.e., human-made) reality. It can also be argued that design works mainly with virtuality, to create artificial reality, especially design fields working with complex materials that have a strong immaterial component because no single representation captures all of the vital information about a material. The representations designers work with are not all design representations, they are also produced by organisations and reflect actual physical aspects of reality, such as data, economical figures, maps, visualised hierarchies, etc. Some representations, however, represent virtuality – aspects of the material that cannot be known but rather have to be imagined based on the available knowledge about reality, or by extrapolating from it. Ethnographic data collection through interviews with actual stakeholder representatives and observations has material components and certainly is based on reality with real humans in real situations and as such has virtuality: it involves elements of reality.

Materials fluctuate between reality and virtuality, in this case between services and representations thereof. We discussed this briefly in Part 1, Chapter 3 in relation to representations in service design. However, the reality of materials can be more or less observable or possible to pin down. Culture (Part 2, Chapter 5) and organisations (Part 2, Chapter 7) consist both of intangible and tangible elements, and of implicit and explicit elements. And since a big part of both culture and organisation is people, and not a person, what is true and real for one individual is not for another. Hence, design research uncovers aspects of reality that might be intangible and implicit, but in documenting and visualising (i.e., representing) that reality, they are creating a virtuality. The same is true for a lot of data that organisations collect about their processes and stakeholders. Subsequent design steps are taken based on the virtuality created and manifested by various people, and the steps lead to additional virtualisation in the form of concept ideas (touch-points, customer journey maps, blueprints). Ideally the concepts are turned into prototypes that are tested in meaningful ways. Meaningful meaning ways in which the virtual representation of a concept (i.e., prototype) can be used to draw conclusions that are connected to reality. Creating representations that allow actors involved in service design and development to understand how reality can change with new concepts is based on the materialisation of aspects of service.

Proxy and para-material

There seems to be materials used in service designing that are formed and manipulated, mostly in order to form and manipulate something else, some other material. Such materials could be seen as *proxy materials*. They work as proxies in the sense that the material that is openly formed and manipulated is deliberately chosen so that some other material, maybe less accessible, is simultaneously formed and manipulated, probably with less precision and openness. A trivial example is the service blueprint. By manipulating what is done frontstage or backstage, one is also manipulating the material organisation. That is, the material organisation is indirectly manipulated. This may well go unnoticed, unless there is a deliberate reflexivity in what it means for that which is indirectly manipulated, when the proxy material is directly manipulated. That is, shifting an activity between the backstage to the onstage may in many cases require reorganisation, layoffs and hiring of new staff. For example, shifting between a closed bistro kitchen to preparing the food in front of the customers requires different skills from chefs and sous chefs, while the prep kitchen may stay the same. The manipulation of activities across the lines in the blueprint indirectly manipulates other materials decisive for the preconditions and structures of making the new service practice possible and successful (Holmlid et al., 2021).

Being conscious about a material's role as a proxy and what is indirectly manipulated is important. From the materials presented in the book a good example of proxy material would be conversations. Conversations are formed by designers to form something beyond the actual conversations, such as progress and influence. One material indirectly formed by forming the material conversations is thinking. By forming and manipulating the conversations, the way that actors think is indirectly formed. Conversations thus are a proxy material for shaping thinking. Additionally, one may assume that beyond materials that are indirectly manipulated there occurs inferred manipulation of yet other materials. In the case of conversations – thinking – one material that is manipulated in such an inferred manner would be organisation. The main point with distinguishing between direct, indirect and inferred manipulation is that the tracing of effects of manipulation becomes less obvious. Moreover, many materials provide these chains of direct, indirect and inferred manipulation, and being aware and sensitive to how this plays out in design situations is important.

A variation on this, but also importantly distinct, is para-materials. A *para-material* would be something behaving like a proper material when it actually isn't. It may work alongside the proper materials, or even work contra to what is expected of and considered to be a proper material. One intriguing aspect of the idea of para-material is that it is dependent on conventions about what could be seen as 'proper material'; the duality this creates is in itself a dynamic and in a state of change.[1] It may also be a material that goes beyond the currently understood materiality of a certain design situation. A trivial example could be a service origami (Stickdorn et al., 2018, p. 238). We may manipulate the service origami in itself, enact and manipulate scenarios through it, giving an impression that the design decisions behind those manipulations are possible to make and will have the enacted effects (but still aware that this may not be either the sufficient or complete set of decisions needed). The assumptions that frame the design process, and all incomplete inferences that are its basis, give the impression that the service origami and its manipulation behave like a material. In the slightly larger context, where the design process is one setting, the origami works alongside many other materials, and sometimes in a counterproductive manner. The 'what if …' and 'how might we …' is instrumental in creating this dissonance, e.g., by the fact that decision making of any substantive, or radical, transformation is played out over long periods of time, and characterised by bounded rationality as well as organic adaptation.

Looking at the materials that are presented in this book, a couple of the materials can be talked about in terms of para-materials. The material time seems prone to be a para-material. In most cases both senses of time are assumption-ridden. This can be seen by the loss of actual time in enactments and visual representations. From a chronological perspective this may be unproblematic,

---

1 Some readers may at this point be searching or waiting for 'patamaterial'. However, the concept of patamaterial is dependent on the existence and possibility of identifying meta-materiality. A tentative definition of patamaterial would be: patamaterial relates to meta-materiality in the same way that meta-materiality relates to the material.

unless one wants to work evidence-based and computationally aggregate time and the use of resources. However, from a kairotic perspective, this chronological loss will affect our possibility to understand other aspects of the service and its other materials. Take as an example waiting times in care processes. They are seldom fully chronologically represented; in Sweden, the service guarantee of waiting for a specialist booking is three months. This is possible to represent on a timeline, but enacting it to share experiences across a design team is difficult. Redesigning the service, so this guarantee could be shortened to one week, will still be difficult to enact in order to understand how the experience (possibly seen as a material) of the service actually changes. Changing the visual timeline could be used as a trigger to have conversations on how that change would be experienced, but that would be of a speculative nature rather than an experiential nature. In this specific example, the handling of Chronos time as a material works in a counterproductive manner to kairotic time (Part 2, Chapter 6). Time behaves as if it is a proper material but operates in parallel with other materials and contra to taking those materials seriously. Through the representations used with their possibilities to afford manipulation, and inferences made on connections to other materials, time is ascribed the character of a para-material. There is also a risk that the representations used induce negative para-material interpretations of materials. In this sense design is a risk practice; any unreflected reuse and creation of templates, tools and ready-mades may shift a material towards counterproductive uses. The material social structures is an important example for this, especially if taken lightly or unsupported, because enactments and materialisations lay bare the manifestations of social structures. However, to change the actual structures the enactments are limited in their effect, unless there are conditions put in place that allow for change, and adapt not only the manifestations but also deal with what lies behind them, little effect will follow.

The character of being, or being used as, a para-material may undermine its trustworthiness outside designing. As the example above shows, the material time should be used carefully together with the material experience so as not to undermine designing. In the worst case the para-material character may undermine designing in itself. During 2022 there was a discourse related to para-materials, but more directed towards the use of design. The term 'theatre' has been used in combination with design, design thinking, user experience, etc., in the form 'design theatre'. This follows a pattern in other areas, e.g., in innovation, where the term innovation theatre is used. The meaning is, for example, that a design process is done for aesthetic reasons rather than for its contribution to substantive goals and effects. This use of the term can create confusion, as theatre and drama are employed as methods and techniques as well as a metaphor in service design. Service design theatre is something that would benefit the field if it had mostly positive connotations. Therefore, it is necessary to find another term for the practice. In Swedish there is an idiom, *spel för gallerierna* (in English: crowd-pleasing, or playing to the galleries), that better captures what is meant. However, what is being done is not design theatre, it actually has as little to do with the rich practice of theatre as it has to do with a rich design practice in a mature organisation. And it is here that the connection to 'para' comes into the picture, as what is done is more like para-design, probably with para-materials.

Ready-mades

Some ways of working with the materials depend on *ready-mades*. A ready-made is an object, or some other artefact, that is picked up as is, from one context to another. It is not made by the user nor heavily adapted for a new purpose or context. It may, however, be understood in a new way by being introduced into a new context.

Ready-mades come in many forms in service design practice. The trivial form of ready-mades is templates and canvases picked up and used, often with little reflection of where they came from, what assumptions and theories are embedded in them and how they relate to the designing at hand.

The actual material formed and manipulated, when using ready-mades, is for example the content with which a template or canvas is filled. Any such ready-made comes with embedded assumptions and theories. Not only will the template in itself force a shape onto the material, but more importantly, so will the underlying assumptions and theories. For example, an actor map canvas forcing the user of the mapping tool to put the customer in the centre does not allow for the customer's perspective to be at the centre of attention. Such a ready-made imposes the assumption onto anyone encountering it that the customer views themselves as being in the centre. This is far from always true, as can be seen in the network mappings in Čaić's work (Čaić et al., 2019).

This does not mean that ready-mades should be totally avoided or always discarded. Rather, it is how we put them to use in designing that matters. While some uses of ready-mades are problematic from the point of view of using them unreflectively, ready-mades do have the potential to be deliberately used to induce reflections. The reflexivity called for with the material social structures is an example where ready-mades and ordinary objects could be used in the work to aid understanding as well as transformation (Tysk & Holmlid, 2022).

For example, by picking up and using a new ready-made every week in a random fashion from a wide array of ready-mades, the influence of those assumptions would be serendipitous, and the bias of one could be reflected through the bias of the next. This would then uncover assumptions embedded in them, or assumptions that are expressed when putting them to use.

Ready-mades could be collected by participants in any work process as *objet trouvé*. Apart from carrying their embedded assumptions and theories, they would also be materialisations of ideas and assumptions of the individual participants. Taken together they would be a materialisation of the assumptions of the collective. Using those ready-mades in parallel, with equal value assigned to them, would give ample opportunity for reflection over many of the assumptions brought in by individuals and through the ready-mades.

Another kind of ready-made is pieces and everyday objects picked up and used in design work. These range from the ready-made pieces used in desktop walkthroughs (Blomkvist et al., 2016) to everyday objects used in constellation work (Tysk & Holmlid, 2022), to props picked up in improvisations and enactments (Blomkvist & Bode, 2012). These ready-mades are given meaning, intentionally, by the persons using them for contextually determined purposes. A plastic brick becomes a mobile phone, a hat denotes a specific feeling, barbed wire shows a difficult relationship, etc. They are materials in themselves, and materialise something that they are not outside the specific design context.

Tool making

Other ways of working with materials depend on designers to create the means to make the material manipulable. That is, we form materials of one kind in order to be able to use that to form some other material. This can be seen as *tool making*. The tools are made, or tailored from existing tools, in order for us to be able to have a process in which the other material can be formed. Whether the tool or the other material is the primary or secondary material is not so meaningful to discern, as they are interdependent on each other, and their materiality plays out in different ways across a longer period of designing. Tools are different from proxy materials, in the sense that the tool is deliberately made as a forming device, while the proxy material is there as the means to access the other material so that it may be formed.

Among the materials presented in this book, some of them highlight tool making. The material clay is used to create tools for reflection in a workshop and a tool for a reminder of the everyday practice. Mediating artefacts are mentioned as central tools for the material conversation. And multiple materials are dependent on visualisations as tools.

Tool making can be done by the designers themselves or in collaboration with many actors. An example of the latter is how participatory backcasting, based on an intervention on cleaner cooking, resulted in a tool for citizens that later was used to achieve transformation towards last-mile electricity connectivity (Lambe et al., 2022). Who the user is of the tool can also vary: sometimes the tool requires designerly knowledge and skill to be used, and sometimes it can be used by layperson designers.

One aspect seldom highlighted with tools in service design are the tool traces that tools make. Think of a saw, and how the saw leaves a trace of sawdust. This sawdust comes from the material worked on, and is subtracted from the total material. Choosing on which side of the line one is sawing is an important decision. A trained eye can also sometimes discern the type of saw used by inspecting the traces on the edge of the material.

One obvious tool trace in service designing is the language that continues to be used in an organisation. Touch-points, ecosystems, etc. – they are all hints towards what tools the organisation has endured, and what materials these tools have been deployed on. Another tool trace often referred to has to do with participatory processes. Organisations are sometimes worried that participation will create anticipation of action, and that participants will be disappointed when the end result is not what was wished for in the process. The worry can be well founded, e.g., from earlier less well-formed participatory work, and probably partly a tool trace. Moreover, all participatory processes leave traces with the participants, if crafted not of broken promises, but of the emancipatory kind.

The most difficult traces, and sometimes the most important ones, are those that are results from non-deliberate subtraction or reduction. The ones that create different kinds of sawdust, and where the decision on how to apply the tool may be difficult to reverse. In some sense, tools (and materials) that change conceptual models are of this kind.

Sometimes tools developed end up in toolboxes that are made available for others. These toolboxes sometimes are done so other designers can use the tools purposefully, tailor them or use them as inspiration for new tools. On the other hand, it is also common that the tools in these toolboxes are used mostly as ready-mades, with little reflection or tailoring. It is important to note that toolboxes often are produced in settings and contexts, and mainly for those settings and contexts. This usually means that the tools are not deliberately made as general tools, or tools that were intended to be used in other contexts.

Another aspect of tool making is that design processes create conditions for service actors and participants to be tool makers in their own service situations. The material certainty artefacts is an example of this, where the design process can focus on making it possible for service actors to make certainty artefacts themselves to support the service. The example above from Lambe et al. (2022) also touches on this. That is, the design process can create conditions within which tools for transformation could be made by the citizens themselves.

Implications of service as hypermaterial

To sum up this chapter, one implication of service as hypermaterial is that representations become central. Working with service development and design involves shaping and interacting with a material consisting of external representations made in the image of a service. Hence, service design creates its own material. The point of creating the material is sometimes to be able to manipulate another material. Proxy materials are used for that specific purpose: to achieve change in a situation that is unavailable in the current situation. Sometimes when using representations this connection is not always clear, as with the blueprint example, where changes in an external representation can have large and difficult to prognosticate implications. Sometimes, as with conversations, a material is not created but rather used for a specific, indirect purpose, i.e., a meeting to ensure a design element is used correctly during service interactions.

By continuing that line of thought we arrive at the conclusion that the material service designers work with is partly virtual – it includes some aspects of reality but is not reality in itself. Part of designing a hypermaterial is then involved with the interplay between reality and virtuality, since service exists in the real world but designers rely on human-made, virtual representations for shaping and working the material into a more finished form. Sometimes, objects from reality also become part of virtuality, as with the example of ready-mades. A Lego piece can then become a customer, or whole information technology systems (Blomkvist et al., 2016). The main point here is not so much that the material moves between reality and virtuality, but rather that design work with service implies working with, understanding and paying attention to those material shifts. Two related challenges are how to move from reality to virtuality without losing track of important elements and how to make holistic external representations of service.

Another challenge is how to go from virtuality to reality. How can design make sure that virtual service representations have any relevance in the real world?

Of course, we don't want all our virtual representations to have an effect in the world. The point of prototyping, for example, is often to explore a situation without connection to reality. In such instances we can think of the material as a para-material – one that behaves like an actual material but without connection to actual services. Of course, the examples earlier in this chapter illustrate the opposite side of this, where designers think they are affecting a situation but in reality are not. This is also an implication of working with hypermaterial services – some aspects are harder to change due to properties in specific materials. Some materials resist change more than others (Part 3, Chapter 1). Designers in service contexts need skills in understanding and ways to deal with various forms of material resistance. Using and creating tools adapted to specific materials is part of that skill. There are not many studies of tool making and tool traces in service design; this is a large area of knowledge that can be explored.

References

Blomkvist, J., & Bode, A. (2012). Using Service Walkthroughs to Co-Create Whole Service Experiences: A Prototyping Technique for Service Design. *Proceedings of ISIDC 2012*. Tainan, Taiwan.

Blomkvist, J., Fjuk, A., & Sayapina, V. (2016). Low Threshold Service Design: Desktop Walkthrough. ServDes2016, 17 May, Copenhagen (pp. 154–166). Linköping: Linköping University Electronic Press.

Čaić, M., Holmlid, S., Mahr, D., & Odekerken-Schröder, G. (2019). Beneficiaries' View of Actor Networks: Service Resonance for Pluralistic Actor Networks. *International Journal of Design*, 13(3), 69–88.

Holmlid, S., Ekholm, D., & Dahlstedt, M. (2021). Practice Occludes Diffusion: Scaling Sport-Based Social Innovations. In A. Tjønndal (ed.), *Social Innovation in Sport* (pp. 57–77). Palgrave Macmillan, Cham.

Lambe, F., Nyambane, A., & Holmlid, S. (2022). Backcasting as a Design Device to Support Grassroots System Change: Insights from a Case Study on Future Energy Pathways in Rural Kenya. Proceedings of Design Research Society Conference, Bilbao, DRS2022, 25.

Simon, H. (1996). *The Sciences of the Artificial* (3rd ed.). MIT Press, Cambridge, MA.

Stickdorn, M., Hormess, M. E., Lawrence, A., & Schneider, J. (2018). This Is Service Design Doing: Applying Service Design Thinking in the Real World. O'Reilly Media, Sebastopol, CA.

Tysk, J., & Holmlid, S. (2022). Systemdesign, labbande och relationalitet. In A. K. Bergman & M. Adenskog (eds), *Den (ut) forskande staden: En FoU-innovation i offentlig sektor*. FoU Helsingborg. https://fou.helsingborg.se/wp-content/uploads/sites/40/2022/07/tysk-holmlid-systemdesign-labbande-och-relationalitet.pdf

4   Layered materials and layered materiality

Several of the materials in Part 2 have some kind of layeredness to them. Some of them are layered as materials in themselves. Some of them are figuring with their materiality as being layered. Some of them are given layeredness through other conceptual models. Some of them are layered in multiple ways, which will only be touched upon here at a surface level.

Materials in layers

There is a trivial approach to *materials in layers*, and one that is a bit less trivial. The former relies heavily on the representation used for the material, and the latter builds on the relationship between the representation and underlying layers that they build on or give access to.

Consider something trivial, a service blueprint, with its swim lanes and 'lines of X'. This indicates layers directly in the representation. Many representations use layers as a feature, and thus structure the access to a possible material. Customer journey maps use layers in a similar manner as service blueprints. Actor maps often use layers in terms of distance (time, spatial or relational) from a central actor, or layers in terms of categories of actors. Persona representations often use layers in terms of more or less detail in descriptions.

A bit less trivial, then, is to consider a persona. A persona is a generalisation, built through analysis over a dataset, which in turn is a deliberate selection of reality (see also the chapter on data in Part 2, Chapter 14). These are layers that are attached to a persona: persona–dataset–reality. Given that there is some analysis made, there may also be layered materiality here – more on that later. Taking the layers a step further, one can easily see that this is in fact true for many of the other representations, a customer journey map is a generalisation, built through analysis over a dataset, which in turn is a deliberate selection of reality. The generic layers would probably be generalisation–dataset–reality.

Turning to the materials mentioned in the book, several of the materials are in layers. The material social structure is described as being in layers. The material time, at least its chronological aspect, is layered. There are the trivial layers of the short and long term, that also influence other materialisations and the way in which we think about details. Another perspective on layers of time is the past, the current and the future. These layers interact in certain contexts; at the time of writing this book, the current is often described as the end of one geological epoch (Holocene) and the start of another (Anthropocene). That is, the long-term epochs are shifting in the current, and thus becoming a concern for the short term.

Layered materiality

The *layered materiality* takes its starting point in that materiality can be seen as something that is becoming and not a given. That is, a material becomes a material when someone interprets it as and uses it as a material, and then ascribes materiality to it. A parallel, in art, is the way in which everyday objects, when placed in art spaces, were interpreted as art, and were ascribed art-world materialities. The classical example of such an art piece is Porte-Bouteille (the bottle rack) by Marcel Duchamp from 1914, that was continued with a rich and diverse development of the use of the everyday in art, e.g., in the Fluxus movement. It is probable that all materials are subjected to these acts of becoming, and the variation of interpretations provides positive richness if handled humbly and with care.

That is, layered materiality appears when different actors assign different materiality to the same material. A straightforward example is a service blueprint, that for one person is a description of the ideal order of actions and activities, while for someone else it is a support for structuring, requiring and recruiting certain competences in different parts of the organisation. In that sense, the service blueprint takes on different materialities that add to it as layers. There is a pluralistic materiality here that has potential in service design practice, that is related to, but not the same as, boundary objects (Star & Griesemer, 1989). The co-designing and catalysing characters of materials in service design practice seem to add to, or go beyond, boundary objects.

Another aspect of this layered materiality is when materials travel through and between contexts, which is closer to the ideas around boundary objects. New materiality is added as layers in every new context, although not all of the earlier materiality travels well between the contexts. That is, the materiality assigned in one context is not necessarily inherited fully in the next. And the materiality that is added in the previous context may not be understood as something that matters in the current context, and does not get the full appreciation it may have had when it was added. In the end, should someone be a travel companion to the material, there will be layers of materiality, like layers of paint or wallpaper. The travel companion could be viewed as a boundary subject, a craftsperson that can uncover pluralistic materialities, similar to a conservator or restorer. An inspiring book that relates to this is Italo Calvino's *Invisible Cities* (2002 [1974]).

Looking at the materials that are presented in the book, a couple of the materials exhibit layered materiality. A *tangible catalyst* like Clay may, for someone, materialise as an insight from a design process. For someone else it materialises as an expression of something directly experienced in the everyday of their life, that is, the basis for the participation in forming with the material. For someone else that same tangible catalyst is assigned a materiality that has to do with how regulations, e.g., of assessing somebody's age, break down into prejudiced judgement. The layering is inherent in the material, but the specific layers added are not. It is not a material devoid of qualities, and it is not a material with only predetermined qualities, to relate to the reasoning about materials without qualities (Löwgren & Stolterman, 2004).

However, at the same time there are mechanisms at play that minimise or limit the variation of material interpretations. There are a couple of mechanisms that are important to highlight here. First, by limiting the professional visions (Goodwin, 1994) used to interpret the materials, the variation will decrease. Second, by routinising the use of tools and materials, the role of those and their place in a sequence of tasks become fixed, and the room for productive use of variations in interpretation will be limited to the space assigned to the routine. Third, by reproducing mannerism in the representations used, e.g., through making templates for representations that unreflected mimic a structure of another representation or material, limits the underlying structural possibilities for varying interpretations. The making of conventions and patterns may also be a mechanism that limits the variation of interpretations, by being prescriptive or by imposing unreflected assumptions.

Conceptual layering

Another aspect of layeredness is how some of the taken-for-granted conceptualisations in service and design are used as materialisations and influence other materialisations, in the form of *conceptual layering*.

For example, the idea that a service system is constituted in micro, meso or macro levels is a conceptual model that creates layeredness to a lot of service designing, and is also a materialisation in itself. However, it is mainly a conceptual model to support our thinking and doing, with no actual phenomena in reality that can be empirically established to make clear distinctions between micro, meso and macro. The distinctions are being made, formed or even made up.

The materiality of micro–meso–macro takes on different forms, depending on what objects are conceptualised on each of the levels. One common materialisation is to view the micro level as consisting of individuals and interactions, the meso level of organisations and relations and the macro level either of clusters of organisations or of norms and policy. The objects shift between the levels and become, in some sense at least, more or less abstract. Another common materialisation is to use the same object for the micro, meso and macro, e.g., individuals and relationships, and instead view them as having different roles in the service system. The levels then become contexts that individuals act within, the same individual can be in multiple contexts and one can zoom in and out and see different people doing different things for different, or multiple, contextual reasons. A third materialisation of the micro–meso–macro, although less common, is to allow participants in design processes to populate the different levels with whatever they see fit, allowing for multiple abstractions in parallel at any given level.

From the perspective of *other* materials of service and in service design, one can approach the micro–meso–macro in several ways. Either one sees it as putting shear stress on the material that at some point will deform it and potentially make it useless for its purpose. Or one sees it as a way of slicing the material so it can be used in different ways and for different purposes on the three levels or scales.

There are other conceptual layerings in the materials that are presented in the book. In the description of time as a material, the two conceptions of time, Chronos and Kairos, provide such conceptual layering. That is, any activity, at a point in time, in a service has a chronological materialisation as well as a kairotic materialisation; it is placed chronologically in relation to others, and it will be experienced in terms of its timing.

References

Calvino, I. (2002 [1974]). *Invisible Cities*. London: Vintage.

Goodwin, C. (1994). Professional Vision. *American Anthropologist*, 96(3), 606–633.

Löwgren, J., & Stolterman, E. (2004). *Design av informationsteknik: materialet utan egenskaper* (2nd ed.). Lund: Studentlitteratur.

Star, S. L., & Griesemer, J. R. (1989). Institutional Ecology, 'Translations' and Boundary Objects: Amateurs and Professionals in Berkeley's Museum of Vertebrate Zoology, 1907–39. *Social Studies of Science*, 19(3), 387–420.

5   A move towards a framework for materials

One of the promising directions we found for categorising, or grouping, materials is shown in Figure 3.5.1. It views materials in terms of who is needed to form them and what is needed to support the forming process. We find this model worth pursuing.

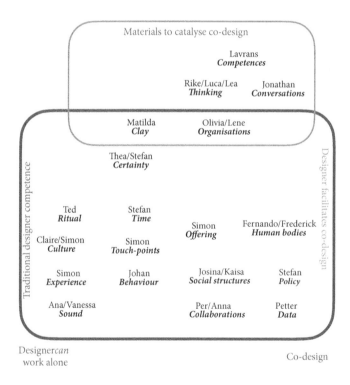

Figure 3.5.1   A suggested structure to position the materials in the book. Although not perfect, it allows us to group and understand the nature of the materials

One group of materials relates to the more traditional design materials, both tangible and intangible. This refers to areas where the designer has a high degree of forming skills and can/could design alone. This may be due to the type of material, aesthetic forming aspects or perhaps have a heritage of historically design domains. However, although they may be something that the designer can carry out alone, many of them will be best carried out as part of a co-design process and together with a project team. A few materials may be an exception to this; for example, culture (broader societal trends as described by Claire and Simon) and ritual (as described by Ted) seem to be easier to form individually by the designer rather than as a co-design activity. This may change as tools improve for these materials.

Another group of materials is co-design materials, and refers to design areas that the designer needs to design together with others in a team. In this context, the designer has a facilitating role in the co-designing activity. This is important since there are most likely other co-design activities facilitated by others (for example, software architecture).

A third group of materials is materials that catalyse co-design. These can be considered meta materials, where the designer works to instil a particular mindset within the co-design group or the organisation(s) in the collaboration. It can also be where the designer brings in the right competences at the right time and in the right way to a co-design process. These materials do not directly form the outcomes, but catalyse and nurture the co-design process. There is an overlap here, for example, clay is a traditional design material that has qualities to make it catalyse the co-design process. Similarly, organisation describes how co-design artefacts both work as part of co-design yet also influence and transform the organisation itself. These direct and indirect outcomes is something that the designer can, by design, choose to influence.

Towards a simplified model

Based on Figure 3.5.1, we developed Figure 3.5.2, which simplifies the categorisation and allows us to understand the materials in relation to their nature. The categories in themselves relate to several underlying factors and are, at this stage, overlapping and based on multiple factors. The term traditional design materials was chosen rather than single-design materials as they have the nature of being materials with a long heritage within design. This is in contrast to co-design materials which are more recent and require or benefit

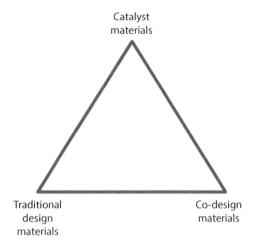

Figure 3.5.2   A simplified model to position materials, related to their characteristics and function

from the application of multiple competences to function. Finally, catalyst materials are materials that catalyse the design process or design outcome. We find the model useful, especially when considering the tensions between the three points. It can be said that there is a repurposing of some materials (e.g., clay) from being a material used solely by the designer to form something to it becoming a catalyst for co-design processes. Further, it can be said that the movement between co-design materials and catalyst materials relates to a stimulus for or support for change. The model has been useful to help with discussions about possible new materials, as well as when attempting to position different schools and their focus.

The model has an analytic as well as generative character to it. Analytically, a material can be positioned in the tension between two of the corners. Clay, as described in this book, can be placed in the tension between traditional and catalyst. It is in many senses formed as a traditional material and used as a catalyst material in the processes. It is both traditional and catalyst at the same time (Figure 3.5.3a). However, a material can also be positioned in multiple tensions. Clay, again, could also be positioned between catalyst and co-design (Figure 3.5.3b).

Another, trivial, analytic usage can be to position a material in relationship to all three at the same time. This could be done by assessment of to which degree it is a traditional, catalyst and co-design material, positioning the

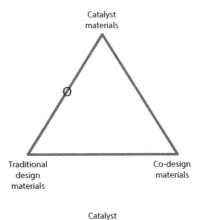

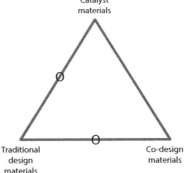

Figure 3.5.3   Two examples of how materials can be positioned in the tensions of the model

material in the balance on every leg of the model (Figure 3.5.4a). Alternatively, a material could be described as a tension field within the frames of the model (Figure 3.5.4b).

However, the model can also be read, and used, to understand the mediating possibilities of materials. That is, catalyst materials can be understood as mediating between traditional and co-design materials. For example, conversations, seen as a catalyst material, mediates in the organisational design work between traditional and co-design materials. By carefully crafting conversations, the organisation may start to understand traditional materials and their multiple meanings as co-design materials.

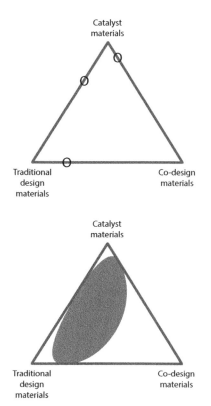

Figure 3.5.4   Two examples of how the model can be used to position materials

One may also view co-design materials as mediating between catalyst and traditional. A view that opens up for materials as mediating between the categories opens up for the organisation to embrace multiple material understandings.

The model is also generative, in the sense that it invites for understanding materials in new ways. What happens if we try to see and use ritual as a catalyst material, or time as a co-design material? Moreover, the model is generative in the sense that it invites inventing and identifying new materials, in tensions, in the radical corners or as mediators between material understandings.

PART 4

A PERFORMER'S REPERTOIRE
(THE SERVICE DESIGNER'S MATERIAL)

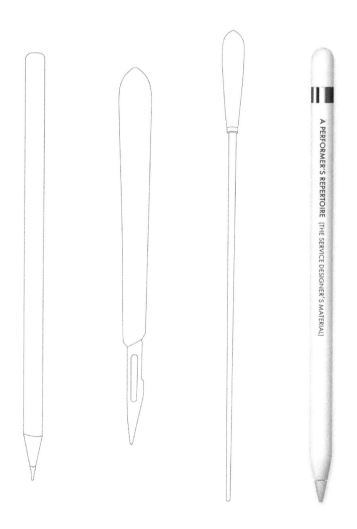

Introducing the finale

The two previous parts of this book have stayed close to the materials, how to describe them, how to understand them and the relationships between them. To some extent the materials' role to service and service design has been weaved into that, holding back on more overarching reflections. Clearly, the renewed senses of material brought forward throughout the book, if adopted, will have consequences on service design practices. The contribution of taking a design perspective on materials of service design, in contrast to service management and marketing perspectives, not only contributes to service design research and practice, but also to the other service fields with new theories and strong concepts of service as a material.

In this final part of the book we deliver three overarching reflections directed to service design practice, research and education rather than focusing on the materials in themselves. One perspective on aesthetics for service design will be covered, among many. The concept of phantasms is introduced to capture the multitude of representational work going on in service design. Service and designing is then connected to the concepts bricolage and rhizomes, as a rewriting of what service and design are engaged in. Finally, we wrap up by returning to the inquiry that was the starting point for the writing of this book.

1 Aesthetics in service design

Simon Clatworthy

> Black and white are the colors of photography. To me they symbolize the alterna-
> tives of hope and despair to which mankind is forever subjected. This kind of pho-
> tography is realism. But realism is not enough – there has to be vision, and the two
> together can make a good photograph. It is difficult to describe this thin line where
> matter ends and mind begins. (Frank, 1952)

This quote from Robert Frank summarises much of what I want to say in this
chapter. He focuses on symbology, vision and how matter and mind create
aesthetic meaning. It could almost be a quote about experiencing a service.

In this chapter I argue the need for service design to develop knowledge of,
and skills in, the aesthetics of service. There are multiple aspects and perspectives that can be taken and this chapter examines aesthetics in a non-material
sense, using input from design and art to view the aesthetics of service design.
The link between aesthetics and experience is identified, and I reflect upon
them based on the materials presented in this book. The chapter concludes
with a discussion of directions that might be considered when further developing research, education and practice while focusing on aesthetics in service
design.

What would Vitruvius think? Materials of aesthetics, function and structure

The area of aesthetics in service design is not discussed or debated to any particular degree. I was invited a few years back to comment on a blog post about
the aesthetics of service design. The interesting thing about the discussion
was that there was really no discussion. There were a few people commenting
that it was an interesting area but little in terms of contributions, analysis or
reflection. Unfortunately there is little within service design research to help

guide us, other than research within customer or user experience, which often comes from business and marketing fields or from interaction design.

In my introductory chapter, I presented aesthetics as one of the three pillars that Vitruvius described for Roman architecture, and showed how they have remained traceable as a central part of design since then. It would be interesting to discuss with Vitruvius the materials presented in this book and to hear his view about them. I would hope that he would see aesthetics in some of the more obvious materials, such as touch-points, but that he would also recognise how social structures contribute to aesthetics.

Moving from beauty in the object to beauty in meaning

In this chapter, I rely heavily on the work by Mads Nygard Folkmann (2010, 2013, 2020) regarding product (and to some extent digital) aesthetics. Folkmann, to my mind, has both a good structure for aesthetics in design and is well supported, argued and reflective.

Aesthetics for a long time has been associated with beauty, and beauty with outward appearance. This was summarised by Adorno using the terms of the true, the beautiful and the good (Adorno, 1970). There has historically been a connection between aesthetics and being cultured and the relationship between aesthetics and taste. Folkmann, however, describes a more recent interpretation of aesthetics as not being about the surface and appearance of something but about its interpretation. He describes this as the epistemology of organising our relationship with the world through design, and the formation of design through imagination. Folkmann regards aesthetics as being about meaning, where meaning is constructed from appearance, how this is sensed, and its conceptual relationship with the world. He does not play down the sensual qualities of material and highlights the notion of the old Greek *aisthetá*, 'that which can be sensed', and its relation to the sensual qualities of the sensed. However, in his interpretation of aesthetics the material and the immaterial are equally relevant.

In Folkmann's view, aesthetics in relation to design is primarily about the creation and communication of meaning. He does not exclude parameters of function, user concerns, materials or technology but proposes aesthetics as an avenue for understanding and investigating design as a medium of meaning construction. His concept of aesthetics connects the sensual with the conceptual, the material with the immaterial. He takes a people-centric view of aesthetics by describing aesthetic experiences as being individual and subjective, whilst clearly recognising the social and cultural influences on individual experiences. Folkmann recognises the interdependence of individual and collective, of design and its context, and shows how these are intertwined and mutually influence each other.

Folkmann describes how the aesthetisation of society has led to aesthetics being central to how we perceive and understand our surroundings and he clearly distances himself from what he terms superficial styling. Folkmann believes that design can have a transformative effect on experience and builds a clear bridge between aesthetics and experience.

Folkmann describes the concept of aesthetics of design as having three facets (Figure 4.1.1):

1. Sensual-phenomenological – primarily sensual communication.
2. Conceptual-hermeneutical – conceptual structure and symbolic coding.
3. Contextual-discursive – negotiation and construction of meaning through discourse and context.

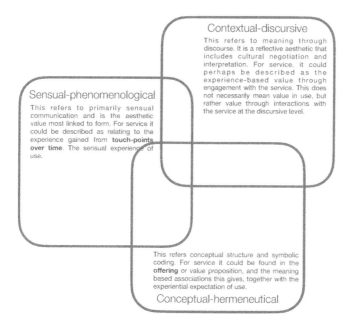

Figure 4.1.1   The three facets of aesthetics, adapted from Folkmann and placed in a service context. It is important to note how important representation is in the expression of aesthetics in service

In his structure, the sensual-phenomenological dimension concerns itself with sensual appearance and conceptual meaning relating to this. It lies more closely to the terms of beauty and form (although Folkmann does not use this term) that is often connected to design, and could be the form of a car or table, for example. The conceptual-hermeneutical dimension relates to aesthetic coding in the concept that is embraced by how design stages meaning in use, where there is a focus on the imaginary in evoking possibility. This relates to the relationship between design and the construction of meaning through the design concept. For example, this could be a new way of paying bills online, or a new computer game concept. The contextual-discursive dimension relates to how design organises meaning by developing a discursive context of organising meaning in a cultural context. The conflict kitchen (an example used in the material description of culture) only serves food from countries that the United States is in conflict with, and works primarily at the contextual, discursive level. It does this by stimulating discussion and reflection through its concept and through use. The contextual-discursive often relates to personal identity, but in a broader cultural context.

A move away from aesthetic objects to experiences?

The move from aesthetics as being the intrinsic beauty of an object towards being a constructed meaning-laden relationship can also be described as a move from aesthetics of the object to aesthetics of the experience. Sabine Döring (2009) connects the aesthetic to the emotional, stating that 'to experience something is to give it emotional value'. She is clear that aesthetics relates to an experienced happening of some kind, and this supports Dewey's phenomenological approach to experience. Dewey states that 'every experience is constituted by interaction between "subject" and "object", between a self and its world, it is not itself either merely physical nor merely mental' (Dewey, 2005, p. 256). Dewey differentiates between experience as being a broad term used by philosophers and directs his interest and focus on people having 'an experience'. In this way, Dewey also differentiates between mundane experiences and memorable experiences. He talks about these as being real experiences, memorable in the way they stand out from the everyday. The temporal aspect of experience and aesthetic experiences in everyday worlds are described by Gumbrecht (2006), who explores how aesthetic experiences are part of the everyday by breaking from the mundane in a noticeable way. Indeed, the dictionary definition of experience as being a happening that leaves an impression on someone fits clearly with Gumbrecht's description. Dewey describes experiences as being an integrated complete experience, composed of parts, or stages, and that an experience is reflected upon afterwards. To Dewey, what he terms the 'esthetic experience' relates to desire beforehand, the practical and the intellectual of the moment as well as sense and meaning afterwards. In this way, he can be said to allude to customer journeys. Folkmann summarises Dewey by integrating the works of Seel (2005) and links aesthetics to the experience by stressing the importance of focusing on the conditions and contexts of experience, together with the means and artefacts that support these aesthetic experiences. This clearly sets the stage for connecting aesthetics, experience and service, since what is the essence of service, other than means and artefacts that support conditions and contexts to encourage experiences? As Herwitz (2008) states, after considering Dewey's and Hegel's views on aesthetics and experience: 'Aesthetics and experience are joined at the hip. Each is part of the other, completes it if you will' (p. 161).

The aesthetics of service design

The connection between aesthetics and experience has not explicitly been made in service design and I would therefore like to make a start in connecting the dots between immateriality, aesthetics and experience. Service design has approached experience from the psychology direction (Norman, 2004) and from marketing (Pine et al., 1999) but has yet to approach it from aesthetics. In the foreword to the service design book by Lara Penin (2018), Clive Dilnot discusses experience and claims that there is little difference between the tangible and the intangible in our experiences. He uses the example of church architecture and comments that no architecture is merely physical. Site is always really a situation, and the design of situations is the core of the aesthetic experience: 'But while experiences are propelled by the material qualities of the thing, it takes place in the mind. It might be better to say then that the tangible *induces* the intangible' (p. 10). He further describes service as a choreographed ensemble of places, things, communications, scripted encounters and so on – in a word, the assemblage, which the subject encounters as a set of experiences over time.

In the following I will use the three facets proposed by Folkmann to identify some elements of service aesthetics and the materials formed in their manifestation. The following descriptions are based on the assumption that aesthetics and experience are closely linked, as described in the previous paragraph.

Sensual-phenomenological – primarily sensual communication

Considering the sensual-phenomenological in a service design perspective, I would place touch-points as the most central material that a service designer forms, or converses with, during service design. In my view of touch-points, I also include the customer/user/service journey, since they form a whole. The design of individual touch-points and their position and use along the journey, together with their interrelations, is one of the central service design activities. Touch-points are also, historically, one of the core parts of service design and the most discussed in research and practice. I think we can add time to the sensual-phenomenological as a material that necessarily integrates with touch-points, and the nuances related to this by Stefan Holmlid, when describing time as a material, are definitely sensual.

I would also like to mention the aesthetics of co-design tools as being important within service design, for example, customer journey maps, giga-maps, tangible tools or simply the visualisations made during workshops. Based on anecdotal evidence, I have seen how the aesthetic qualities of co-design tools have a significant effect on their success. The sensual-phenomenological qualities encourage acceptance, collaboration, playfulness and ideation and their conceptual, symbolic and cultural aspects add to this. This suggests that the aesthetics of co-design are therefore a relevant area to pursue.

Conceptual-hermeneutical – conceptual structure and symbolic coding

Moving to the conceptual and symbolic, many of the materials that are described in this book fit within this category. However, it is difficult to separate the meaningful/symbolic from the discursive in service design, since services are co-produced, contextual and necessarily relate to dialogue and meaningful interactions. So, there is a clear overlap between the conceptual and the discursive, particularly within service.

Folkmann describes the conceptual-hermeneutical as dealing with issues of meaning and understanding. For him, this relates to rich layers of meaning that a design might have at a conceptual level, but also how this meaning is staged. Taken in a broader sense, this could describe service design itself, the design of an offering and how it is experienced over time (through touch-points).

The stand-out material in the conceptual-hermeneutical aesthetic category to me is that of the offering or value proposition. I discuss this more in detail later, since it is clear to me that the service concept/offering/value proposition has a strong aesthetic experiential quality to it. The addition of the unfolding of an experience brings time and timing into play as an important material, and the richness of meaning also means that we have to add social norms, cultural trends and ritual/myth/the sacred.

Contextual-discursive – meaning through the discursive context

The field of discursive design suggests viewing aesthetics as a vehicle for the expression of ideas, with discourse, discussion and social debate as desirable outcomes. If we look more broadly at discursive materials, Foucault and Nazzaro (1972) described that discourse constructs a topic, governing the way it can be talked and reasoned about. Therefore, it can be argued that discourses make it possible for us to perceive the world in a certain way (Burr, 2003). Thoughts immediately come to Dunne and Raby's conception of non-commercial electronic and interactive solutions that aim to engage speculation, reflection and outrage. Core to the contextual discursive aesthetic according to Fokmann is based on Ranciere's discussion regarding aesthetics and the 'rearrangements of signs and images, relationships between what is seen and what is said, between what is done and what can be done' (Ranciere, 2013, p. 35). Timo Arnall, in interaction design, describes discursive design as being about reflexive conversations about immaterial materials in which sociocultural concerns are addressed through 'dialogical, material, and communicative modes of design, that requires both practical and analytical intersections in designing and reflection' (Arnall, 2014, p. 226). Balsamo highlights the opportunities that design and technology offer in shaping culture, stating that they enable 'the development of new narratives, new myths, new rituals, new modes of expression, and new knowledges' (Balsamo, 2011 p. 237). Arnall suggests using a broad range of design fields such as photography, animation, filmmaking and social media to do this and shows how interaction design can 'transform tacit, obscure, and technical knowledge into communicative, discursive material'.

In my view, service design has taken a discursive turn in recent years, adding sociocultural aspects to the core of the field. When considering the materials of discursive aesthetics, I think that all of the materials suggested in the book can be placed here. This is not surprising since, as I have mentioned, service is discursive in nature. There are, however, some materials that I would like to highlight here in a service design perspective. Conversations are obviously relevant, so too are thinking, culture, rituals, social norms and practices. This is not to exclude other materials, and the description of how service design tools influence and organisation can also be described as the use of a discursive design material. I would like to stress here that the discursive has enormous relevance to the design of commercial but also particularly public service. In commercial terms, innovative services create new discussions and conversations, which become central to brand equity. The recent Nike adverts featuring Kaepernick, who famously took the knee in protest and subsequently lost his playing career, show how cultural discourse builds brand equity. In public service, there has for a long time been a focus on the functional, about consistency and fairness. However, cultural change, together with technological change, has led to the need to change our behaviours and logics. For example, the recent service design focus within healthcare which is attempting to move the concept of healthcare from a focus on curing illness to a societal imperative promoting health is constructing meaning through discourse. As designers, the discursive aesthetic is therefore key to innovation in service. Although there is discussion about service design relating to policy and the social, there is little directly about culture and meaning, or discursive service design.

What does this mean for service design?

This section identifies some consequences that Folkmann's three facets of aesthetics might have for service design. In many ways they are a continuation of earlier comments, but they are framed in an applied service design context. They are not intended to be exhaustive, rather initial reflections of what the service design field can do to develop a field of aesthetics in service.

Focus on aesthetics in service design

There is clearly a need for the service design community to direct its focus on the aesthetics of service design through education, coordinated research and application in practice. The aesthetic categories described here do not come from service design literature, but instead come predominantly from art and design. It is therefore important that service design aesthetics is identified, discussed and described within service design research and practice. The link between aesthetics and experience in service design might be the first step, and we need to clearly connect aesthetics, experience and service design together. Not only this, we need it from a design perspective. At present, the research within marketing about customer experience does not adequately focus on the conceptual, cultural or meaningful and lacks a design perspective. Following on from this, I think we need some tools to assist with integrating this into the service design process. The existing core service design books do not give attention to service design aesthetics and this needs to change.

In the following subsections, I will highlight a few areas that I find immediately obvious as a consequence of these findings. I hope they can start a discussion regarding a new facet of service design.

The experiential journey

During the past years, the customer journey has evolved to become more and more focused on the experience that the customer (the user and also the employee) has at each stage of the journey and from the journey as a whole. The experiential aspect of the journey is therefore a natural place to focus on the aesthetics of experience, and I would expect it to increasingly reflect on this. Claire Dennington has found a promising way of doing this by relating to cultural references and associations that the journey elicits, in addition to describing the desired (target) experience at each stage (and as a whole). She has experimented with what she calls the stylistic journey (Dennington, 2021), in which each stage of the journey is accompanied by mood boards that not only describe the expected experience but also give an immersive view into its culturally related symbology. In this way, the journey map gives an increased cultural and meaning-based context. Ted Matthews has experimented using the graphic novel as a way of describing expected experiences, in what he describes as graphic experiential evidencing (Matthews, 2016). This uses the language of the graphic novel to give an increased immersion in the experience, and is something that is well described in the excellent book *Understanding comics* by Scott McCloud (1993). At The Oslo School of Architecture and Design (AHO) we have been experimenting with using video segments to further build on Dennington's mood board-based version. Initial trials as part of courses show promise and we would like to develop a combination of graphic mood boards and video mood boards for the whole experience and the individual journey steps. In this way, the dramaturgy, narrative and different cultural references could come into focus as part of the journey.

The aesthetic offering/value proposition/experiential value proposition

I consider it important to focus on the offering as an important part of the aesthetics of service design. This might seem odd, since the offering is intangible and difficult to pin down from a design perspective. The offering relates to the symbolic and discursive aesthetics of service and also to a 'promise' of the sensual, yet it is still not discussed as a core element of service design. Since the aesthetics of service can be linked to the user experience, we should explore in more detail how the experiential value proposition relates to service aesthetics. Recent work within neuropsychology by Lisa Feldman Barrett (2018) identifies how our experiences are primed by our emotions, and how we are continually creating 'experiential scenarios':

> We usually think of predictions as statements about the future, like it's going to rain tomorrow or the Red Sox will win the series. But here I am focusing on predictions at the microscopic scale as millions of neurons talk to one another. These neural conversations try to anticipate every fragment of sight, sound, smell, taste, touch that you will experience, every action that you will take. These predictions are your brain's best guesses at what's going on in the world around you, and how to deal with it to keep you alive and well.
>
> Through prediction, your brain constructs the world you experience. It combines bits and pieces of your past to estimate how likely each bit applies in your current situation. Right now, with each word that you read, your brain is predicting what the next word will be, based on probabilities from your lifetime of reading experience. In short, your experience right now was predicted by your brain a moment ago. Prediction is such a fundamental activity of the human brain that some scientists consider it the brain's primary mode of operation. (p. 59)

Barrett explains how our experiences are undeniably constructed from predictions and expectations. In the service context, we might consider that this links to a synthesis of the perceived offering, the projected offering (from the service provider), together with a cultural negotiation. The offering is therefore sensorial, conceptual (in terms of framing the holistic experience of the service) and discursive (through the cultural negotiation about experiential meaning). If we accept this view of the offering, then we can conclude that the offering is an aesthetic material of service. It can be designed and formed as a projected offering, it is a promise of experiential value (a primer for predicted experience) and thereby strongly influences the lived and remembered experience. It is therefore worthwhile to explore the aesthetic nature of the service offering to develop a better understanding of it, and this can have consequences for teaching, practice and research.

From user to users

The contextual-discursive aspect of aesthetics highlights cultural negotiation as being central, and this requires that the service designer relates to communities and culture. Whilst the user (singular) has increasingly become a central part of service design through qualitative approaches, the cultural negotiation suggests understanding users as a community or culture. This not only relates to behaviour and nudging, but also to aesthetics and the collective experience. Ted Matthews states that 'a perspective shift from user to users is required, that achieves new forms of collective experiences rather than just tailor-made individual ones' (Matthews, 2021, p. 177). Matthews focuses on how design can use cultural meaning through the use of ritual, the sacred and myth in his work (see the material description earlier in the book). A broader view of culture and its use in service design is described by Claire Dennington both in this book and in her PhD (Dennington, 2021). Further, design for behavioural change, described in this book by Johan, and the suggestion of social norms as a material by Josina Vink and Kaisa Koskela-Huotari suggest that a cultural turn is perhaps happening in service design. Together, they can supplement the user-centric approach with a broader user-centric view as part of aesthetics.

Storytelling

The focus on meaning and experience described in this chapter indicates that storytelling is an important part of aesthetics and service design. This implies that storytelling should be a natural competence for service designers to master. The combination of experience over time that storytelling embodies, together with meaning and culture, should make storytelling a core part of any service design curriculum. However, it is often not focused on, nor is it particularly visible within service design research. There is therefore a need for a service design approach to storytelling and time, as Stefan Holmlid discusses.

Aesthetics as part of speculative service design

Speculative design presents possible futures, and as part of this integrates all three facts of aesthetics. Speculative design requires a deep cultural understanding and reflection, since speculative solutions cannot be communicated without creating a future cultural context. Further, speculations need to be accessible and appealing, which requires aesthetic and artistic sensibilities. Finally, speculations often question meaning and context, and therefore demand a meaning-laden cultural context to position them.

There are multiple projects that have worked with scenarios and forecasting within service design, and these identify the need for major structural change in, for example, public services. What we do not see so much is critical service design projects that have a goal to provoke thought and discussion. Dunne and Raby (2013) describe how speculative design uses design proposals to challenge narrow assumptions, preconceptions and givens about the roles played by products in everyday life. The field of speculative design has until recently been product- and interaction-focused, and I would like to see service design projects that aim to challenge assumptions, preconceptions and givens about services in everyday life as a means to reflect upon society and upon service design itself. It therefore seems logical to develop speculative service design as a focus area within service design. In the context of this book, speculative service design will utilise and explore multiple materials and discover new ones. Since the majority of these materials seem poorly understood from an aesthetics perspective, speculative service design will also contribute to a material understanding.

It seems that we do not provoke ourselves or others enough within service design, and service design is rarely provocative in a cultural context, even though the potential is huge to do so. Services are central to our everyday lives, and provoking reflection on our everyday lives, our culture and its trajectory through service design would be beneficial for all, and would evolve the role of the designer as cultural intermediary. Firstly, it adds a reflective discursive layer to service design and the directions of service development. Secondly, it adds a playful element to service design. Now that service design is established as valuable to service providers, we can allow ourselves some provocative thinking, at the societal level but also within organisations, to push the boundaries of change. It is therefore a good development and exposition of the service design skillset.

Culture and the semantic transformation

The focus on meaning in relation to aesthetics, when taken together with the contextual discursive layer, suggests that aesthetics and service design demands a cultural orientation. Claire Dennington has suggested culture as a material, and her work in translating popular culture into services and the service design tool that she has developed are an excellent way to do this (Dennington, 2021). Claire built on work by Karjalainen from product design (Karjalainen, 2004) and my work in brandslation (Clatworthy, 2012) by looking in detail into how cultural phenomena (for example, trends) can be analysed for their meaning and how this can be translated into a design solution. This is something that Karjalainen describes as the semantic transformation, and Claire shows that there are three translations that occur when translating a cultural phenomenon into a service. Her approach includes a cultural relevance and aesthetic into service. Matthews offers a similar approach when designing with myth/ritual and the sacred (Matthews, 2021). Common to both of these approaches is that an understanding of cultural meaning and its translation into service is central to service aesthetics.

Design historians are needed in service design

A few years ago, Apple tried its interaction style against Samsung in court using an argument based on design history. They argued that designers create styles that have a particular fit with the culture of the times (the zeitgeist) and that this creates enormous value, deserving protection as intellectual property. This connects design history to commercial value and shows that design has 'periods' of design, in the same way that art has movements and epochs. A particular 'style' or approach becomes linked to the culture of the time and a piece of design can be placed on a timeline based on its aesthetic. I wonder if the same can be said of service design? Are there service design styles that are design-driven, and that can place a service within a period? If so, what distinguishes such a service from a similar service from a different period? Is it a touch-point style, a kind of offering, an interaction style or simply the visual look of the service that places it on a timeline? I suspect that it is aspects of all of these, although it might not be related to the final design, but the representations during the design process, or through co-design approaches. This is just supposition and I would like to have a design historian's view of service design. Perhaps the criteria that design historians have used need to be updated to be able to adequately cover service design, and if so, I am intrigued to understand what that update would include. Design history has mostly related to aesthetics and products, and has only recently started to approach interaction design. I would relish it if design history engages in a discourse around service design, and I think it is needed to help us understand ourselves in a way we obviously cannot understand ourselves right now.

The importance of representation

I will not go into detail about the importance of representation in service design, since Johan is the master of this and has covered it in the book. I would, however, like to mention one aspect of representation, and that is the representation of aesthetics. In service this could be equated to experience prototyping (Buchenau & Suri, 2000) and there are multiple techniques available to experience the experience as a prototype. The three-facet model of aesthetics raises an aspect regarding how to prototype the experience. The sensual is something that design has a long tradition in prototyping and the term negotiotyping (Capjon, 2004) is a good term to describe prototyping as a way of negotiating a solution within a project team. Negociotyping generally relates to the sensual aspects of a service, and we have not adequately cracked the experience prototyping aspect in terms of negotiotyping the conceptual-hermeneutical or the discursive-contextual. Here, I believe that we need to start a discourse to bring together research and practice to develop some basic experience prototyping approaches that can be utilised to prototype all three facets of aesthetics. Here, I am not talking about speculative service design, but rather developing a means of successfully representing all facets of aesthetics at an early stage of development.

Conclusion

Aesthetics is central to how we experience services and is poorly understood as part of service design. In this chapter I suggest a structure for a discussion about the aesthetics of service, and show how it has interconnections with seemingly disparate materials such as organisation and social norms and practices. This means that we need to complement the historical aesthetic approach by adding meaning, cultural relevance and social practices to the beauty of an object. In my mind, this can only be seen as being a positive contribution to service design. I strongly believe that the approach towards materials taken in this book can contribute to a design-based view on aesthetics in service design and the aesthetics of service. I look forward to further developing the experiential user journey, experiential offerings and to experiencing the aesthetics of critical service design. I look forward even more to a future conversation with a design historian, about how service design embraced aesthetics.

References

Adorno, T (1970). Aesthetic theory. University of Minnesota Press.

Arnall, T. (2014). Exploring 'immaterials': Mediating design's invisible materials. International Journal of Design, 8(2), 101–117.

Balsamo, A. (2011). Designing culture. Duke University Press.

Barrett, L. F. (2018). How emotions are made. Mariner Books.

Buchenau, M., & Suri, J. F. (2000). Experience prototyping. Proceedings of the 3rd Conference on Designing Interactive Systems: Processes, Practices, Methods, and Techniques, 424–433.

Burr, V. (2003). Social constructionism. 2nd edition. Routledge.

Capjon, J. (2004). Trial-and-error-based innovation: Catalysing shared engagement in design conceptualisation. Unpublished PhD, Arkitekthøgskolen i Oslo.

Clatworthy, S. (2012). Bridging the gap between brand strategy and customer experience. Managing Service Quality, 22(2).

Dennington, C. (2021). Refashioning service design: Designing for popular cultural service experience. Unpublished PhD thesis, The Oslo School of Architecture and Design (AHO).

Dewey, J. (2005). Art as experience. Penguin.

Döring, S. A. (2009). The logic of emotional experience: Noninferentiality and the problem of conflict without contradiction. Emotion Review, 1(3), 240–247.

Dunne, A., & Raby, F. (2013). Speculative everything: Design, fiction, and social dreaming. MIT Press.

Folkmann, M. N. (2010). Evaluating aesthetics in design: A phenomenological approach. Design Issues, 26(1), 40–53.

Folkmann, M. N. (2013). The aesthetics of imagination in design. MIT Press.

Folkmann, M. N. (2020). Post-material aesthetics: A conceptualization of digital objects. The Design Journal, 23(2), 219–237.

Foucault, M., & Nazzaro, A. M. (1972). History, discourse and discontinuity. Salmagundi, 20, 225–248.

Frank, R. (1952). València Spain. Steidl.

Gumbrecht, H. U. (2006). Aesthetic experience in everyday worlds: Reclaiming an unredeemed utopian motif. New Literary History, 37(2), 299–318.

Herwitz, D. (2008). Aesthetics: Key concepts in philosophy. Continuum.

Karjalainen, T. M. (2004). Semantic transformation in design: Communicating strategic brand identity through product design references. University of Art and Design Helsinki.

Matthews, T. (2016). Introducing graphic experiential evidencing (GEE). 10th International Conference of Design and Emotion, 26–29 September, Amsterdam.

Matthews, T. (2021). Exploring sacred service design. Unpublished PhD, The Oslo School of Architecture and Design (AHO).

McCloud, S. (1993). Understanding comics: The invisible art. William Morrow.

Norman, D. A. (2004). Emotional design: Why we love (or hate) everyday things. Civitas Books.

Penin, L. (2018). An introduction to service design: Designing the invisible. Bloomsbury Publishing.

Pine, B. J., Pine, J., & Gilmore, J. H. (1999). The experience economy: Work is theatre and every business a stage. Harvard Business Press.

Rancière, J. (2013). The politics of aesthetics. Bloomsbury Publishing.

Seel, M. (2005). Aesthetics of appearing. Stanford University Press.

2   Service phantasms

Johan Blomkvist

We have looked at different states and types of representations in Part 1, Chapter 3 and further developed the idea of virtual service representations and their role as material in design in Part 3, Chapter 3. In this chapter we will elaborate further how design relates to external and mental representations. The chapter will start by further exploring the distinction between reality and virtuality of external representations and consider how people can understand and be included through external representations. Further, the chapter will consider groups of people working together with representations in co-design situations. In this, we suggest the concept of service phantasm as a way to understand how service can be perceived and formed as part of design. Phantasm here should be understood as a mental representation of something, with an (illusory) likeness with that something that is influenced by our imagination and other internal and collective activities.

Material affinity

Judging by the long and varied list of materials, any one designer will struggle if the ambition is to work with all of them. Some will get used to and comfortable with working with digital interfaces, and they will have a tendency to see service from that perspective. Some might be more inclined to look at the behaviours or emotions more carefully, and some yet might be drawn towards business-related elements of service. With such a wide and disparate space of materials, no single designer can master all, and the materials known and mastered will shape the designer.

Service is not something you can see or touch in its entirety. Instead, service designers depend on external representations to understand and make sense of service (see Part 1, Chapter 3). As an example, organisations are difficult to capture in one representation but through the different documents produced by, and about, organisations it becomes possible to build up an understanding of it. As shown in Part 2, Chapter 7, different disciplines capture and describe different aspects of organisations, but they also use different forms of representation to capture similar aspects. As we saw in Part 3, Chapter 3 on hypermateriality, designers work a lot indirectly with materials. In the process of doing so, they generate a variety of external representations relevant to projects or goals. These materials form a kind of material patchwork where each patch tells a story about the material from a specific perspective. To continue the example with organisations, the patches include sales numbers, design artefacts, worksheets, (digital) whiteboards, stories and so on. These patches are not reality but rather interpretations or imaginations. Even data collected within a service or in relation to customer segments will have flaws and bias (Part 2, Chapter 14). A customer journey map builds on impressions and interpretations of sequences of interactions. Interviews, as well as their summaries, are subjective recollections of events or preferences. Prototypes are imaginations of future service elements. Together, all of these patches of external representations form a simulacrum of service.

Some materials are easier than others to represent as part of a design process. Some are constantly changing and some are more static (i.e., definite representations and ongoing; see Blomkvist & Segelström, 2014). Methods, approaches and processes have also been suggested as being particular to design. Given that, and maybe a bit surprisingly, no one involved in this book has suggested that a process or method is an essential material in design. Probably due to the multitude of contexts of service (e.g., commercial, digital, healthcare, hospitality, etc.), there is little point in proposing a single unified process of design for service.

Many types of materialisation are also essential for bridging the gap between reality and virtuality. A mix of modelling, mapping and enacting provides the basis for materialisation. Each has its own merits and blind spots. What is materialised is mostly what is available to designers to shape in the real service. Modelling waiting time makes time a component of service that can be shaped and moulded to improve service. This is true for any element of service because internal representations are individual, but service design depends on collaboration and coordination and thus requires external representation.

Enacting a face-to-face interaction between two stakeholders brings a potential future situation into the design process. Left untouched, that interaction is hidden from the people working with design. Enactments are performed and perceived in different ways depending on the members. The performers' background, knowledge and expertise are a way of bringing reality into a virtual representation. The same goes for any perceiving participants – they too have perspectives that influence how the enactment is understood and evaluated. For the facilitator of an enactment, it is vital to understand what and how to bring reality into play, and to help the participants understand how the material virtualisation relates to reality. Being able to see and touch service also helps with understanding and creating an internal representation of a service. In addition, it serves as tangible evidence for progression. In a sense, enactments then create trust in a similar way to other certainty artefacts (Part 2, Chapter 10).

Representations can allow participants to engage with and immerse themselves in service situations through, e.g., enactments. On the surface, enactments can seem like straightforward design activities, but in reality there are a lot of issues that influence knowledge generation from enactments. An enactment is in itself a virtuality, one of many plausible ones. So how do you know if you have created a representation that is relevant to the service that is being worked on? How and what material should be included? Who should be in control?

Diagetic prototyping

What does it mean for knowledge creation that participants often are feigning their roles, or at least contribute without motivation? And the associated question of believability or immersion, and how to achieve it through materialisation? In this context, it is relevant to borrow the term diagetic from the world of movie making. The word originally referred to sound that comes from within the context of the movie and that can be heard by the characters. For instance, if a movie character is driving a car and the car stereo plays music that both the viewer and the character can hear, that sound is diagetic. The meaning has been expanded in the context of design to include elements of 'reality' included in prototyping, leading to the term diagetic prototyping. When we view this term from the perspective of the book this becomes difficult to parse, to say the least.

Since prototyping builds on our imagination about what a future situation might look like, there should be no diagetic elements to bring in to prototyping. However, placing a hospital bed in a room where participants enact a healthcare scenario can be seen as a diagetic element. Another term, possibly more suitable here, is trans-diagetic prototyping, since the material in itself is virtual. Diagetic representations require participants to be immersed, to treat and act like a service is actually happening. Taking representations seriously is one big challenge for service design.

Designing includes understanding both the current situation and the future. It has been suggested that representations of the current situation are visualisations, while representations of the future are prototypes. All prototypes are fictional, because they describe imaginary futures. Many are also virtual, since they contain some elements or resemblance of reality.

In terms of designing service, this book emphasises the role of a service designer as a translator of communication, thought, virtuality and reality. Design of service involves observing organisations, relations and behaviours to be able to translate them into representations that capture vital aspects of reality. Those representations then need to be translated into a future virtuality and based on those representations translate back to reality. The virtuality needs to be given a form that people outside of design can react to in a realistic way, and their reactions then need to be understood and translated into useful knowledge about service. Furthermore, this view emphasises humans as essential components of service materiality.

Simulacrum as emergent image of service

Simulacrum can have different meanings but is considered here as an image with a likeness to the thing it represents. Simulacra and individual experiences help construct mental representations of service that can be thought of as service phantasms. Of course, all representations to some degree are simulacrum, since they are not copies. This is especially true for service which is ever changing and complex. In this chapter, however, simulacrum is the resulting image of service, from a patchwork of external representations available to designers. This simulacrum can be thought of as Frankenstein's monster, pieced together by body parts from different humans. In a similar way, an image of service grows out of several different representations.

There are two main aspects of a service simulacra: interpreted reality and imagined future. None depict reality, they are rather emergent service phantasms. In the case of imagined future simulacra, there is not even anything in the physical reality that serves as a model for likeness – the image refers to ideas about what service could be in the future.

Interpreted reality simulacra

Interpreted reality is a patchwork of different documents and models of the current situation: who are the users, what is the service supposed to do, where can design have the largest impact, what customer journeys can be identified, etc.? This includes representations produced by design, mainly during a research stage, as well as documents produced by organisations to, e.g., manage operations, predict trends or assess risks.

Imagined future simulacra

An imagined future simulacrum is a patchwork containing all the prototypes and representations of hypothetical service materials. Desktop walkthroughs, experience prototypes, but also ideas or questions asked about what the future might look like help build up representations of imagined futures. The main difference from interpreted reality simulacrums is that it does not represent something in the real world, but rather something that might be in the future, something that is becoming, as part of the design process.

Mental representations of service are phantasms

To summarise this far, a service simulacrum is a perceivable, Frankensteinian collection of external representations. As such, it is ambiguous and complex. Designers working with service need to understand and make sense of service, and the simulacrum is a valuable resource for that. Other actors involved in the design work can share the collection and construe their own simulacra. Each individual also has their own experiences from design research, conversations, collaborations, etc., as well as previous life experience and background which influences how a simulacrum is perceived. Individual experiences and simulacra are building blocks of mental representations. Also, if a designer has not been taking active part in a service, their mental representations of service are based on simulacra which are in themselves ambiguous and imprecise.

External representations connect designers with service

Following this line of reasoning it becomes apparent that there is a lot of room for each individual to fill in the gaps. Service phantasms are what designers have available at any time, a partially co-constructed internal representation of service. That is, the material designers are trying to shape. Changing the material involves both a reinvention of the phantasm and additions to the imagined future simulacrum; they are in a constant state of dynamic interplay/action where each one influences the other.

Schooled designers are especially good at adapting and adding to imagined future simulacra, through prototypes, sketches, scenarios, etc. The representations that designers make of service (elements) are what links design to service (or any other material). For service design, a simulacrum is especially important, since the service itself cannot be captured without several interconnected external representations. The flip side is that working with simulacrum can lead to a service becoming its representation, in the eye of a designer. The representation can either be a proxy for service or it can be a para-material (see Part 3, Chapter 3). In the minds of the designers the simulacrum is the service, and since it is reality, any changes made to it is also an actual change in reality.

What is brought into a simulacrum is also what designers are able to work with. If some aspect of service is left out of the mix of representations, it is also unavailable or hidden for design. If a system-level representation is missing, it does not matter if the interface and each touch-point is polished and well designed, you might still miss, e.g., redundancies or waste on the system level, making the service unsustainable. Roleplaying as a representation of a call centre conversation reveals experiential, social and emotional qualities of a situation. For instance, it can lay bare the emotional work involved in specific types of calls. Revealing those qualities and types of situations makes them available and actionable for design. This is why, in the words of Josina Vink and Kaisa Koskela-Huotari (Part 2, Chapter 2) making the invisible visible is so important.

Designers and designing simulacra and phantasms

A service phantasm is built also from previous encounters with similar services. It continues to grow based on interactions with, and representations of (elements of), the service itself. Designers then add to the representations and an image, a simulacrum reflecting the service, starts to take shape through the many external representations. The simulacrum and the service is interpreted through a lens of previous experiences, background and knowledge. Through that process the service phantasm becomes more elaborate and multifaceted (see Figure 4.2.1). The more the service simulacrum grows, and as design starts to move from the current situation, what is, into the future, what could be, the more important the simulacrum becomes for shaping the service phantasm.

Service
representations

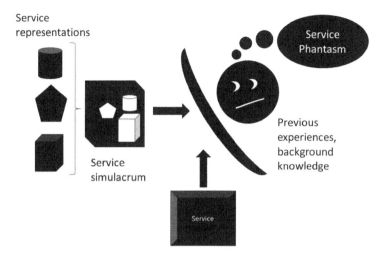

Service
simulacrum

Figure 4.2.1 A service and its simulacrum is interpreted by an individual that interprets and imagines a service phantasm

The simulacrum takes over the role of the service and becomes the material that is shaped by design.

Each individual designer has their own service phantasm: an abstract, vague and ambiguous version of the service that can be called upon to test ideas or suggest changes. As a designer you also have to be able to share your phantasm with others. This is a form of representation that makes it possible to verify that the shared mental representation of service overlaps between individuals.

Together, designers create and refine simulacra, and since each simulacrum is so important for building up an understanding of service, designers have a huge responsibility to make fair representations. This often fails, as design projects do not represent minorities or edge cases, thus excluding people from taking part. This is not necessarily reflected in the individual phantasms, however, since each designer has their own background and experiences. These experiences are also what designers rely on when making judgements and decisions about how to transform or develop a service. In turn, this can mean that the resulting service is filled with cultural stereotypes rather than actual individuals. Representations along the way that are created and tested using a multitude of backgrounds help add useful pieces to the shared mental representation of a service. Representing service in a realistic way also helps design be impactful and create better service in general.

To summarise, a service can never be fully known or exhaustively described. Many different external representations form a simulacrum – an image of service. The image together with collective activities and previous experiences combine into a service phantasm: a mental, flawed, representation of service that need to be consistently renegotiated. To a large extent, the simulacrum *is* the service in the eyes of the designer, and the phantasm is how the designer understands it. We would argue that far too little effort has been put into understanding what it means to design a represented material, and much more needs to be done to support designers' ability to represent service, both internally and externally.

Reference

Blomkvist, J., & Segelström, F. (2014). Benefits of external representations in service design: A distributed cognition perspective. The Design Journal, 17(3), 331–346.

3   Service and design as bricolage and rhizomes

Stefan Holmlid

The idea that service design is possible to comprehensively and unambiguously define is a figure of thought based on ideals of reductionism and essentialism. Not only is service in practice complex, and a constant designing and becoming, service design is also complex. Designing can, as pointed to in Part 1, Chapter 2, be described in terms of balancing, synthesising and integrating. The desire to define and categorise may lead to misdirected efforts. The many materials and perspectives put forward in this book support a different, pluriversal, conception, where a singular definition is a question worth asking, but a goal not valuable to reach.

The assertions about service as a material in Part 1, Chapter 4, combined with the multiple ways in which design depends on multiple representational practices (Part 1, Chapters 2 and 3) are foundational for the ongoing transformation of service design. The many materials in Part 2, with all its variation and disparity, combined with the multiple ways that materials can be understood in Part 3 (Chapters 3, 4 and 5), support this from a practice and theory point of view.

As a consequence of this, the critique towards service design for lacking a definition of service design becomes part of a discourse around what service design is for different disciplines. Moreover, whose ideals about what it means that a concept has theoretical and phenomenological validity, are part of such a discourse. In practice, sometimes we need to make and agree on a definition, to be able to work towards specific purposes. In research, for example, one may need to show how one understands design, positioning the way in which design is approached, in order to be able to claim certain knowledge contributions. To be clear, this does not set design apart from other sciences; in physics, it is of major importance to choose between light being a particle or a waveform when devising and interpreting results from experiences. Hence, there is not one definition to rule them all, and there never will be.

One approach to such a pluriversal conception is to build on ideas from Gilles Deleuze and Felix Guattari. Here, two of the concepts emanating from their work will be connected to an understanding of materials in service and service design. The first concept is *bricolage*, in the sense of different entities that are combined together with the ways in which they are joined together and understood. The second concept is *rhizome*, understood as an organically developing, often networked, relational structure (Figure 4.3.1).

Bricolage

There are multiple theories of service, with their own concepts and frameworks. Some of these provide an understanding of service from multiple perspectives, or as being composed of multiple disjunct elements. One way of approaching service, then, is to view service, or service systems, as a bricolage (Deleuze, 1994). A bricolage of theories and frameworks, a bricolage of concepts and perspectives, a bricolage of practices, places, actors and resources.

The service research concept 'resource integration', when seen from a design perspective as deliberate action (Part 1, Chapter 4), can easily be understood as bricolaging. The resources, that are typically very disparate elements, are pieced together by acts of integration, often by multiple people and disjunct practices. The resulting values and new resources that come out of this are typically disparate and only loosely held together. For example, a professional practice acts together with an everyday practice, with a policy system and technology artefacts, to make public transport happen. In part this will depend on preparation, in part on improvisation. Many customer journey maps are visual manifestations of this bricolage.

From a design perspective, paying attention to the joints, seams, cracks and counterforms created when the different resources are joined together over time would be as interesting and important as the individual elements and the larger, or high-level, outcome of integration. A couple of aspects of counterforms in service, such as time, social white space and control, have been discussed (Holmlid, 2006; Holmlid & Hertz, 2007). Moreover, developing a designerly understanding of seamfulness (Weiser, 1994) is dearly needed, as an aesthetic competence and as opposed to the too limited idea of seamlessness. This is especially important given ambitions of service design to influence the everyday life of people, e.g., self-care with chronic diseases (Murray et al., 2006).

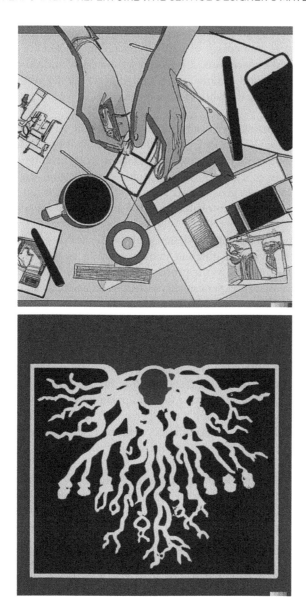

Note: Prompts: 'The hands of a designer working with a bricolage of material objects and photos, table seen from above, in line drawing style' and 'A rhizome representing a multilevel system consisting of talking heads, as an album art cover in blue note style no text'.

Figure 4.3.1 DALL-E generated images of bricolage and rhizome

The same reasoning goes for service design and materials in designing. Design and designing is a bricolage of partly overlapping practices, a bricolage of frameworks and conceptions, a bricolage of materials and purposes, a bricolage of methods and techniques. Designing in the service realm becomes a work with bricolages, the work of a bricoleur.

Although not focusing specifically on the materials, the Visualtiles framework (Diana et al., 2012) is an early suggestion that supports such a view; giga-mappings is another (Sevaldson, 2011), as is the work on prototypes and proto-typing (Blomkvist & Segelström, 2014). Multiple visualisations are put together more or less loosely to give a richer picture, however, this is not necessarily a fuller or more complete representation of the service or service system.

In such a view of designing, a designer explicitly analyses and explores the materials themselves and different joining practices as well as their promi-nence, potential and role in the process ahead. This is a knowledge-intensive practice, where theory, experiential knowledge and aesthetic knowing all play a role in the systematic and organic work of material bricolaging. Sometimes only a few materials are used, alongside the ways in which they may be pieced together. Sometimes a wider complex array of materials and joining tech-niques are used. Clay (Part 2, Chapter 15) is combined with conversations (Part 2, Chapter 8) in curated sequences of participation that directly articu-late experiences (Part 2, Chapter 13) and indirectly bring social structures (Part 2, Chapter 2) to the surface, to manipulate certainty artefacts (Part 2, Chapter 10) of the design team, time aspects (Part 2, Chapter 6) moved of the future imagined service and form policy framing (Part 2, Chapter 19) moved that needs to be in place for a successful service.

One role of the designer is to negotiate how we want the outcome and the pro-cess of designing to be experienced, and therefore to negotiate which needs and materials can be formed, and to what extent. That is, this is not static, and the mix changes over time, as for example suggested by Lavrans Løvlie on identify-ing, combining and directing competences dynamically during a project.

For some, the materials that will be used and mixed can be seen from the system transformation project as a whole, while for others certain materi-als can be added and taken away at different points in time organically. For an organisation a specific bricolaging practice can be seen as a competitive advantage expressed through their organisation and method package, given ideas about what materials to use and join together and ideals about the competences and processes applied. For an individual designer, the mix of materials mastered, and the bricolaging mastery, form their competence and a knowledge-intensive, creative and aesthetic practice. For an educational institution the mix of materials introduced, learned and applied materialises their ideas about service design itself. That is, seen across different aspects of designing, this has relevance both in terms of how materials are combined and formed, but also in terms of the central role of the designer in facilitating such bricolaging.

If we view service as bricolage, and design as bricolage, it invites a couple of framings, with a couple of consequences.

First of all, the bricolages are already there, and are becoming at the same time. The current service system, and any specific service situation, is a bricolage, hence it is already there. And every service action is making, or adapting, more bricolage, hence it is constantly becoming. This means that, even when some of the bricolaging is done in the design studio, preparing some resource to be used in a service situation or laying out a process to be followed, this will build on the material of the service system that is brought into the studio. The service system, later influenced by the results from the studio work, will bear evidence from the mixing and bricolaging of materials done in the studio.

Second, through participatory processes the understanding of the current bricolage in practice can be highlighted and shared. Moreover, the transformation of this into something new can be done as collective creation, devising the balance and the understanding of the action spaces it affords between what is prepared for and what is improvised in service situations.

Third, to make these bricolages in and of service systems and service situations, the resources, structures and preconditions for such situated making needs to be in place. This means that the organisation needs to have structures in place that allow for changes at multiple levels to be employed (Sangiorgi, 2011), and there needs to be preconditions that do not hinder transformation (Holmlid et al., 2021). Put differently, there needs to be transformation readiness. The designers also need to have readiness to work in the contexts, as part of the system in transformation (Part 2, Chapter 2). Those resources, structures and preconditions are themselves a bricolage. They have also been the subject of design and development through a multitude of disciplines, across multiple organisations, including a bricolage of design practices. It would be naïve to expect that this would have been done in a coordinated and deliberate effort.

Rhizomatic

The multiplicity and the many layers of bricolages points to an understanding of the structures and relationships as *rhizomatic* rather than rational and predictive. Rhizomatic structures are non-linear networks where there is no overarching hierarchical ordering principle exerting power over what connections can and cannot be made (Deleuze & Guattari, 1987). It is also common to understand rhizomatic structures to be emergent and to grow organically, and it is difficult to say where that growth started and whether there is an end point. This means that designing also is emergent and contributes organically to its contexts. It does not matter where designing starts, as long as it continues exploring, connecting, varying and questioning. This would also mean that designing has no obvious end. There is no perfect first material to start out with, and there is no discernible final material that ends designing.

For service design this would mean that the designing going on by service actors in a service situation through situated action may be a start and an end of designing. At the same time it would mean that the forming of conversations (Part 2, Chapter 8) with management, or tangible catalysts (Part 2, Chapter 15) with lone-coming migrant youth, may be starting points and end points of designing. All at the same time. Design is already ongoing, design is timeless. This transcends ideas about design being involved early or late. Failing to recognise this would be to repeat failures that have led to overuse of simplified models such as double-diamond and design thinking, and oversimplification of patterns and design operations. The ideal of being involved early or late has its reference to the project process models use, and a chronological understanding of those.

Furthermore, with a rhizomatic perspective designers (and others), as agents of a system, through our actions, are matters of the system as well as being practitioners materialising the system. Seeing and describing the system, being part of influencing and acting in the system and being influenced by the system transforming. At the same time they are part of organisational practices in different organisational contexts, with distributed mandates and initiatives, enacting multiple policies, norms and social structures. They are all places to start, and places to end. Again, all at the same time. Which one of these is the starting point becomes irrelevant, while creating the conditions for growth and development of one or multiple becomes a relevant situated approach. However, if designing lacks initiative to start somewhere, that combination of place and initiative may be one place to start, exactly where designing is seeing itself contributing, but it should not be the end.

As a consequence of bricolage and rhizomes, education of service designers is not a single thing; there is room for many kinds of things. Moreover, it is necessary to step away from modernist notions of being able to define what service design is, and instead educate service designers in relation to an explorative mindset, and in relation to bricolages and rhizomatic systemic structures. As designers they need to develop skills, understanding and attitude that their own practice is part of a bricolage of practices, and that their design work is to work with bricolages as a design approach rather than a predetermined sequence of tools.

References

Blomkvist, J., & Segelström, F. (2014). Benefits of external representations in service design: A distributed cognition perspective. The Design Journal, 17(3), 331–346.

Deleuze, G. (1994). Difference and repetition. Columbia University Press.

Deleuze, F., & Guattari, D. (1987). A thousand plateaus: Capitalism and schizophrenia. Trans. B. Massumi. University of Minnesota Press.

Diana, C., Pacenti, E., & Tassi, R. (2012, September). Visualtiles: Communication tools for (service) design. ServDes2009, 24–26 November, Oslo (59, pp. 65–76). Linköping University Electronic Press.

Holmlid, S. (2006). Introducing white space in service design: This space intentionally left blank. Emergence Conference, Carnegie Mellon.

Holmlid, S., & Hertz, A. (2007). Service-scape and white space: White space as structuring principle in service design. European Academy of Design Conference, Dancing with Disorder: Design, Discourse and Disaster.

Holmlid, S., Ekholm, D., & Dahlstedt, M. (2021). Practice occludes diffusion: Scaling sport-based social innovations. In A. Tjønndal (ed.), Social innovation in sport (pp. 57–77). Palgrave Macmillan.

Murray, R., Burns, C., Vanstone, C., & Winhall, J. (2006). RED report 01: Open health. Design Council.

Sangiorgi, D. (2011). Transformative services and transformation design. International Journal of Design, 5(2), 29–40.

Sevaldson, B. (2011). GIGA-Mapping: Visualisation for complexity and systems thinking in design. Nordes, 4.

Weiser, M. (1994). Creating the invisible interface. Proceedings of the ACM SIGCHI Conference on User Interface Software and Technology.

4 Returning to the foundational question

We started out with what seemed to be straightforward questions: if design is about forming materials, then what are the materials of service design? Other design fields engage heavily in material exploration, wouldn't it be strange if the field of service design didn't engage in such explorations too?

In this book we have had the privilege of being able to give room to a service design perspective on materials, which is not something that any of the other design fields has done. Some of what is presented in the book will be recognised from these other fields. For example, approaching the design material as time-based is prevalent in interaction design as well as landscape architecture, although with different framings. Focusing on the immaterial as an object is part of the foundations of participatory design, e.g., through its focus on workplace democracy. Symbolic values as a material are key to product design and graphic design. This is just to mention a few possible connections. We hope you as the reader will see connections based on your background and make it possible to explore them in your work. We encourage that. We actually would love that.

The making of this book turned out to be a material exploration of sorts, shared with some brilliant minds of the service design field. Or framed differently as transformative learning, from a focus on forming materials as matter, to focusing on forming materials that matter.

A contribution to service

Through this exploration of materials we believe we have shown that service, when considered as a design material, goes beyond a way to explain transactions and markets, and beyond forming touch-points as a service interface.

Service, as a material, may be difficult to grasp as a concept. It might seem illogical to devote a whole book to the material of the immaterial. However, we feel that by starting to articulate how service is manifested in design work and in service co-creation, we may form a starting point to go beyond reductionist ideas of the material–immaterial dichotomy, and open up new constructivist perspectives.

Service is situated action, has aesthetics, is a hypermaterial that is bricolaged and rhizomatic. Service design is a practice participating in forming development processes and cultures, as much as it forms the foundations and possibilities for a well-made service system and the making of value in service. Service designers are a knowledge-intensive practice community that apply their competence in those settings, together with others, through a pluriversal set of materials that are organically developing.

This is as much a contribution to service as it is to design. While there may be no actual grand theories developed, or claimed, in the book, there are models and concepts proposed that are firmly rooted in design, not to mention the 18 materials, that bring new possibilities to service research and practice.

Towards a service design language

In the same manner as in other design fields, through the articulation of materials, their characteristics and how they relate to service and service design, we see that there is a language for service design developing. Not that there was no language before, but, by focusing on the materials that are at the core of service designing, the language gets richer in the sense that there is dedicated space to develop it, and it becomes more precise in the sense that it is developed in and of service design as a field. The service design field, and practice, has relied heavily on language, metaphors and analogies from totally different fields. This book is a contribution to continue to develop a language of service design, in its own right, as a design field, where we can depend less on metaphors from areas remotely related. This development needs to continue, where focus is on what service and service design is, beyond what it is metaphorically like, or analogic to be.

This language is in constant development, and a discourse around materials of service design needs to go beyond trivial tangible design outcomes. Well-designed touch-points are important for service, but are not in themselves the key to understanding service as a material for design. Not only experiential aspects of time and collaboration become integral, but also how agents, resources, institutions and integrative actions interact to form service. Moreover, aspects such as how initiative is structured, how power is shared and distributed and levels of engagement become central. Instead of focusing on instants, we could focus on pluralistic value creation, dynamic integration of evolving resources as well as actors as resourceful interpreters of assumed service.

The contributions of this book come at a time when design in general is at a point where institutionalisation is ongoing with conservative ambitions, and at the same time radical questioning and transformation is asked of design. On the one hand there is institutionalisation through design thinking and similar ambitions. On the other hand, the future of design to renew itself comes from, for example, decolonisation. Service design education needs to develop into resilient holding spaces, where transformation and novelty is valued and knowledge already developed is advanced and built on.

For service design research, multiple avenues of research open up, from descriptive historical accounts of service design language, to experimental work around language use, to generative work based on strong concepts expressed through language.

Materials as repertoire

One of the aspects related to the definition of material is that of material as repertoire. This begets the question of the service designer's material. In design it is common to refer to a repertoire of examples that a designer knows of and deliberately or non-deliberately refers to in their work. This is of course also true when it comes to the materials that are formed when designing. What are the materials that a service designer should know and master? What is feasible for a service designer to master as a repertoire, and at the same time master an accompanying set of methods and tools?

The number of materials and the competences needed to form the materials has reached a stage where we believe that service design is becoming specialised and is subdividing into subspecialities. We also believe that there may be other forces driving specialisation, as mentioned elsewhere (Holmlid et al., 2017; Sangiorgi et al., 2022).

We don't feel able at this stage to identify these groups, but it seems that one direction of specialisation is that of granularity. Some designers are interested in the micro scale, as zoomed-in service designers, focusing on the detailed interactions with touch-points along a service journey. Some are macro focused, zoomed out, focusing on the details of a wider system scale. Others take on a role to transform the development culture. There could also emerge other specialisations, cutting through the matters of service design in totally different ways with other guiding principles. Some could be focused on a collective, through social, participation and joint behaviours, whilst others could be focused on the instrumental, through the individual, interactions and beneficiary value. This is not to imply that these are independent or incongruable areas, and it is possible to have a plurality of competences taken from all.

However, it seems like areas are starting to crystallise within service design and, for a service designer, this means critically identifying and regularly re-reviewing your own skills, choosing which materials you feel most comfortable with and the materials you need to further your development as a service designer. For an educational institution, it becomes a question of finding the area and level of ambition; generalist, and over what area, or specialist, and specialist in what. Hopefully, the materials, the foundations and the discussion around the materials presented in this book can help by allowing you to consider alternative clusterings as part of education solutions.

Our only wish is that we retain service designers that have the ability to both zoom out and zoom in and to synthesise between the two, be it between meaning and solution, context and detail or any other shift in scale or level. The core design skill of being able to move between the macro to the micro should not be underestimated, especially together with the skills of engaging others and their aesthetic and experiential knowing, and the skills of representation and expression.

Materials that challenge existing education

It seems to us that some of the materials, maybe even the approach to understand what we mean by materials, is challenging current design education. This is particularly true for studio-based teaching, where skills and competences are built through practice. Linked to this is the understanding that the materials introduced into education have affordances for forming. In studio education, students often get to explore and learn these affordances through practice, and we think some of the materials of service design challenge existing design education. In a trivial sense the challenge is that the materials are not readily available to be explored within the studio.

It is accepted that one of the key aspects of service design is that the service designer asks important and fundamental questions – questions that others don't dare to ask, or indeed don't think about asking. This relates to social structures in which the inherent logic of an organisation and its behaviour lie and to something that Lavrans Løvlie mentioned in his interview about designers identifying the core of a problem or problem area, particularly during co-design. Conversations can be seen to fit well with visualisation and representation skills in service design and how a visualisation often highlights the core of a problem area. We believe that finding a way to teach the forming of and nature of conversations will be an important addition to service design going forward. These materials are difficult, but not impossible, to explore and develop skill outside the service context.

Social structures and behaviours are materials that deserve mentioning here. This is because of their relation to the dynamics of a team, the organisation and a service itself. The materials are interesting in this respect because they move forward from identifying stakeholders/actors towards understanding and forming the roles, assumptions and beliefs that they have. Behaviours are perhaps becoming a key material in both a co-design context but also in terms of service provision. This leads to a need to focus on how behaviours are formed and possibly changed, and opens up an area of moving from user-centred design to users-centred design. In other words, a move from not just individuals but groups of individuals, right up to national and global contexts with policy and culture. Service design has a need to bring social structures into its core, and this opens up a cultural view of service in its broadest sense. The challenge to studio-based education here is, as we see it, to introduce this knowledge into the critical reflexive work on and during designing.

We also consider time to be an interesting material with implications for research, education and practice, both in itself but also due to it being implicit in almost all of the materials in this book. The service designer needs to understand Chronos as well as Kairos. During our conversations we realised that through representations the service designer is essentially a time traveller. By this we mean that they design for future use situations, they prototype these and evidence them. Not only this, the service designer has importance when it comes to the design process and timing of activities and stages therein. Time and timing, and the ability to place oneself in a future time, are all skills that time-based media relate to, and imagining future experiences is a core service design competence, we believe. This suggests incorporating more experience and knowledge of narrative and dramaturgy into service design education. Another challenge with time being implicit is how representations of service can be used and adapted to deliver understanding of the experience of time in a service, and opening up time as material for forming.

Data have already been mentioned as an important material, and we mention them again here to flag that data as a material is not a central part of many service design courses, yet has enormous and increasing importance. One of the challenges here is to develop a skill set whereby the service designer can use data in a transformative manner, focusing on what could be, right from the start of a project. Developing fluency with data as a material is surely a challenge for traditional design-based education, and will bring the question of exactly how much knowledge is required to be able to do this. Chris Downs, in his interview, is optimistic, and we should perhaps integrate his approach into service design going forward.

A call for material explorations

With a bird's eye view, we can note that it is not only possible to talk about materials in service design, but also that materials in service design have features, usages and relationships to practice that are distinct for service design as a field of knowledge. However, whether the main takeaway from the book is the specific material descriptions or the frameworks that point out possibilities to develop and explore variations of materials is up to each reader.

This book specifically establishes a discourse around the materials of service design. The intention is not to develop an exhaustive list of materials but rather to discuss it as a means to explore what service design is, might be and might not be. Such a discussion gives new insights into service, since something has to be combined, formed, customised and produced to provide service. We believe that these 'somethings' have not yet been fully identified and that a discussion about them might provide new insights into design for service. During the writing of the book we've had wonderful dialogues with many service designers. While this book is now finished, it is more of a starting point for exploration, other journeys through the landscape of the materials of service design. It's about time to continue the dialogue, and you are invited to do that on the companion website (servicedesignmaterials.ep.liu.se). What is the material you would like to explore and share with the service design community? Where do you want to go now?

To rephrase what we said earlier in the book: there is a lot of learning to be made by exploring the forming of materials as matter, as well as by exploring the forming of materials that matter.

References

Holmlid, S., Wetter-Edman, K., & Edvardsson, B. (2017). Breaking free from NSD: Design and service beyond new service development. Designing for Service: Key Issues and New Directions, 95–104.
Sangiorgi, D., Holmlid, S., & Patricio, L. (2022). The multiple identities of service design in organizations and innovation projects. In B. Edvardsson & B. Tronvoll (eds), The Palgrave Handbook of Service Management (pp. 497–529). Palgrave Macmillan, Cham.

Index

Printed and bound by CPI Group (UK) Ltd, Croydon, CR0 4YY

25/09/2024

14563400-0001